THE WORLD OF ZEN

Head and torso of the "Buddha of the Future" (Maitreya Bodhisattva). This suavely contoured wooden statue, about four feet three inches in height, dates from around 650 A.D. and belongs to the Chuguji, a temple in Nara. In this figure, which is noted among early Japanese sculpture for the nobility and radiant sweetness of its expression and gesture, one can trace the waves of influence accompanying the flow of Buddhist philosophy across Asian lands. The melting roundness of the torso reminds us of the Golden Age of Gupta India, and the tranquil wave-like drapery (not shown here) speaks strongly of the late days of Chinese Wei.

The World of Zen

AN EAST-WEST ANTHOLOGY

Compiled, Edited, and with an Introduction by

NANCY WILSON ROSS

VINTAGE BOOKS
A Division of Random House
NEW YORK

VINTAGE BOOKS
are published by Alfred A. Knopf, Inc.
and Random House, Inc.

To
my distinguished contributors
who have aided understanding
between East and West

Preface

The material in this book was not assembled by way of presenting a handy kit of Asian panaceas for contemporary Occidental troubles. Certainly no philosophy of "self-knowledge" can be acquired by merely turning a printed page. Yet as one who for a number of years has been a serious student of Zen Buddhist philosophy and has derived very special pleasure and insight from the Zen-inspired arts of the Far East, I came gradually to a belief that a comprehensive anthology on the subject—from Western as well as Eastern sources—might serve a useful purpose. The understanding of Zen, currently a matter of interest to many Americans, very few of whom will ever have the opportunity, or even the desire, to pursue the strict meditative disciplines of a devotee, is not easily come by. Still it remains my belief that an East-West exploration of Zen's unique philosophy is capable of shedding some light on the enduring dilemma of human existence, and deepening an awareness of mankind's spiritual brotherhood. It is even possible to hope that in the scale of some long-term historic equation, the present American-European attraction for an ancient but still dynamic Eastern "way of liberation" may, to some degree, balance the mechanization and materialism which have been, and still are, our dubious gifts to Asia. (Gary Snyder, an American contributor to this anthology, in describing his recent experiences in a Zen monastery in Kyoto, tells us that his Japanese associates eagerly question him about young America's interest in a philosophy to which Japan's postwar generation appears to pay scant heed.)

As to just how enduring, per se, Zen's influence on the West, and on America in particular, will be—that is not easy to appraise. Influences are intangibles, and, as such, do not lend themselves readily to specific analysis or summation. We Americans have a way of "using up" ideas at a rapid rate. The gigantic maw of television, forever agape and forever unfilled, is the classic example of this national characteristic. Certainly it would be unfortunate if, now that the word Zen has reached common currency in the West, the idea got around that America had "had" Zen and nothing remained except to nod appreciatively and drop it as a passé cult. But perhaps we can safely assume that a philosophy which has endured with unbroken vitality and continuity for hundreds of years can hardly be pigeonholed within a decade—in America or anywhere else. It is encouraging to realize that although Zen is indubitably Far Eastern in origin, its singular range of perception and expression is not, nor has it ever been, confined to one geographic part of the globe. Zen-like intuitions have been experienced and expressed by men and women in all parts of the world, throughout recorded history—a fact I have been at some pains to indicate in a section of this book called "Universal Zen."

The major contributor to *The World of Zen* has been D. T. Suzuki—and properly so, as it was Dr. Suzuki's many books that first brought Zen's paradoxical teachings within seeming reach of the sceptical, "logical" Western mind. Now in his nineties—serene, humorous, wise, diligent, and dedicated—this venerable philosopher and East-West "bridge-builder" confesses that he has but one ambition: to live to be a hundred in the hope of making further contributions to translations from old Zen sources.

Since this anthology was designed for the general reader, the main emphasis has not been placed on original scriptures. These demand a special interest, knowledge, and vocabulary beyond the scope of an introductory study. A few, however, have been included, among them some of the brilliantly readable discourses of Huang Po, translated by an Englishman, John Blofeld, who is currently on the Faculty of Arts of Chulalongkorn University in Bangkok. Also included are excerpts from the *Shaseki-shu* and the *Mumonkan*.

The first contributor to this volume, following on my own introductory chapter, is Ruth Fuller Sasaki, an American by birth, who now occupies virtually the position of an abbess at a Zen temple and training center in Kyoto. (See photograph section.) The attainment of such a position by a woman is indeed remarkable, though two thousand years ago the Indian founder of world Buddhism declared that women were quite as capable of "enlightenment" as men: a revolutionary viewpoint which helped to contribute—if one can believe the Buddha's own prophecy—to the eventual decline of Buddhist power in the land of Hinduism!

A number of selections have also been made from the writings of well-known psychologists who have adapted Zen techniques to their special requirements: Erich Fromm, a German-born American; Robert Linssen, a Belgian; Hubert Benoit, a Frenchman; Akihisa Kondo, a Japanese. Among these four contributors I cannot resist speaking particularly of Dr. Benoit, a surgeon by profession and a musician by avocation who, while serving as an army doctor in the last war, was severely injured during a bombardment. Torn practically limb from limb, he miraculously survived, though he lost two inches in height and sustained permanent damage to his back and his right hand. Neither surgery nor violin-playing was any longer possible for him. Out of agonizing years of self-adjustment (about which Dr. Benoit is not inclined to talk readily) he became what a colleague has wryly described as "that most unfashionable phenomenon, a metaphysically grounded psychologist." Through Aldous Huxley, Dr. Benoit heard about D. T. Suzuki and, in his subsequent personal discovery of Zen, he came to feel what so many people have—that here were profound and subtle truths he had always known, not consciously but intuitionally.

A few further points should perhaps be briefly mentioned for general orientation. First, I would like to make clear that there are two main schools of Zen training: the Soto and the Rinzai. This volume is almost entirely taken up with the method of the Rinzai followers, for it is to this method that most Westerners have been drawn—due in large measure to Dr. Suzuki's writings and also to the unfortunate fact that the works of Dogen—Soto Zen's greatest philosopher—have, up to now, been very inadequately translated. In the present volume Chang Chen-chi has, however, contributed a section on the "Serene Reflection" meditation which is typical of Soto training as contrasted to the Rinzai with its use of the *koan* or irrational "riddle" technique.

In the interest of simplicity, and again because this book was designed for the general reader, it was decided to omit from the editor's own text the diacritical marks above certain consonants which indicate phonetic stress in the Japanese language: as for example, Bashō, Nō, Sōtō, kōan. Some contributors to the present volume have employed these stresses, others have not. Current usage of the Japanese-English Language Press tends to omit them, although this does not necessarily meet with the complete approval of all scholars. Hyphens sometimes used in words like Daitoku-ji, Ryoan-ji have also been omitted in the editorial sections.

Finally, the editor's contributions, as well as her footnotes, are signed. Unsigned footnotes are those of the original author (with occasional amplification of sources by the editor).

[N.W.R.]

Nancy Wilson Ross, who was born in the Pacific Northwest, where Oriental people have long been a familiar part of the local scene, made her first trip to Japan, Korea, and China in 1939. Since that time she has traveled extensively in Asia and has written on Asian subjects for many magazines, including the *Atlantic Monthly*, *Harper's Bazaar*, *Horizon*, *Mademoiselle*, the *New Yorker*, and *Vogue*. "What is Zen?," an article recently written by Miss Ross, has been widely distributed by the Japan Society to universities, schools, and libraries in this country. Her latest novel *The Return of Lady Brace* (1957), used a Buddhist priest as a principal character in an American setting. As Mrs. Stanley Young, Miss Ross serves on the board of the Asia Society of New York City. And in the spring of 1964, she lectured on Zen at the Jungian Institute in Zurich, Switzerland.

I wish to express my sincere gratitude to Ruth Fuller Sasaki, D. T. Suzuki, Professor Chang Chen-chi, Will Petersen and Alan Watts for the warm personal interest they have taken in the preparation of this book. I want also to thank personally William Barrett, Dr. Hubert Benoit, John Blofeld, R. H. Blyth, Harold Henderson, Donald Keene, Dr. Akihisa Kondo, Robert Linssen, Ivan Morris, Paul Reps, Gary Snyder, Arthur Waley and Langdon Warner for their valuable contributions.

In the art section I am deeply indebted to Mr. Sazo Idemitsu of Tokyo for graciously permitting the reproduction of so many Sengais from his notable collection, and for his generosity in having several of these paintings specially photographed for this volume. I wish also to thank Mr. Douglas Overton and Mr. Eugene Langston of the Japan Society of New York City, the executive staff of the International House of Japan in Tokyo, and Mr. C. Nagakura of the Idemitsu Kosan Company in Tokyo for their help in arranging details of the Sengai transaction. For the Reps "picture poems" I wish to thank Paul Reps himself, the Charles E. Tuttle Company of Tokyo and Mr. Meredith Weatherby—who also very kindly supplied the page of No masks. For valuable suggestions and immediate and generous response on a number of occasions, I wish to thank Mr. Perry Rathbone and Mr. Robert Treat Paine, Jr., of the Boston Museum of Fine Arts, Mr. Harold P. Stern of the Freer Gallery of Art in Washington, D. C., Mr. Alan Priest of the Metropolitan Museum of Art, New York City, Mr. Laurence Sickman of the William Rockhill Nelson Gallery of Art in St. Louis, and Dr. Richard Fuller of the Seattle Art Museum. To Mr. Paul Mills, curator of the Oakland Art Museum, I also owe thanks (along with Mr. Idemitsu) for permission to use excerpts from the catalogue of a show held in Oakland in 1956 as part of a Japan Cultural Festival. I want also to express my keen appreciation to Mr. James Cahill of the Freer Gallery of Art in Washington, D. C. for his part in a lively and highly enjoyable correspondence on the subject of Zen in art and Asian art in general.

For unusual photographs of archery and *kendo*, I am indebted to the *Kokusai Bunka Shinkokai* of Tokyo, and again I owe thanks to Mr. Douglas Overton of the Japan Society for his part in procuring these pictures. Most sincere thanks are also due Mr. Frederick L. Hamilton of Old Saybrook, Connecticut, for the several photographs he so generously and promptly supplied from his outstanding collection of Far Eastern subject matter.

It is a pleasure to express publicly my long-standing gratitude to the general staff of the New York Public Library; in particular, in this instance, to the personnel of the Art and Oriental Departments, and specifically to Mr. Francis W. Parr. For their gracious cooperation on a number of occasions thanks are due Mr. Hirozo Ushida, of the Consulate General of Japan in New York, Mr. Y. Enomoto of the Japan Tourist Association, and Mrs. Mary Farkas of the First Zen Institute of America in New York City. I take this opportunity to thank also four New York bookshops for their diligence in searching out special material: The Gotham Book Mart, Orientalia, The Paragon Book Gallery and E. Weyhe and Company.

I am grateful to my publishers, Random House, for their generous support of this complex project, and although I owe thanks to too many people in the firm to list them all here, I cannot omit certain names: Mary Heathcote, whose conscientious and intelligent attention to many details has put me eternally in her debt, Nan Talese, who hovered so faithfully over the galleys, and members of the production department, under Ray Freiman, who gave so much care to the book's design.

Last, but by no means least, I make a low Oriental bow to my agent, Ivan von Auw, Jr., of Harold Ober Associates, and my husband, Stanley Young, who both patiently and painstakingly read every word of what was—to begin with—a veritable mountain of manuscript.

ACKNOWLEDGMENTS AND COPYRIGHT NOTICES

For permission to use the following material grateful acknowledgment is extended to:
George Allen & Unwin, London, England, for permission to quote Gordon Bottomley's poem "Dawn" and for excerpts from the works of Christmas Humphreys, Robert Linssen and Arthur Waley (further identified in footnotes).

Merle Armitage for permission to use "The Marionette Theatre" by Heinrich von Kleist from *Five Essays on Paul Klee;* contributors: Merle Armitage, Clement Greenberg, Howard Devree, Nancy Wilson Ross, James Johnson Sweeney; distributed by Duell, Sloan and Pearce.

R. H. Blyth for permission to quote from *Eastern Culture* and *Oriental Humor*, both published by Hokuseido Press, Tokyo, Japan.

Charles T. Branford Company for permission to use quotes from Gustie Herrigel's *Zen in the Art of Flower Arrangement.*

The Bollingen Foundation for generous permission to quote from D. T. Suzuki's *Zen and Japanese Culture*, Mai-Mai Sze's *The Tao of Painting*, seven lines by Solomon Trimosin quoted in C. G. Jung's *Psychology and Religion*, and for securing permission to use a section from Dr. Suzuki's "The Awakening of a New Consciousness in Zen" published in the *Eranos Jahrbuch*, 1952, Band XXIII.

Cambridge University Press for generous permission to quote from E. N. Butler's *Rainer Maria Rilke.*

Bruno Cassirer, Oxford, England, for generous permission to use quotations from *Buddhist Texts Through the Ages*, 1954, edited by E. Conze, I. B. Horner, D. Snellgrove and A. Waley.

City Lights Bookshop and Mr. Lawrence Ferlinghetti for permission to use excerpts from Alan Watts' *Beat Zen, Square Zen and Zen.*

Chicago Review for permission to quote from the Summer, 1958 Issue, volume 12, #2.

Dodd Mead & Company for use of material from Okakura's *Book of Tea.*

Doubleday & Company, Inc. for permission to quote from Harold Henderson's *An Introduction to Haiku.*

Grove Press (and *Evergreen Review*) for permission to print excerpts from John Blofeld, Donald Keene, Will Petersen, Arthur Waley, Langdon Warner and Alan Watts (further identified in footnotes).

Harcourt Brace & Company for permission to quote from T. S. Eliot's "The Hollow Men" from *Collected Poems, 1909–1935* (copyright 1936 by Harcourt Brace & Co.), and for E. E. Cummings' poem "When God Lets My Body Be." (Copyright 1923, 1951 by E. E. Cummings). Reprinted from *Poems, 1923–1954* by E. E. Cummings by permission of Harcourt Brace & Co.

Harper & Brothers for permission to quote from Erich Fromm in *Zen Buddhism and Psychoanalysis* and from Chang Chen-chi's *The Practice of Zen.*

Harvard University Press for generous permission to quote from Langdon Warner's *The Enduring Art of Japan* and from the *Harvard Theological Review;* also to the President and Fellows of Harvard College and the Belknap Press for the use of seven lines from Emily Dickinson's poem, "A Bird Came Down the Walk" in *The Poems of Emily Dickinson*, edited by Thomas Herbert Johnson, 1955.

Henry Holt & Co., Inc. for permission to quote from A. E. Housman's *A Shropshire Lad* and lines from Robert Frost's "Lost in Heaven" (*A Further Range*), copyright Robert Frost, 1936.

Horizon Magazine for permission to use excerpts from "The Square Roots of Zen" by Nancy Wilson Ross, July, 1959, and for the use of their color print of the Kano Tanyu painting from Miss Ross's collection.

Houghton Mifflin Co., for generous permission to use four lines from Amy Lowell's "Shooting the Sun" published in *The Complete Poetical Works of Amy Lowell;* eleven lines from Archibald MacLeish's poem "Ars Poetica"; (*Collected Poems, 1917–1952*); and fourteen lines from M. Anesaki's *Buddhist Art in its Relation to Buddhist Ideals.*

The Hutchinson Group, London, England, for permission to quote from D. T. Suzuki's book *Introduction to Zen Buddhism*, published by Messrs. Rider & Company.

Alfred A. Knopf, Inc. for generous permission to quote from "Thirteen Ways of Looking at a Blackbird" from *The Collected Works of Wallace Stevens.*

The Macmillan Co. for permission to quote from "Among School Children" by William Butler Yeats (*Collected Poems*); from Vachel Lindsay's "The Chinese Nightingale" (*Collected Poems*) and Marianne Moore's "To a Snail" (*The Collected Poems of Marianne Moore, 1935*).

Mademoiselle Magazine for permission to quote from "What Is Zen?" by Nancy Wilson Ross, January, 1958.

Massachusetts Institute of Technology Press (and John Wiley & Sons) for permission to quote from R. G. H. Siu's *The Tao of Science.*

John Murray, London, England, for permission to quote from Alan Watts' *Spirit of Zen* in the *Wisdom of the East* series. (See also Grove Press)

The National Broadcasting Company and Mr. James Nelson of the *Special Projects Department* for permission to quote from Dr. D. T. Suzuki and Dr. Huston Smith, speaking on its "Wisdom Series," April 19, 1959.

New American Library (See Vedanta Society)

New Directions for permission to quote from *The Cantos of Ezra Pound* and from *Personae, the Collected Poems of Ezra Pound;* from *The Collected Earlier Poems of William Carlos Williams;* from *Selected Poems by Muriel Rukeyser* (copyright 1935, 1938, 1939, 1944, 1948, 1949, 1950 and 1951 by Muriel Rukeyser); from Thomas Merton's *Seeds of Contemplation* (copyright Our Lady of Gethsemani Monastery, MCMXLIX).

W. W. Norton & Company, Inc., for generous permission to quote from Rainer Maria Rilke's *Duino Elegies.*

Oxford University Press for permission to quote from *A Search for Man's Sanity* by Trigant Burrows.

Pantheon Books, Inc., for permission to quote from Dr. Hubert Benoit's *The Supreme Doctrine;* from *Zen in the Art of Archery* by Eugen Herrigel; and from Alan Watts' *The Way of Zen.*

Princeton University Press for generous permission to quote from Earl Miner's *The Japanese Tradition in British and American Literature,* 1958.

G. P. Putnam's Sons for permission to quote from Simone Weil's *Gravity and Grace,* copyright 1952 by G. P. Putnam's Sons.

Dr. Frederick Spiegelberg for his permission to quote an original translation from Rainer Maria Rilke published in his *The Religion of No Religion,* Stanford, California, 1948 (copyright by James Ladd Delkin).

Swami Nikhilananda of the Ramakrishna-Vivekananda Center of New York City for giving permission to quote, and kindly identifying a reference from, the *Upanishads* in an article by Swami Madhavananda in *The Cultural Heritage of India,* volume 1, published by the Ramakrishna Centenary Committee, Belur Math, Calcutta.

Vanguard Press for permission to quote from Edith Sitwell's *A Book of the Winter.*

The Vedanta Society of Southern California (and Christopher Isherwood) for permission to quote from the translation of the *Bhagavad-Gita* by Christopher Isherwood and Swami Pravhavananda, originally published by Harper & Brothers, now a Mentor Religious Classic of the New American Library. (Copyright by the Vedanta Society.)

John Wiley & Sons (See under Massachusetts Institute of Technology Press)

Contents

I do not need to burn the Gospels in order to read Hui-Neng.

—HUBERT BENOIT, in *The Supreme Doctrine*

One can tell for oneself whether the water is warm or cold. In the same way, a man must convince himself about these experiences, then only are they real.

—I-CHING

As thou knowest not what is the way of the spirit, nor how the bones do grow in the womb of her that is with child, even so thou knowest not the works of God who maketh all.

—*Ecclesiastes XI : 5*

The great path has no gates,
Thousands of roads enter it.
When one passes through this gateless gate
He walks freely between heaven and earth.

—MUMONKAN

It seems proper to comment briefly on the artists, Sengai and Reps, whose work has been used throughout the text.

Sengai, a famous Zen priest who was also a gifted painter, was born in 1750 and entered Zen training at the age of ten. He became in time the superior of Japan's first Zen temple, of which he was the one hundred and twenty-third abbot in direct line from the legendary Eisai. In spite of his high position, and though living in a time noted for its formality and strict social distinctions, Sengai made friends with "wise and foolish, noble and humble, old and young." When he died in 1837, at the age of eighty-eight, all classes of society—the priesthood, the peasants, nobility, samurai and merchants—mourned the passing of a rare friend.

Of the typically Zen "painting-poems" of Sengai, a modern Zen master, Sogen Asahina of Engakuji Temple in Kamakura, has commented: "Even for the Japanese, it is very difficult for the uninitiated to understand Zen paintings or poems. This difficulty is greatly increased when Zen transcendentalism and humor are presented in translation. But though (or perhaps because) you do not *intellectually* understand Sengai's works, you may catch something of the Zen spirit with which they are suffused."

Paul Reps is a contemporary who first made his place in Zen's East-West annals back in the 1930's with his translations (along with Nyogen Senzaki) of old Zen anecdotes and dialogues under the English titles of *The Gateless Gate* and *101 Zen Stories*. In 1952 Reps first started his now famous "picture-poems," offering them as "weightless gifts" to his many friends as he moved about the world. In 1957 a Japanese friend to whom he had given a number of them started the first of the Reps shows in Kyoto. At this immensely successful exhibition, as in all the later ones, the "poems," on rice paper of various sizes, were Scotch-taped at their tops to horizontal bamboo poles strung from the ceiling at different levels, where electric fans blew them gently. There they fluttered "like washing in the breeze, or moving banners." Meredith Weatherby in his introduction to a volume of these sketches, *Zen Telegrams*, has said that Reps is, "in a sense, trying, through the medium of these shapes, to give the English word some of that pictorial flashing quality which the ideographs of China and Japan possess in their own right, the quality that breathed that magical life into their calligraphy."

[N. W. R.]

CHAPTER 1

Introduction

By NANCY WILSON ROSS

During the past few years in America a small Japanese word, with a not inappropriate buzzing sound, has begun to be heard in unlikely places: on academic platforms, at cocktail parties and ladies' luncheons, and in campus hangouts. This word is "Zen." Sometimes called a religion, sometimes "the religion of no-religion," sometimes identified simply as a "way of life," Zen is ancient and alien in origin, its philosophy paradoxical and complex. Its sudden Western blooming is therefore something of a phenomenon.

The applied tenets of Zen—formulations and adaptations of original Buddhist principles—lie at the root of the most unique elements in Japanese life. Zen's influence, implicit or explicit, can be traced through almost every aspect of Japan's culture from garden planning to architecture, ceremonial swordsmanship to Judo, flower arrangement to archery, poetry composition to the formal tea ceremony, painting techniques to the conventions of the theater. So complete has been Zen's infiltration for centuries that it is by now quite impossible to understand the contradictory and long-enduring civilization of this small island country without some understanding of Zen itself.

Traveling a long distance in space and time from its origins in India in the sixth century B.C., to reach Japan via China and Korea in the twelfth and thirteenth centuries A.D. (although other forms of Buddhism reached Japan as early as the sixth century A.D.), Zen Buddhism first touched American shores about 1900. After some fifty years of incubation—and ironically enough, since the war in the Pacific—it has suddenly begun to attract a

3

growing number of enthusiastic supporters in this country, among them distinguished scientists, artists, and psychoanalysts.

Although Zen in America has become generally associated in the public mind with the "beat" generation, it may not finally matter that the present advance of this philosophy in the Western world has such unorthodox associations. Trained Zennists are notably tolerant people. The West Coast's beloved *roshi* (venerable teacher), Nyogen Senzaki, who died in 1958, liked to quote an old saying: "There are three kinds of disciples: those who impart Zen to others, those who maintain the temples and shrines, and then there are the rice bags and the clothes hangers."

From Japan some pertinent remarks on the fad side of Zen were recently offered by Chicago-born Ruth Fuller Sasaki, who has been ordained a Zen priest and is now in full charge of a Kyoto subtemple—a quite extraordinary honor for a Westerner and a woman. In an interview given at the time of her ordination in 1958 she commented: "In the Western world Zen seems to be going through the cult phase. Zen is not a cult. The problem with Western people is that they want to believe in something and at the same time they want something easy. Zen is a lifetime work of self-discipline and study." Mrs. Sasaki went on to describe how, during her period of training, she learned to spend seven days at a time in a monks' hall sleeping only one hour a night, and sitting in meditation or contemplation for as long as eighteen hours without a break.

Disciplines similar, though by no means as rigorous, are not altogether unknown among Zen followers in this country. Members of New York's First Zen Institute have been meeting to practice meditative exercises for almost three decades. Each summer for a number of years Los Angeles Zennists have held a week of strict training in group meditation. A recent session was led by a Zen *roshi* from an old and noted Japanese monastery. The printed invitation to the *sesshin* (a Zen word for a special period devoted to meditation and study) read, "Bring your sleeping bag and toothbrush. There is no charge." Alongside the week's Spartan schedule appeared a sketch of fierce-eyed Bodhidharma, the legendary First Patriarch who brought the Great Teaching from India to the Sino-Japanese world, and the notice: "Let us keep the promise of complete SILENCE during our *sesshin*." This meant silence for seven full days—a rule faithfully adhered to by a mixed group of disciples: social figures, teachers, college students, artisans and artists, housewives and businessmen.

Now what is it that these people from diverse backgrounds are seeking so earnestly outside the bounds of their own religious, philosophical, and aesthetic orientation, and that has led the more serious among them to submit to difficult and puzzling disciplines? The answer would seem to lie in the basic qualities that distinguish Zen as a way of life, and these may be very loosely summed up as follows: Zen, although considered a religion by its followers, has no sacred scriptures whose words are law; no fixed canon; no rigid dogma; no Savior or Divine Being through whose favor or intercession one's eventual salvation is assured. The absence of attributes common to all other religious systems lends Zen a certain air of freedom to which many modern people respond. Furthermore, Zen's stated aim of bringing about—through the employment of its special methods—a high degree of self-knowledge with a resultant gain of peace of mind has caught the attention of certain Western psychologists, among them Carl Jung, Erich Fromm and the late Karen Horney. Other Western names included in modern discussions of Zen range from Korzybski to Kierkegaard, Sartre to Jaspers, Kerouac to Kafka, Heisenberg to Martin Buber. When the existentialist German philosopher Martin Heidegger encountered Zen writings he professed to discover in them the very ideas he had been independently developing.

The gravest obstacle in discussing Zen's possible meaning for the West is the difficulty of explaining "How it works." In its own four statements, Zen emphasizes particularly that its teaching lies beyond and outside words:

> A special transmission outside the Scriptures;
> No dependence upon words and letters;
> Direct pointing to the soul of man;
> Seeing into one's nature and the attainment of Buddhahood.

To know Zen—even to begin to understand it—it is necessary to practice it. And here Westerners come to a dilemma. Ruth Sasaki believes it is not possible to get at Zen's deepest roots or to rightly utilize its unique method without the aid of a master, a *guru*, to use the Indian term.

To reach the state of illumination—*satori*—and the "spiritual equilibrium" that follows, certain definite techniques are used by the Zen master and pupil. There is a form of question and answer known as the *mondo* by which ordinary thought processes are speeded up to the point of the hoped-for abrupt breakthrough into "awareness." And then there is the *koan*, a formulation in words not soluble by the intellect alone—indeed, often quite senseless to the

5

rational mind, a veritable "riddle." But the *koan* contains the possible seeds of the shock that may also break open the sealed door of ordinary consciousness, which is forever caught in the contradictory bonds of dualism, forever balancing this with that, unable to take hold of "reality" because always immersed in a series of distinctions, discriminations, and differences.

To work on a *koan* necessitates a sincere and enduring eagerness to solve it, but also—and here comes the twist, and one of the many paradoxes in which Zen abounds—you must *face it without thinking about it*. This point is stressed in the unbending effort to force the student beyond the eternally dualistic and dialectic pattern of ordinary thinking. Again and again it is emphasized that one cannot take hold of the true merely by abandoning the false, nor can one reach peace of mind or any final "answer" by argument or logic. Science might be cited as a prime example of the failure to bring solace or release through "facts." Scientists reduce matter to molecules, molecules to atoms; they present the theory of the infinite divisibility of matter. They also assert that all life is merely force or energy. The sum total of their brilliant findings remains almost totally incomprehensible to the average mind, even to the exceptional mind that happens to be unscientific. How, then, in the modern world, ruled by conflicting theories, with global problems and personal problems forever presenting themselves for solution, can the individual ever "come to rest," struggling as he still is—but in an ever more complex environment—with the very same basic questions of individual meaning, of the riddle of life and death, that Siddartha Gautama, the historic Buddha, faced in the sixth century B.C.?

Once you have taken up this ancient basic question of "meaning," you are on your way to an impasse which your so-called "rational" mind cannot solve for you. And it is at this point that the Zen *koan* is presented as a sort of spiritual dynamite. But one cannot, alas, "explain" a *koan. Koans* are meant to be directly experienced. They are formulations on which to practice that famous "law of reversed effort" by which results are often mysteriously obtained in the hidden, unconscious depths of one's being.

A subject for meditation might be these lines from an old Japanese poem: "The cherry tree blooms each year in the Yoshino Mountains. But split the tree and tell me where the flowers are." Or the last line from another famous Japanese poem: "Now I know my true being has nothing to do with birth and death."

An instructor giving this line as a *koan* might question: "How can you free yourself from birth and death? What is your true being? *No! No! Do not think about it! Just gaze at it closely.*" Perhaps a few hints would be offered: "Zen, it is asserted, has the aim of enabling you to see directly into your own nature. Very well. Where *is* your true nature? Can you locate it? If you can locate it you are then said to be free of birth and death. All right, you have become a corpse. Are you free of birth and death? Now do you know where you are? . . . . Now your body has separated into its four basic elements. Where are you now?"

Doshin asked Sosan: "What is the method of liberation?" The master replied: "Who binds you?" "No one binds me." "Why then," said the master, "should you seek liberation?" Replies of this type, says Alan Watts, "seem to throw attention back upon the state of mind from which the question arises, as if to say: If your feelings are troubling you, find out who or what it is that is being troubled. The psychological response is therefore to try to feel what feels and to know what knows—to make an object of the subject." Yet this is not easy. It is indeed "much like looking for an ox when you are riding on it" or "like an eye that sees, but cannot see itself."

Carl Jung has been at some pains to point out that the master-pupil relationship is not easy for the average Occidental to accept. In his introduction to one of Dr. Suzuki's books, Dr. Jung wrote: "Who among us would produce such implicit trust in a superior master and his incomprehensible ways? This respect for the greater human personality exists only in the East." Even were it not for the ordinary Westerner's psychological resistance to the notion of a personal master, other difficulties arise in the passing on of strict Zen training. There are, for instance, far from enough English-speaking *roshis* to go around. Most people who take on a partial—or total—dedication to Zen's "heterodoxical transformation process" must perforce seek the way for themselves.

Just how far the ordinary, unaided seeker can penetrate toward the core of Zen is difficult to assess, but whichever way he seeks it—either under direct personal guidance or alone—the key to realization lies in the words "direct immediate perception," or "direct seeing into." The condition of enlightenment itself, and not words *about* that condition, are what matter in Zen. Zen masters sternly reject all the speculation, ratiocination, and verbalism so dear to the intellectual Westerner. Overemphasis on the brain, at the expense of other parts of the total consciousness, can seem both amusing and amazing to Asian teachers. A Zen abbot once set before an American aspirant two sets of small legless Japanese dolls, one pair weighted in the bottom part, the other in the head part. When the pair weighted in the head were pushed over, they remained on their sides; the ones weighted in the bottom bounced back at once. The abbot roared with laughter over this illustration of the plight of Western man, forever stressing the thinking function at the expense of his totality.

Some extremely useful hints on this point in particular and Zen training methods in general, as well as the possible rewards for a Westerner who submits to them, may be found in Eugen Herrigel's *Zen in the Art of Archery* (see Section VI of this volume). This little book describes in detail the agonizing, bewildering five-year trials of a European pupil—a college professor and a crack marksman with pistol and rifle—who attempted to learn archery, Zen style, while in Japan. The mastery of this ancient sacred sport turned out to be much more than the mere acquiring of new techniques. In the mind of the Zen master who acted as Herrigel's instructor it was nothing less than "a profound and far-reaching contest of the archer with himself." The contest had little to do with learning to hit the target in successful, professional style—a paltry goal held to be "sheer devilry," leading to the unfortunate state in which a man could "get stuck in his own achievement." Instead, day after day for five years, with few words yet unswerving intention, the master's emphasis was placed on acquiring a condition called "waiting without purpose but in a state of highest tension"—*not* physical tension, but with a body at once *aware* yet *relaxed*. The pupil was not to be braced for "failure"—the natural result of a competitive viewpoint—but to think in terms of "fulfillment." When at long last the patient but puzzled Westerner had learned how "not to shoot," but simply to "let the shot fall from him" with the ease and naturalness of ripe fruit from a tree or snow from a slowly bending bamboo, he felt that he was finally in possession of a great secret of enlightened human behavior.

To get at the underpinnings of the Zen way of life, it is helpful—perhaps even essential—to go behind the Taoistic Chinese influence which flavors it, back to Buddhism's beginnings in India more than two thousand years ago, for Zen considers itself to be nearer the original doctrines of Siddartha Gautama, the Great Teacher, than any other of the many sects belonging to the two main Buddhist branches, Mahayana and Hinayana. Zen's emphasis on self-reliance, on effort towards discovery of "the 'light' man can find in himself," recalls the Buddha's revolutionary challenge to his first disciples, "Look within, *thou* art the Buddha"—a tacit denial of any special divinity in his own person not also shared by all men.

The birth of the Indian founder of Buddhism, around 560 B.C., occurred in a period not unlike our own, a time when the minds of thinking men were torn with warring philosophies and conflicting theories on the origin, meaning, and purpose of life. Siddartha Gautama, destined to become the Buddha—which simply means the Enlightened One—was the son and heir of a wealthy rajah of the military caste in what is present-day Nepal. From birth—so legend says—the young prince was zealously protected by an overdevoted father who hoped to prevent the eyes of his adored son from ever falling on any gloomy or tragic scene. But after Gautama reached young manhood he made a series of forbidden and secret journeys outside the gates of the family palace and there saw three unhappy sights which forever altered his destiny: an abject beggar, a corpse surrounded by weeping mourners, a hopelessly diseased cripple.

His peace of mind shattered, Gautama began to ask himself certain serious questions. What was the possible meaning or value of human life when suffering lay at its root, when poverty and sickness were not exceptional but universal—as he had just learned from the palace servant who accompanied him on his forbidden journeys? What purpose had individual human existence since it must be terminated inevitably in the mysterious oblivion of death?

Unable, in the face of these racking questions, to endure any longer his protected and luxurious life, Gautama finally stole away in the middle of the night, leaving behind a beautiful wife and first-born son, to undertake seven years of wandering from teacher to teacher in search of answers to his inescapable Why's. He at last attained illumination while sitting alone in deep meditation under a sacred fig tree. This figure of the contemplative man seated cross-legged, hands in lap, eyes directed within—so often seen in Asian sculpture and paintings—is to the Eastern world what the figure of Christ on the crucifix is to the Western.

Having attained enlightenment, Gautama—now become "The Buddha"—went forth to preach up and down the Indian roads for forty-nine fruitful years. His aim was not to save others but to help them to save themselves: this is the differentiating crux of Mahayana Buddhism from which Zen stems. Buddha preached a doctrine of a Middle Way between the Opposites. The teaching was essentially psychological, a training in discipline of mind and body aiming at self-mastery and nonattachment. Its principles were embodied in an Eight Fold Path of Right Thought and Right Behavior that would, if earnestly followed, enable a man to rid himself of his greed, his desire for possessions, his "clinging" to objects and persons (claimed as the chief cause of suffering). Finally it would bring him to complete freedom from the restrictive and—to the Buddhists—totally false sense of a separate "self," or individual ego, walling him off from the rest of life. When he had reached this state of being, all fear of inadequacy, of deprivation, and also of death would inevitably be conquered.

Although the direct, pragmatic, and at the same time serene and immensely tolerant teaching of the Buddha lost out in the land of its birth to the more sensual Hinduism, it has flourished for centuries throughout the rest of Asia taking on coloring from the various cultures through which it passed much as a moving river reflects different scenes from its ever changing banks. Zen— or Ch'an, as the Chinese called it—is, then, the Sino-Japanese expression of this ancient teaching, and it was the Chinese with their Taoistic outlook who developed Zen's peculiar form of dynamic meditation, that "stilling of the self," that condition of full awareness, neither passive nor aggressive. When the young and eager country of Japan took over China's already highly developed civilization—not by war or conquest, but voluntarily and with the fullest enthusiasm—it also acquired Chinese Buddhism. Then, true to their practical yet basically aesthetic and mystical natures, the Japanese applied Ch'an's (Zen's) subtle dynamic laws in many original ways to their own indigenous culture.

The question inevitably arises whether the present American response to things Japanese—and specifically to the paradoxical subtleties of Zen—may have its root in our recent occupation of Japan. Although it is unlikely that more than a handful of GI's ever heard the word "Zen," it is certainly plain that many were affected by a milieu so completely unlike anything they had ever known. An initial interest in Zen might have come to them through quite indirect stimuli. Old Chinese and Japanese landscape paintings, whose values and virtues differ so markedly from our own, have been the entrance into the Zen world for many people. In the Chinese and Japanese aesthetic, emphasis falls on asymmetry rather than on symmetry, on space seen not merely as something to be "filled in" but as something *positive in itself*. These deceptively simple works of art, often rendered only in ink strokes of varied styles and weights, manage to suggest, with incomparable nuance, both life's mystery and its reassuring homely quality: the bird resting on the bough; the tree bent with snow; the distant mountains, half-veiled, half-revealed by mist;

man always presented small, not set forth as the "master" of all he surveys but instead as a *related part of the whole.*

The experience of the Japanese tea ceremony has also been known to rouse sensitive Westerners to an awareness of something truly unique in the spirit of this contradictory people. The tea ceremony, stressing as it does the virtues of silence, a quiet exchange between friends, the contemplation of one or two simple but beautiful objects, takes place in a small garden structure whose interior is meant to be seen as "the abode of vacancy." The traditional Japanese garden—exemplifying laws of abstract composition unpracticed in the West until the work of some modern painters—has its most famous expression in the raked sand–and–rock garden of Ryoanji, described in an essay in Section III of this volume. The sense of timelessness implicit in the tea ceremony may be caught again at a performance of the stylized ancient drama called the No. Even the more spectacular and popular Kabuki affords fleeting glimpses of Zen's way for those prepared to catch them. A stage silence prolonged past Western limits of pleasure or comfort, when not impatiently resisted but simply "gone with," can finally register with the force of a great sound; the slight movement of an actor's fan, a barely perceptible shift of an arm or a foot, other unstressed gestures that produce from a Japanese audience mysterious cries of approbation—these delicately sustained moments could conceivably lead a puzzled Occidental into new avenues of insight. And finally, a first step into Zen's paradoxical pleasures can lie through poetry, for in the stripped, evocative brevity of a *haiku* or a *tanka* there often lurks the very essence of Zen.

> The wild geese do not intend to cast their reflections,
> The water has no mind to receive their image.

To account fully for the present enthusiasm for Zen may not be possible, but there is no denying its growing American and European popularity. Zen seems to be serving as one of a number of fresh elements in a more dynamic exchange between East and West. This long-desired rapprochement, quietly developing despite appearances to the contrary, may contribute in time to the realization of that old-new vision—a general World Culture, a Civilization of Man. A minor aspect of the new and properly paradoxical Japanese-American exchange was touched on by Sabro Hasegawa, a gifted Japanese painter and Zen disciple, in a piece written not long before his recent death: " 'Old' Japan was newer than the new Occident, while new Japan is apparently more old-fashioned than either the new Occident or old Japan itself." He went on to describe the contemporary Japanese painters' growing concern with photographic realism in art, while at the same time so many Western artists are turning to abstraction.

Perhaps also it is not too far-fetched to assume that some of the same disillusionment, the same disturbing sense of things gone awry in a familiar world, that has affected the intellectual climate of Japan is turning many Westerners toward less familiar philosophies, attracting them to un-Western, non-Aristotelian ways of regarding life and the meaning of personal existence.

When Aldous Huxley wrote his little book *The Doors of Perception*, a description of the effects of a scientific experiment with carefully controlled dosages of the drug mescaline, he referred specifically to one of the famed bits of classic Zen dialogue with which aspirants to enlightenment are sometimes confronted. This passage, which had puzzled Huxley very much when he read it in one of D. T. Suzuki's books, tells of a young novice who asks his master, "What is the Dharma-Body of the Buddha?" (in our Western terminology, "What is Universal Mind or the Godhead?"). The master replies, "with the prompt irrelevance," says Huxley, "of one of the Marx Brothers, 'The hedge at the bottom of the garden.'" When the bewildered novice pursues the problem further, he may get for his second answer a real Groucho whack on the shoulder with the master's ever ready staff, and a second seemingly nonsensical reply: "A golden-haired lion."

Huxley reported that under the effect of the drug—which had thoroughly relaxed the grip of the rational top brain and the insistent habitual separativeness of his own personal ego—he saw, with delighted amusement, just what these fantastic Zen replies really meant. They now appeared not in the least nonsensical, for in this moment of freedom and illumination, all life stood revealed to him as a totality, a great "One-ness." Thus any answer made to a question about Universal Mind would, of necessity, be as true as any other.

A passage of this nature serves to recall the dadaists and surrealists of Europe who, after World War I, attempted to bring about a "general and emphatic crisis in Western consciousness." This they tried to do by a number of unusual devices. In painting they played the game of *trompe l'oeil;* on their canvases one frequently finds two or more objects presented as one. Dali's early painting of his old nurse is a familiar example, with her spine shown as a crutch-propped aperture through which one gets a view of sea and sand. In writing as well as painting the dadaists delighted in unlikely juxtapositions of images and ideas: "the cave bear and the lout his companion, the *vol-au-vent* and the wind his valet, the cannibal and his brother the carnival, the Mississippi and its little dog . . ." or "beautiful as the chance meeting on a dissecting table of a sewing machine and an umbrella." It was thus, acting as Breton's "modest registering machines," that surrealists expressed themselves—to the pleasure of their compeers and the bewilderment of outsiders. At dadaist gatherings speakers would sometimes sit in silence or ring bells or "make poetry" by poking holes through bits of paper. (Zen behavior, not entirely dissimilar though differently motivated, is described in other parts of this volume.) Lines from Eluard, Breton, and Rimbaud often have a Zen ring. Among Eluard's *Proverbs* one reads, "Make two o'clock with one o'clock," "I came, I sat, I departed," "A crab by any other name would not forget the sea," "Who hears but me hears all." Among Zen sayings one finds: "When Tom drinks, Dick gets tipsy," "Last night a wooden horse neighed and a stone man cut capers," "Lo, a cloud of dust is rising from the ocean, and the roaring of waves is heard over the land," "Who is the teacher of all the Buddhas, past, present and future? John the cook."

Zen enlightenment, which carries with it a deep and lasting comprehension of one's place in the totality of the universe, is not easily gained—contrary to the impression of "immediacy" that many people have taken away from their cursory reading of Zen literature. Although illumination may come in a sudden flash, during which one perceives one's "self" and the rest of the world as they really are, this galvanic charge is unlikely to occur short of an extended period of disciplined personal effort. The seeker, as one Zen master asserts, must pursue for a very long time the problem of final "knowing" with a single-purposed ferocity and all the attendant frustrations of a "mosquito trying to bite on a bar of iron."

Those who, to begin with, find Zen not only paradoxical and puzzling but annoying, even enraging, might profit from an old story of a certain learned man who came to a Zen master to inquire about this rare philosophy. The master politely invited his visitor to share a cup of ceremonial tea while they discoursed together. When the master had brewed the tea by the strict procedures of the tea ceremony, he began to pour the whisked green liquid into the visitor's cup and continued pouring until the cup had overflowed. Even then he went on pouring until the discomfited guest, unable longer to restrain himself, cried out in agitation, "Sir, my cup is already full. No more will go

13

in." At once the master put down the teapot and remarked, "Like this cup, you are full of your own opinions and speculations. How can I show you Zen unless you first empty your cup?"

CHAPTER 2

Zen: A Method for Religious Awakening[1]

By RUTH FULLER SASAKI

FOREWORD

In the autumn of 1958 I was invited by Dr. Huston Smith, Professor of Philosophy at the Massachusetts Institute of Technology, Cambridge, to deliver a lecture on comparative religion to faculty members, students of the Institute, and their friends. During his visit to Kyoto the previous year, Dr. Smith had become acquainted with the work of the First Zen Institute of America in Japan, of which I am the Director, and with my long association with Japanese Rinzai Zen.

When I received Dr. Smith's invitation I had only recently returned to the United States after an absence of nearly four years, and was quite unaware of the degree of interest being taken in Zen in the West and even less aware of the various interpretations to which Zen was being subjected and the uses to which it was being put. I was happy, therefore, to have the opportunity Dr. Smith's invitation afforded me of clarifying certain important points in Rinzai Zen and of correcting some of the mistaken views so obviously rife.

The text of my lecture that evening is here reproduced with a minimum of change. . . .

This much I should like to add, however. In Japan today there are two major Zen sects, the Rinzai and the Sōtō. The Rinzai Sect represents the Zen current in the Chinese Lin-chi school of late Sung, at which time (13th century)

---

[1] *Zen: A Method for Religious Awakening*, by Ruth Fuller Sasaki. First Zen Institute of America in Japan, Kyoto, 1959.

it was brought to Japan by a number of Chinese masters and Japanese monks who had studied under Lin-chi masters in China. At that period the *kōan* system, which I have described in the text, had already become the distinguishing teaching method of the Lin-chi school. Present-day masters in Japanese Rinzai Zen, the lineal descendants of those early teachers, in instructing their students continue to use approximately the same method as that used in the Chinese Lin-chi school in the days of Sung.

On the other hand, Japanese Sōtō Zen represents the Ts'ao-tung school of Zen,[2] also current in China in the Sung dynasty. The masters of the Ts'ao-tung school, however, did *not* use the koan as a means of bringing their disciples to enlightenment, but depended almost entirely upon the practice of *zazen* (meditation). The great Japanese priest Dōgen Zenji, after studying under a Ts'ao-tung master in China, brought the method of this school back to Japan, also in the 13th century. Moreover, Dōgen greatly modified both the teaching and the teaching method of the school to accord with his own highly personal views, so that the Japanese Sōtō Zen of today has lost much of its resemblance to the Zen of the Ts'ao-tung Sect in China from which it sprang.

The goals of both the Sōtō and Rinzai sects in Japan today are not different, but the teaching methods in use in the two schools are, and should not be confused. It is in the method of Rinzai Zen that I myself have had many years of training and which I have described in the following text.

I sincerely hope that, after reading this short exposition, much about Rinzai Zen teaching that has seemed difficult to understand may have become somewhat more clear. Other aspects of Zen, including its relationship to Buddhism as a whole, as well as to the Kegon (Hua-yen) school of Chinese Mahayana, have already been taken up in *Zen—A Religion*, an earlier publication of mine which the present lecture in some ways supplements.

Ryōsen-an, Daitoku-ji
Kyoto, Japan
May 15, 1959

I am a Zen Buddhist and have been one for over twenty-five years. So I speak from within Zen, not as one who observes it from the outside. Though brought up in a strict Presbyterian family, I became a Buddhist in my twenties. The study of early Buddhism, into which I soon plunged, brought me to the

---

[2] See Section V, pages 217–219, of this volume. [N. W. R.]

conclusion that the pivot of that religion was Awakening and the Buddhist life a life lived in accordance with Awakening. Meditation was the means through which Śākyamuni, the historical Buddha, had come to his enlightenment. The forty-nine years of his life after his great experience were spent in trying to show other men how they, by following the path he had pursued, might attain this awakening for themselves. Therefore, to find a teacher who could give me correct instruction in how to practice Buddhist meditation became my aim. Also, I wanted to see if meditation methods that eastern people had for centuries found successful would work equally well for a westerner. At forty I first had the privilege of practicing under a famous Rinzai Zen master or *rōshi*, Nanshinken of the Nanzen-ji monastery in Kyoto, Japan. Later, as the obligations of a normal family life permitted, I continued my practice and study in Japan under Nanshinken, and in America under the late Sōkei-an Rōshi. For the past ten years, free of household responsibilities, I have lived almost continuously in Kyoto, devoting myself to Japanese and Chinese language studies as they relate to Zen, and to Rinzai Zen practice under my third Zen teacher, Gotō Zuigan Rōshi. Though I have not yet completed my Zen study, perhaps I can share with you a little of what I have learned. But please do not expect a learned discourse. During these years, I have had little time to keep up with the latest developments in philosophy, psychology, and science. Furthermore, though Zen does not necessarily outlaw books—contrary to what you may have heard about it—gradually I have found that just living life every day, fully and awarely, is so fascinating and rewarding that the majority of books that come my way hold little of interest for me.

Many people say to me, "Zen is so difficult to understand. I have read a lot about it, but, though I think I understand what it's about while I am reading, afterwards I realize I haven't understood at all." Of course there are others who, without having read a single primary Buddhist or Zen text, think they know all about it. How many hours have I not spent in my Kyoto temple listening to people, usually Americans recently come to Japan, tell me just what Zen is. To such visitors I have nothing to say; to those who do not understand, I am always searching for a way to give a clue to what Zen is about.

Perhaps for westerners the primary hindrance in understanding Zen, even intellectually, lies in the fact that the great verities that Zen, with Buddhism, takes as basic are diametrically opposed to those the Hebraic-Christian religions have always assumed to be absolute. It is difficult to put aside one's way of looking at even an inconsequential matter and to observe it from a totally new and different standpoint. How much more difficult to do so with religious concepts and beliefs with which we have been inculcated from earliest childhood. But unless you can put aside your usual viewpoint, you will never be able to understand what Zen is concerned with, and why, and who. Try, now, for a few minutes to clear your minds of all your previously held notions and read what I am going to say with what, in Buddhism, is called a "mirror mind."

Zen does not hold that there is a god apart from the universe who first created this universe and then created man to enjoy, or even master it—and these days it seems not to be enough to master the planet Earth; we must now master the universe as well. Rather, Zen holds that there is no god outside the universe who has created it and created man. God—if I may borrow that word for a moment—the universe, and man are one indissoluble existence, one total whole. Only THIS—capital THIS—is. Anything and everything that appears to us as an individual entity or phenomenon, whether it be a planet or an atom, a mouse or a man, is but a temporary manifestation of THIS in form; every activity that takes place, whether it be birth or death, loving or eating breakfast, is but a temporary manifestation of THIS in activity. When we look at things this way, naturally we cannot believe that each individual person has been endowed with a special and individual soul or self. Each one of us is but a cell, as it were, in the body of the Great Self, a cell that comes into being, performs its functions, and passes away, transformed into another manifestation. Though we have temporary individuality, that temporary, limited individuality is not either a true self or our true self. Our true self is the Great Self; our true body is the Body of Reality, or the Dharmakāya, to give it its technical Buddhist name.

Buddhism, and Zen, grant that this view is not one that can be reasoned about intellectually. Nor, on the other hand, do they ask us to take this doctrine on faith. They tell us it must be experienced, it must be realized. Such realization can be brought about through the awakening of that intuitive wisdom which is intrinsic to all men. The method for awakening this intuitive wisdom is meditation. Zen, among the various schools of Buddhism, is the one which has emphasized over everything else the attainment of this realization in this very body, here and now, and provided a method, tested through the centuries, for accomplishing it.

It is the generally accepted view today that, as far as doctrines are concerned—and, as you see, Zen does have them, contrary to what you may have heard—Zen is developed Mahayana Buddhism as the Chinese mind, steeped in the Chinese world view and classical Taoism, realized it. In fewer words, we might say that Zen is Indian Buddhism dyed with the dye of Chinese Taoism. Japanese Zennists, however, while conceding this, consider Zen to be rather a return to the Buddha's Buddhism. By that they do not mean a return to Hinayana or Theravada Buddhism, the Buddhism of the monkish schools that arose after the Buddha's death, but rather a return to Śākyamuni's basic teaching that every man can and should attain this transforming religious experience of awakening for himself. Śākyamuni, as the embodiment of his total teaching, is the central figure for Japanese Rinzai Zen, and Śākyamuni's image is always the main image in its temples.

From the very beginning of its history the first aim of the followers of the Zen Sect has been the attainment of awakening. The founders of the sect left to other schools the writing of dissertations on methods, descriptions of progressive stages along the way, discussions and treatises on the doctrinal implications of the experience. The old Zen masters said: "Get Awakening yourself! Then you'll know what it is." In other words, if you want to know the taste of water, drink it.

Meditation, the method the Buddha had followed, was the method the old masters of Zen themselves pursued and urged upon their students. It is not too clear whether the meditation practices of developed Chinese Zen were those directly transmitted from Indian teachers to their Chinese disciples, or whether they owe something to the Taoist meditation practices current in China in the earlier days. It has been stated by the eminent scholar Dr. Hu Shih that Chinese Zen discarded the classical sitting meditation of Indian Buddhism as a method of attaining enlightenment, and that Chinese Zen monks practiced, rather, "walking meditation," that is, they preferred to gain their realization through contact with nature on long walking trips from one mountain temple to another and through their sharp verbal give and take with the Zen masters they visited. While I do not deny that Chinese Zen monks were great travellers afoot, my own reading leads me to believe that the younger monks undertook these pilgrimages in order to search for a suitable master, one with whom they had *innen*, as we say in Japan, true rapport or true relationship; and that the older monks set out upon their pilgrimages after they had, or thought they had, attained enlightenment, in order to test their own understanding against that of the famous masters of the day. I am inclined to believe that classical sitting meditation was as basic a practice in Zen throughout its history in China as it is in the monasteries of Japan today.

In the early days of Zen in China, that is, in the seventh and eighth centuries, an enlightened Zen monk would settle himself on a remote mountainside in a little hut, often made by his own hands. There earnest students would seek him out and, having built their own huts close by, pass their days meditating, serving the master, and receiving such instruction as he deigned to give them. As the group of disciples increased in number, permanent buildings to house them would be constructed. Thus a temple was founded. Or, a master accompanied by his immediate disciples would take up residence in some already well-known temple. If he was famous, student-monks would flock from everywhere, their numbers sometimes swelling to two or three thousand. Such a body of monks lived in their own quarters and their mode of life was ordered by fixed rules and regulations. Meditation and physical labor were the main forms of activity. At regular intervals the master gave talks to the monks, talks called in Japanese *jōdō*, meaning literally "ascending the hall." For this talk the master seems to have taken a raised seat in one of the temple halls or in a courtyard. There he discoursed on Buddhism in a decidedly informal way, often employing the colloquial speech of the district. At the conclusion of the talk, the master's own students or a visiting monk would come forward and question him about the problems that troubled them. The ensuing exchange of question and answer between master and monk was known as a *mondō*, literally "question and answer." The mondos seem always to have taken place in the presence of the assembly of the monks. The master appears to have given little private instruction except to his more immediate disciples.

During this jodo or talk, the master was accustomed to hold a stick in his hand, three feet long or thereabouts. This he flourished from time to time to emphasize important points in his sermon. Sometimes he would deal the questioning monk a blow with it. Perhaps he recognized that, through his meditation, the monk had reached a state where his mind was frozen, as we say. At such a moment there is nothing like a good hard whack to break the mental impasse. Perhaps the monk was just plain stupid, or perhaps he was trying to show off before everyone. Then the blow might be given in hope of waking the stupid monk up or to indicate the master's displeasure with the smart aleck.

Far too much has been made of the Zen stick in some western expositions of Zen. In the hands of the old masters it served primarily as a teaching device, as it still does in the hands of the Japanese masters today. As for the long stick held by the head monks as they patrol the meditation hall during the periods of sitting, all practitioners of zazen, or Zen meditation, regard it as the sword of Mañjuśrī, the Bodhisattva who represents the doctrine of intuitive wisdom. After the head monk takes the stick from its customary hook, he bows deeply before the shrine of Mañjuśrī, a shrine in every Zen meditation hall. From that moment on until he bows again and lays the stick on the altar before the Bodhisattva, the head monk represents Mañjuśrī himself. If the head monk must use the stick to rouse a drowsy or inattentive monk, after the blow has been struck both bow politely to one another. There is no personal rancour on the part of him who strikes the blow and only gratitude on the part of him who has been struck.

In the early days of Zen, the monks and laymen who came to the mountain temples to receive instruction from the master had burning spiritual problems to solve. They strove with the greatest ardor to attain awakening. For many the attainment of awakening was a life and death matter and they gave themselves over body and soul to it. The students' zeal and the profound religious understanding of the great masters of T'ang and early Sung produced a body of brilliant mondos, "questions and answers," which cover the entire range of Zen doctrine and experience. These mondos were recorded in writing by the close disciples of the masters, as were also many of the masters' talks and sermons.

But as time went by, the fires of enthusiasm began to die down. Though hundreds and hundreds of monks still surrounded the masters, and laymen in large numbers continued to come for instruction, the urgency to solve spiritual problems came to seem less pressing and the spontaneous exchanges of question and answer took place less often. The masters, their own originality flagging, began to use the sermons and mondos of the great masters of earlier days as texts for their sermons, commenting upon these as they had heard their teachers comment before them. To spur on students who lacked their own strong "spirit of inquiry," the masters gave the old mondos as problems to be solved through meditation. To these were added statements from some of the sutras (scriptures) and stories from the lives of the masters of the past, stories containing seed words or phrases the masters had uttered. Thus was gradually built up a body of "problems for meditation"—in Chinese *kung-an*, in Japanese *kōan*—a large part of which the Japanese Rinzai masters use today with identical intent. At what period the masters ceased instructing their disciples through public interchanges before the assembly of the monks and placed full dependence upon the somewhat artificial device of the koan, I do not know. Today, however, all instruction in Zen takes place in private interviews between the student and the master, and what transpires during *sanzen*, as this interview is called in Japanese, is considered a matter for absolute secrecy on both sides.

The word "koan" was originally a Chinese legal term meaning "case," that is, a legal case that had been decided and thereafter was used as a precedent for decisions in cases of the same kind. In Zen, koans are used both as a means of opening up the student's intuitive mind and as tests of the depth to which it has been opened. Koans are not solvable by the rational mind or intellect. To solve a koan the student, through meditation upon it, a particular kind of meditation we call in Japanese *kufū*, must reach the same level of intuitive understanding as that from which the master spoke the words of the koan. When the student has reached this level of understanding, his understanding and, therefore, his answer to the koan will be approximately the same as that of all the Zen students who have solved it in the past. Each koan has what may be called a "classic" answer. Against this classic answer the master tests the student's answer. When the two agree, the student may be said to have "solved" or "passed" the koan.

Originally there seems to have been little system in the sequence in which koans were given to a student. Each master had mondos and stories that had come down in his teaching line or "house," as it was called, and apparently gave to each student such of these as he felt were needed at the time to awaken or deepen the student's insight. But already in *Mumonkan*, the late Sung collection of koans known to many of you as *The Gateless Gate*, a definite progression is discernible to one who has studied them.

In the Sung period, Japanese Buddhist monks began going to China to study under Zen masters there and Chinese Zen masters began coming to Japan. Both the Chinese masters and the returning Japanese monks brought to Japan with them the koans they had studied under their respective masters, and in their turn used them in instructing their Japanese disciples. Toward the end of the seventeenth century, by which time Japanese Zen had suffered a serious decline, Hakuin Zenji, a brilliant and energetic Japanese Rinzai priest, journeyed from one part of the country to the other, studying under all the remaining authentic teachers the Chinese koans previously transmitted to them. These he made into a collection which he arranged in a systematic progression.

To the perhaps seven or eight hundred Chinese koans he had gathered, Hakuin Zenji added a few of his own making, the only koans in modern use that did not originate with Chinese masters. Hakuin Zenji transmitted these koans to his numerous immediate disciples, and it is they that make up the body of koans used by all Japanese Rinzai masters today. Though present-day Zen roshis do not slavishly follow the order Hakuin Zenji established, since individual students have individual needs and the masters individual preferences, on the whole, koan study today follows the ordered, progressive system handed down from him.

Now who are these Zen masters or teachers and what is the role they have played throughout the long history of Zen and continue to play today? From the very beginning, as strongly as it has emphasized meditation as the basic practice, Zen has emphasized the necessity for the direct transmission from teacher to disciple of the intuitive understanding of THIS. Traditionally it is said that Śākyamuni Buddha transmitted his Dharma—his understanding of THIS or of Ultimate Truth, to use the technical Buddhist term—to his disciple Kāśyapa; Kāśyapa, in his turn, transmitted his understanding to Ānanda, and so on down through a long line of Indian teachers and disciples until, through Bodhidharma, it was eventually transmitted to Hui-nêng (Enō), known as the Sixth Patriarch of Zen in China. Hui-nêng had a number of immediate disciples to whom he transmitted his Dharma. To two of Hui-nêng's Dharma-heirs can be traced back all the major lines of Zen teaching and Zen teachers throughout the history of Chinese and Japanese Zen up to the present day.

What is this transmission? When the disciple has reached the same profound depth of intuitive understanding and realized completely the same deepest truth as his master, when both see inner eye to inner eye, or when they "lock eyebrows together," as the old texts put it, then only does the master put his seal on the disciple's attainment, guarantee it, as it were. And only when the disciple has had his attainment "sealed" is he properly prepared to teach others and may he, in turn, transmit the Dharma to another, "transmit" meaning, of course, "acknowledge the attainment of his disciple."

The same holds true in Japanese Rinzai Zen today. The only person who is considered to be a teacher of Zen is he who has received the authentic transmission from his teacher. Teacher or disciple may be either monk, priest, or layman, provided that the transmission is authentic. In Japan such teachers have the title *rōshi*, "old master." It is such a teacher only who is called a Zen Master. Today, the authentic Zen roshi, or master, guides his students to the experience of awakening by means of koans and the special type of Zen lecture or sermon known as *teishō*. Monks or priests or laymen who have studied and practiced Zen but have not received the transmission, who are not authenticated roshis and therefore never called by the title "Zen Master," often write and lecture and talk about Zen, but they may not give koans to their students or followers. If people go to hear them talk or read what they write, it is with the knowledge that such a person is talking or writing from an incomplete understanding of Zen. So, in Japan today, all men and women who wish to study authentic Zen in the authentic way, study it under a roshi or teacher belonging to a direct line of transmission. It is quite easy to determine who these authentic Zen masters are.

As I have said before, the student may be a monk who hopes to become a temple priest, if not a Zen master; or he may be a layman or laywoman who seeks no more than personal religious experience. Though there may be some difference in details of procedure, the study and practice are identical in every case. I might add that today—and perhaps the same has been true throughout Zen history—not everyone whose understanding of Dharma has been acknowledged by his teacher becomes a roshi or Zen master. Some disciples may have attained true enlightenment yet lack certain qualifications necessary for teaching others. In actual practice, permission to teach koans is a step beyond acknowledgment of attainment, and is a matter on which the teacher has final decision. Not a few persons receive the master's seal on their attainment but do not receive the title of roshi.

Now how does one go about studying and practicing Zen today? A would-be student goes to a Zen roshi, one for whom he has deep respect, in whom he has faith, and with whom he has a distinct feeling of relationship. In a polite and humble manner the student requests to be accepted as a disciple. If the roshi consents, he will turn the student over to his head monk or senior disciple to be instructed in zazen, or meditation practice. The student will be told how to sit and how to breathe; he will be given certain concentration exercises to practice. For a considerable period the student pursues these elementary practices at home several hours a day, or sits with a group of other students who meet for zazen practice at certain specified times. When the head monk or senior disciple decides that the student has acquired a "good seat," that is, can sit in the correct posture for a considerable length of time and is proficient in concentration, he will inform the roshi that the student is now prepared to begin his koan study.

The student then goes to the roshi and, during the private interview known as *sanzen*, an interview conducted in a formal and specifically prescribed manner, the master gives the student a koan which he is now to meditate upon. At definite times from then on the student is expected to go to the roshi for a like interview, and during each interview to express to the master his view at the moment of the inner meaning or content of the koan on which he has been continuously meditating. When the student attains correct insight into the koan, the master, to test his understanding still further, will ask him to bring a word or phrase, preferably from some old Chinese proverb, pithy saying, or poem, that conveys in secular words the inner meaning of the koan. These words or phrases are known in Japanese as *jakugo*. I have yet to find a suitable English word for this expression, though perhaps "capping verse" might do. When the student has brought the correct jakugo—and almost every koan has a fixed jakugo—the master will give him another koan to meditate upon. And thus the student's Zen study will continue—hours and hours of meditation upon koan after koan for years and years. The constant supervision of the master throughout the course of this study assures that the student's own personal views and his mistaken and deluded notions are discarded one by one, for, in order to pass a koan, he must reach the traditionally correct understanding of it. No other understanding is acceptable or accepted. It is undoubtedly due to this teaching method that Rinzai Zen has continued to flow in so pure a stream in spite of the many hands it has passed through in the course of so many centuries.

Since each koan deals with some aspect of Truth as it is held in Zen Buddhism, little by little the student is brought to realize the total of Zen doctrine which is wholly concerned with the THIS, of which I have spoken earlier, and its relative, or manifested, aspects. The doctrines of Zen are not stated specifically either in written or spoken words, but, through long-continued meditation upon the succession of koans, deeper and deeper levels of the student's intuitive mind are opened, levels where these unspoken doctrines are realized as truths. For the Zen master teaches his student nothing. He guides him in such a way that the student finds everything he would learn within his own mind. As an old Chinese saying has it, "The treasures of the house do not come in through the gate." The treasure of Truth lies deep within the mind of each one of us; it is to be awakened or revealed or attained only through our own efforts.

You may be somewhat surprised that I have spoken at such length and not once used the word "*satori.*" This word, I fear, has suffered as much abuse as the word "Zen," and what it connotes and implies has been as much misconstrued. Recently, after a conversation with an American visitor who considered himself a well-informed Zennist, a conversation in which the word "satori" had appeared innumerable times, I said to my old teacher, Gotō Rōshi: "I have studied Zen for nearly thirty years under three Zen masters, and I don't believe I have ever heard any one of them use the word 'satori'." "Well," Rōshi replied, "I doubt if you have ever heard it from my lips."[3]

The Chinese character for "satori" is composed of the character for "mind" and the character for "myself." When "myself" and "mind" are completely united, there is satori. Really, the solution of each and every koan implies a satori. For without becoming one with the koan, without attaining the state of mind of which the koan is an expression, one cannot solve it. To be sure, satori is sometimes experienced without formal meditation upon a koan, or by persons not engaged in Zen study. But every satori is unquestionably the result of the intense occupation of the mind with some deep problem. In the case of Zen students it seems seldom to occur while actually practicing formal meditation; most often it takes place when least expected.

There are, however, greater and lesser satoris. Some of the koans of Zen are great or basic koans, through which realization of great basic truths is attained. The satori that usually accompanies the solution of one of these great koans is termed "Great Satori." Around each of the basic koans are many, what I like to term, satellite koans. Since their underlying truth is the same as that of the great koan with which they are associated, when the great koan has once been realized, the dependent koans can be fairly easily solved. My first teacher, Nanshinken Rōshi, once told me that when, after spending three years of meditation upon his first koan, the koan "MU,"[4] he finally attained the realization of it, he was able to pass through forty minor related koans in a few days.

The attainment of the realization of the first koan is undoubtedly the most difficult and usually takes the longest time to accomplish. Two or three years, or even more, is not unusual. The satori accompanying the realization of this first koan is often so momentous and transforming an experience that many people consider this to be THE satori, the one and only satori, beyond which

---

[3] See, however, pages 41-47 of Section II of this volume. [N. W. R.]

[4] A monk asked Master Jōshū: "Has the dog Buddha-nature or not?" The master answered: "Mu!" *Mumonkan.*

In Japanese "good" is
yoshi and "bad" is *ashi*.
Both these words also
mean reeds or rushes. A
crab is shown walking
along the waterside among
the reeds. The poem says:

SENGAI

"The crab makes his world
The harbor of Naniwa.
And goes sideways
Through the reeds of good and evil."

This would seem to be a play on the idea of the ambivalence of human
beings as compared to the consistent behavior pattern of the crab. (Naniwa
is the old name for Osaka.)

there can be nothing more. How wrong they are! The old masters were constantly inveighing against this idea. Ceaselessly they urged their students to continue on and on. Ta-hui (Daie), a famous master of Sung, used to say: "I have had eighteen great satoris and lost count of all the small satoris I have had." It is only after the first satori that true Zen study may be said to begin. Please do not forget this.

Though you have now heard something about Zen and Zen practice, undoubtedly you still wonder why, through the centuries, people have continued to pursue this curious study. What can they hope to get through all this effort? The classic Zen answer, and the Buddhist answer as well, is "Nothing."

I don't profess to know clearly what is causing so many Americans and Europeans to interest themselves in Zen today. In fact I should like to have someone tell me. I know they are said to be unable to have faith in traditional religious doctrines, to find in scientific materialism poor nourishment for their spirits, to feel that modern life, with its multitude of machines, is an exhausting and unrewarding way of life for them as human beings. And, of course, there are always the few who don't like to conform and who seem to think that perhaps in Zen they will find justification for their own personal interpretations of freedom.

I have indicated to you why I began to study Zen. Certainly, however, many persons in the past and in Japan today, have been driven to this practice by a consuming urge to discover the answers to such difficult and profound questions as: What is the nature of man and of the universe? What is life? What is death? I don't know if you will find satisfactory answers to these problems through Zen or not. Certainly you will not unless, through your Zen practice, through seeing into your own deepest mind, you attain intuitive insight into the THIS within which all the answers lie. . . .

In the course of studying and practicing Zen for a long, long time . . . the small personal self gradually dissolves and one knows no self but the Great Self, no personal will, only the Great Will. One comes to understand the true meaning of the term *wu-wêi*, or in Japanese *mui*, "non-action," for one knows that, as a separate individual, there is nothing further to do. One does not cease to act, but one's actions arise spontaneously out of the eternal flow of the activity of THIS, which one is not only in accord with, but Is. The man of Zen is clearly aware that he is abiding in and will eternally abide in, THIS AS IT IS; that the world in which he is living his everyday life is indeed THIS in its myriads of manifestations, forever changing, forever transforming, but forever

THIS. In the words of the sutras: "Nirvāna is none other than Saṁsāra[5]; Saṁsāra is none other than Nirvāna."

But in Zen, when we must speak, everyday words are preferred to quotations from the scriptures. So, in conclusion, let me put more simply what I have just said. The aim of Zen is first of all awakening, awakening to our true self. With this awakening to our true self comes emancipation from our small self or personal ego. When this emancipation from the personal ego is finally complete, then we know the freedom spoken of in Zen and so widely misconstrued by those who take the name for the experience. Of course, as long as this human frame hangs together and we exist as one manifested form in the world of forms, we carry on what appears to be an individual existence as an individual ego. But no longer is that ego in control with its likes and dislikes, its characteristics and its foibles. The True Self, which from the beginning we have always been, has at last become the master. Freely the True Self uses this individual form and this individual ego as it will. With no resistance and no hindrance it uses them in all the activities of everyday life, whatever they are and wherever they may be. . . .

---

[5] *Saṁsāra* is a Sanskrit word meaning "faring on" or coming-to-be, *i.e.*, the world of becoming or existence here on earth as contrasted to *Nirvāna*, the annihilation of the personal as we understand it. [N. W. R.]

CHAPTER 3

A Few Statements About Zen[1]

By D. T. SUZUKI

(1) Zen discipline aims at attaining enlightenment (or *satori*, in Japanese).

(2) *Satori* finds a meaning hitherto hidden in our daily concrete particular experiences, such as eating, drinking, or business of all kinds.

(3) The meaning thus revealed is not something added from the outside. It is in being itself, in becoming itself, in living itself. This is called, in Japanese, a life of *kono-mama* or *sono-mama*.[2] *Kono-* or *sono-mama* means the "isness" of a thing. Reality in its isness.

(4) Some may say, "There cannot be any meaning in mere isness." But this is not the view held by Zen, for according to it, isness is the meaning. When I see into it I see it as clearly as I see myself reflected in a mirror.

(5) This is what made Hō Koji (P'ang Chü-shih), a lay disciple of the eighth century, declare:

> How wondrous this, how mysterious!
> I carry fuel, I draw water.

The fuel-carrying or the water-drawing itself, apart from its utilitarianism, is full of meaning; hence its "wonder," its "mystery."

(6) Zen does not, therefore, indulge in abstraction or in conceptualization.

---

[1] From *Zen and Japanese Culture*, by D. T. Suzuki. Bollingen Series LXIV. Pantheon Books, New York, 1959.

[2] *Kono* is "this," *sono* "that," and *mama* means "as-it-is-ness." *Kono-mama* or *sono-mama* thus corresponds to the Sanskrit *tathata*, "suchness," and to the Chinese *chih-mo* or *shih-mo*.

In its verbalism it may sometimes appear that Zen does this a great deal. But this is an error most commonly entertained by those who do not at all know Zen.

(7) *Satori* is emancipation, moral, spiritual, as well as intellectual. When I am in my isness, thoroughly purged of all intellectual sediment, I have my freedom in its primary sense.

(8) When the mind, now abiding in its isness . . . and thus free from intellectual complexities and moralistic attachments of every description—surveys the world of the senses in all its multiplicities, it discovers in it all sorts of values hitherto hidden from sight. Here opens to the artist a world full of wonders and miracles.

(9) The artist's world is one of free creation, and this can come only from intuitions directly and immediately rising from the isness of things, unhampered by senses and intellect. He [the artist] creates forms and sounds out of formlessness and soundlessness. To this extent, the artist's world coincides with that of Zen.

(10) What differentiates Zen from the arts is this: While the artists have to resort to the canvas and brush or mechanical instruments or some other mediums to express themselves, Zen has no need of things external, except "the body" in which the Zen-man is so to speak embodied. From the absolute point of view this is not quite correct; I say it only in concession to the worldly way of saying things. What Zen does is to delineate itself on the infinite canvas of time and space the way the flying wild geese cast their shadow on the water below without any idea of doing so, while the water reflects the geese just as naturally and unintentionally.

(11) The Zen-man is an artist to the extent that, as the sculptor chisels out a great figure deeply buried in a mass of inert matter, the Zen-man transforms his own life into a work of creation, which exists, as Christians might say, in the mind of God.

CHAPTER 4

The Religion of Tranquility[1]

By SOKEI-AN

Zen is a religion, but a religion with a unique quality. To understand Zen you must understand this quality.

Zen makes a religion of tranquility. Zen is not a religion which arouses emotions, causing tears to roll from our eyes or stirring us to shout aloud the name of God. When the soul and the mind meet in a perpendicular line, so to speak, in that moment complete unity between the universe and the self will be realized. This realization will brand itself upon our intellect with a brand which, like a secret word, will ever hold our enlightenment.

You do not come to this moment through logic or philosophy. If you come to an understanding of reality by reading, or biting the tip of your pencil, such understanding will not be religion. It is through meditation that what is called, by your [Western] term, Reality is to be realized. To that force we refer all the activities of life. To us this is religion.

Our religion has its own atmosphere. . . . When we come into the meditation hall where all our brothers sit in meditation, we are absorbed into the quietude. Therefore you will find our temples where the music of pine trees is to be heard, or the murmur of running brooks. . . .

You have heard the story of the monk who was cutting the weeds in the garden of a ruined temple. A piece of tile he cast aside struck against a bamboo tree. At the sound he was enlightened. Do you think perhaps you will be en-

---

[1] "The Religion of Tranquility," from *Cat's Yawn*, by Sokei-an. First Zen Institute of America, New York, 1947.

lightened if you strike a chair with your broom-handle while you are sweeping the kitchen floor? You must not forget the quietude of the silent vale between the mountains where this monk had been meditating day and night alone. When the stillness of the valley was rent by the sharp crackle of the tile, in that moment he awakened to his intrinsic wisdom.

These days human beings have forgotten what religion is. They respond to the taste of food, to luxurious living, to beauty, to the drama. They understand science and philosophy, arguing from morning to evening in terms which have been used for generations. They have forgotten a peculiar love which unites their human nature to Great Nature. This love has nothing to do with human love. Standing in the midst of nature you feel this love of Great Nature. Then art becomes sterile, words become dry. Zen students must experience this peculiar love. This is religion.

The Three Types of Religious Method[1]

By SOKEI-AN

There are three devices—three steps—by means of which every religion is explained. And there are three different methods of practice by which religion is comprehended.

The first type employs metaphor. This metaphorical device assumes many different forms. Sometimes it assumes the form of mythology, as in Greek mythology, Japanese Shinto or Mantrayana Buddhism. Christianity also employs the symbolic or dramatic form. It pictures Heaven as a celestial city surrounded by a wall of gold whose great pearly gates are guarded by Saint Peter. A shining golden staircase, upon which angels ascend and descend, leads upward to the throne of God. And on this throne, in the center of Heaven, God is seated with Christ on His right hand. Such an allegory was invented to explain the religion. The explanation, however, is not of itself the religion. What it signifies is the religion.

The second type of device employs not the metaphorical but the philosophical method. This form of representation does not picturesquely arrange heavens and hells, gods and angels. It appeals to man's intellect. He forgets, however, that theology and philosophy are merely devices by means of which he may realize religion, forgets that their purpose is to make him think philosophically in order that by this thinking he may awaken to Reality.

The third type of device is this: to handle Reality Itself, and by handling It to awaken to the state of Reality. It is action, the same kind of direct action as

---

1 "The Three Types of Religious Method," *ibid.*

you use in your daily life. When you are merely hotly discussing with your friend you say, "I will smite you!" But in direct action you hit him without a word.

Bodhidharma employed no reasoning and gave no explanation. To him every act from morning to evening was religion—swallowing water, eating food, sleeping, tending shop, talking to one's neighbors—every act was religion. Action was his way of practice. And you—either you are in this state, or you are not in this state.

But to attain this state we must abandon our customary conception of religion. When we come to this state and are in this state from morning to evening we do not need to explain anything. For that reason Bodhidharma said, "Devise no word!" Men of Zen devise no explanation. As the first act of their daily life they get up and put their feet into their slippers. But to realize this act as religion the mind must be enlightened.

Nansen was a famous Chinese Zen Master. One day he was in the woods near the temple cutting down trees with a huge axe. A monk who had come from a distance to pay homage to the Master passed through the woods and came close to the wood-cutter. "Is the Abbot of Nansen at home?" he asked the wood-cutter. The wood-cutter replied to the monk: "I bought this axe with two pieces of copper." And, lifting the axe above the astonished monk's head, he added, "It is very sharp!" The monk fled in dismay. Later he discovered that the wood-cutter was Nansen himself.

He who truly attains awakening knows that deliverance is to be found right where he is. There is no need to retire to the mountain cave. If he is a fisherman he becomes a real fisherman. If he is a butcher he becomes a real butcher. The farmer becomes a real farmer and the merchant a real merchant. He lives his daily life in awakened awareness. His every act from morning to evening is his religion.

II

THE ESSENCE
OF ZEN

The calligraphy reads:

"The spring color all over the fields."

II THE ESSENCE OF ZEN

CHAPTER 1

The Sense of Zen[1]

By D. T. SUZUKI

Zen in its essence is the art of seeing into the nature of one's own being, and it points the way from bondage to freedom. By making us drink right from the fountain of life, it liberates us from all the yokes under which we finite beings are usually suffering in this world. We can say that Zen liberates all the energies properly and naturally stored in each of us, which are in ordinary circumstances cramped and distorted so that they find no adequate channel for activity.

This body of ours is something like an electric battery in which a mysterious power latently lies. When this power is not properly brought into operation, it either . . . withers away or is warped and expresses itself abnormally. It is the object of Zen, therefore, to save us from going crazy or being crippled. This is what I mean by freedom, giving free play to all the creative and benevolent impulses inherently lying in our hearts. Generally, we are blind to this fact, that we are in possession of all the necessary faculties that will make us happy and loving towards one another. All the struggles that we see around us come from this ignorance. Zen, therefore, wants us to open a "third eye," as Buddhists call it, to the hitherto undreamed-of region shut away from us through our own ignorance. When the cloud of ignorance disappears, the infinity of the heavens is manifested, where we see for the first time into the nature of our own being. We now know the signification of life, we know that it is not blind striving, nor is it a mere display of brutal forces, but that while we know not

---

[1] From *Essays in Zen Buddhism, First Series*, by D. T. Suzuki. Published for the Eastern Buddhist Society, Kyoto, by Luzac and Company, London, 1927.

definitely what the ultimate purport of life is, there is something in it that makes us feel infinitely blessed in the living of it and remain quite contented with it in all its evolution, without raising questions or entertaining pessimistic doubts.

CHAPTER 2

Satori, or Acquiring a New Viewpoint

SUZUKI ON SATORI[1]

The object of Zen discipline consists in acquiring a new viewpoint for looking into the essence of things. If you have been in the habit of thinking logically according to the rules of dualism, rid yourself of it and you may come around somewhat to the viewpoint of Zen. You and I are supposedly living in the same world, but who can tell that the thing we popularly call a stone that is lying before my window is the same to both of us? You and I sip a cup of tea. That act is apparently alike to us both, but who can tell what a wide gap there is subjectively between your drinking and my drinking? In your drinking there may be no Zen, while mine is brimful of it. The reason for it is: you move in a logical circle and I am out of it. Though there is in fact nothing new in the so-called new viewpoint of Zen, the term "new" is convenient to express the Zen way of viewing the world, but its use here is a condescension on the part of Zen.

This acquiring of a new viewpoint in Zen is called *satori* (*wu* in Chinese) and its verb form is *satoru*. Without it there is no Zen, for the life of Zen begins with the "opening of *satori*." *Satori* may be defined as intuitive looking-into, in contradistinction to intellectual and logical understanding. Whatever the definition, *satori* means the unfolding of a new world hitherto unperceived in the confusion of a dualistic mind.

---

[1] From "Satori, or Acquiring a New Viewpoint," in *An Introduction to Zen Buddhism*, by D. T. Suzuki. Eastern Buddhist Society, Kyoto, 1934. Also published for the Buddhist Society of London by Rider and Company, London, 1949.

ALAN WATTS ON SATORI[1]

Satori is a definite experience in so far as the manner of its coming and its effects upon character are concerned; otherwise it is indefinable, for it is the sudden realization of the truth of Zen. Essentially Satori is a sudden experience, and it is often described as a "turning over" of the mind, just as a pair of scales will suddenly turn over when a sufficient amount of material has been poured into one pan to overbalance the weight in the other. Hence it is an experience which generally occurs after a long and concentrated effort to discover the meaning of Zen. Its immediate cause may be the most trivial event, while its effect has been described by Zen masters in the most astonishing terms. A master wrote of his own experience, "It was beyond description and altogether incommunicable, for there was nothing in the world to which it could be compared. . . . As I looked round and up and down, the whole universe with its multitudinous sense-objects now appeared quite different; what was loathsome before, together with ignorance and passions, was seen to be nothing else but the outflow of my own inmost nature, which in itself remained bright, true and transparent." Another wrote, "Whatever doubts and indecisions I had before were completely dissolved like a piece of thawing ice. I called out loudly, 'How wondrous! How wondrous! There is no birth-and-death from which one has to escape, nor is there any supreme knowledge after which one has to strive.' "

Some descriptions are even more vivid than these; in many cases it seemed as though the bottom had fallen out of the universe, as though the oppressiveness of the outer world had suddenly melted like a vast mountain of ice, for Satori is release from one's habitual state of tenseness, of clinging to false ideas of possession. The whole rigid structure which is man's usual interpretation of life suddenly drops to pieces, resulting in a sense of boundless freedom, and the test of true Satori is that he who experiences it has not the slightest doubt as to the completeness of his release. If there is anywhere the least uncertainty, the least feeling of "this is too good to be true," then the Satori is only partial, for it implies the desire to cling to the experience lest it should be lost, and until that desire is overcome the experience can never be complete. The wish to hold fast to Satori, to make sure that one possesses it, kills it in just the same way as it kills every other experience.

---

1 From *The Spirit of Zen*, by Alan Watts. John Murray, Ltd., London, 1948.

HUBERT BENOIT ON SATORI[1]

Behind everything that man experiences there is debated within him the illusory question of his being or his nullity. Man's attention is fascinated by the fluctuations of this dispute, and these appear to him unceasingly important and new; and he is unconscious of the dispute itself and of its constant monotony. Man is attentive to the forms of his psychosomatic states, to their qualitative variations which are always new; he does not see, behind the formal manifestations of his momentary state, the quantitative variations of what we will call the in-formal sensation of his existence. If, at any moment, I wish to perceive, by means of an intuitive inward movement of perfect simplicity, the in-formal impression that I have of existing more or less, I can do so; but as soon as I cease to wish it I cease to do so and my attention is seized once again by formal perceptions. When I voluntarily perceive my in-formal sensation of existing (quantitatively variable), my mind is active concerning the ultimate reality of my condition at the concrete moment that I am living, and then my intellectual centre is insulated, and I experience no emotion. As soon as I cease this voluntary perception, which is unnatural, my intellectual centre ceases to be active, ceases to be insulated, and my emotions begin again.

My in-formal sensation of existing varies quantitatively, from annihilation to exaltation, but without a special effort I do not pay attention to that, though it is nevertheless that which is in question for me in my actual egotistical-dualistic condition. I am attentive to the mental forms which reveal my state, annihilated or exalted.

My mental passivity, seduced and held captive by the forms of my humour, constitutes a non-insulation of this centre which exposes it to emotional short-circuits, to jumps, to agitation (what the Hindus call "the mad monkey").

The man who desires some day to obtain satori should train himself progressively to insulate his intellectual centre in order to protect it against emotional agitation. And he should do so, without eliminating or modifying artificially the circumstances which concern his Ego and which try to move him fully in the course of his natural life as it comes to him. In order to do that he

---

[1] From *The Supreme Doctrine, Psychological Studies in Zen Thought*, by Hubert Benoit. Pantheon Books, New York, 1955.

43

must unceasingly reawaken the possibility that he has (and which tends unceasingly to fall asleep again) of perceiving, beneath the forms pertaining to his states-of-mind, his in-formal sensation, more or less positive or negative, of existing. This attention does not lead to turning his back on concrete egotistical-dualistic life, but, on the contrary, to keeping himself in the very centre of his being, accomplishing it by living it in the motionless inner point at which appears the very first dualism, that of existence—non-existence. When man's attention is fixed exactly on this source of all his agitation, then and then only, tranquility begins for him. When this tranquility is firmly established the inner conditions are at last favourable for the opening of satori in which dualism is conciliated by integrating itself in a ternary synthesis.

It is clearly impossible to describe this presence within oneself which is the immediate and in-formal perception of the degree of existence at the moment, precisely on account of the in-formal character of this perception. Let us suppose that I ask you: "How are you feeling at this moment?" You will ask in reply: "From what point of view? Physically or morally?" I answer: "From all points of view together, how do you feel?" You are silent for a couple of seconds, then you say, for example: "Not so bad," or "So-so," or "Very well," or something else. . . . Of the two seconds during which you were silent the latter does not interest us, for you were using it in order to put into a form of expression your perception of your total state-of-mind; you had then already slipped away from the inner presence which interests us. It is during the first second that you perceived what is really in question for you all the time, and of which you are habitually unconscious, being conscious only of forms which derive from this unconscious perception or of forms in connexion with which this unconscious perception exists. If someone, after having read this, tries to obtain the in-formal perception of which we are speaking, let him beware; there are a thousand ways of believing that one has it, whereas one has it not; in any case the mistake is the same and consists in one complication or another which comprises forms; one is not simple-minded enough. *Informal and immediate perception of existence is the simplest kind of perception there can be.* Correctly carried out it can be obtained in the middle of the most intense external activity and without disturbing that; I do not have to turn away from what I am doing, but rather to feel myself existing in the very centre of the formal world of my activity and of the attention that I pay to it.

HISAMATSU ON SATORI[1]

... The awakening of Zen is *satori* (self-awakening), and the *satori* of Zen is recognizing the real noumenon of a person, his original feature, not necessarily recognizing the real substance of various acts. The *satori* of various acts is simply the *satori* in the domain of specific acts, and not the total and universal *satori* of the person himself. The *satori* of various acts may be unhindered freedom as far as the acts are concerned, and yet not be the unhindered freedom of the person himself. However free one may become in painting, the minor arts, singing and dancing, and archery, this freedom is not in itself the *satori* of Zen. To realize the *satori* of Zen is to become one who is unhinderedly free, released from all chains, one who recognizes himself truly, being no longer attached to the forms of matter and spirit, one who faces the present world of existence and non-existence, life and death, good and evil, pro and con. The *satori* of Zen is not the *satori* of any particular act of a person, but the *satori* of the original self of a person, regardless of who he is. It is not the *satori* of the visible and special phenomena, but the *satori* of the original, formless, undifferentiated, and noumenal self.

To explain with an analogy, the *satori* of various acts is like an individual wave awakening to the individual origin of the wave, and though it may be the origin, it is simply the individual phenomenal origin. This kind of *satori* is no release from the phenomenon of the wave. The *satori* of Zen is like all individual waves awakening to water, their noumenal origin. Water is the noumenon of all individual waves; water is the original feature of waves. Water raises all waves and goes over all waves, and water raises the waves and goes over them at the same time. There are many different kinds of waves, different forms, but water has neither form nor difference; water is homogeneous and formless and yet the origin of waves of all forms. . . . Waves form and vanish, but water is eternal and indestructible, and it remains so even when it appears and disappears. . . .

... The masters of various acts in Japan turned to Zen in order to free themselves in their acts, to pass beyond the boundaries of their acts. . . . When various acts are performed, and yet remain various acts, this is not the attitude of Zen: there is no freedom in them. The freedom of Zen is the freedom of water to wave and not the freedom of wave to wave.

---

[1] From "Zen and the Various Acts," by Shinichi Hisamatsu (Hoseki), translated from the Japanese by Hyung Woong Pak. *Chicago Review*, Volume 12, Number 2, Summer 1958.

CHRISTMAS HUMPHREYS ON SATORI[1]

. . . I was having tea alone with the cat on my lap, and a "tea-time" programme on the wireless to relax my mind after a session of writing this book. I suddenly felt very happy, an unusual state in my intensely active and imaginative mind, then, as it were, I felt about me a steadily rising tide of enormous joy. I wanted to sing, or to dance to the music. The warmth of the tide was glorious, as of a huge affectionate flame. I remained intellectually conscious; that is, I was critical of my own condition, considering it, comparing it, wondering what it might mean. Never before had I attained this discriminate consciousness which functions on a plane where all discrimination seemed absurd. Then the tide ebbed slowly and I was left exhilarated, rested, refreshed.

A far more prolonged experience took place in Kyoto. I went for the weekend from my work in Tokyo, and only on a return visit a fortnight later did I realize the condition of mind in which I had spent the entire week-end. It was the climax of an attempt to draw together various Japanese sects on the "Twelve Principles of Buddhism," the birth of which I described in *Via Tokyo*. I was probably worked up to the importance of the occasion, but when I arrived at the all-important meeting, and was faced with fifty distinguished Buddhist abbots and monks from all over Japan, I suddenly dropped all mental content, all emotion, and sat, without thinking what I was to say, in a state of almost absurd serenity. I was no longer interested in results, nor anxious, nor proud, nor at all concerned with self. I was utterly happy, perfectly serene, and above all magnificently certain. I *knew* what I had to say and do; I *knew* that it was right. I felt but a cog in an infinitely complex process of becoming, wherein I just played what I knew to be my part. There was neither emotion nor thought; all differences were healed in wholeness. There was a light within me as well as the sunlight filtering through the bamboo curtains onto the golden floor. When I spoke, I am told that I spoke "as one having authority." In the end all agreed to what I had asked, but I did not react to any victory. I just went on to the next appointment, a pleasant dinner with friends which I enjoyed enormously. Only a fortnight later, when I met the same group of men and tried to settle details with them, did I find that I was arguing. The vision was gone, and with it the certainty. I was back in the world of the opposites and I was on one side.

---

[1] From *Zen Buddhism*, by Christmas Humphreys. William Heinemann, Ltd., London, 1949.

A third type of experience, and indeed my first, had no immediate "background" and I was in fact in a Turkish bath. Suddenly, as I lay at physical and mental ease, there was a blinding flash of vision, a lightning flash that "held" for several seconds of time. I understood at last, completely and beyond all argument, the whole problem of self and selfishness, of suffering and the cause of suffering, of desire and the ending of desire. Like a fool I tried to explain the vision to myself, and of course it fled.

None of these examples, of famous men or my own, has any concern with God. Satori is utterly impersonal, draws all its powers under a central wing and stands like a rock on its own foundation. It is sufficient unto itself, its own authority. It is utterly here and now and "this," and takes no thought for the morrow. Without any sense of separateness there is no need of benevolence, or of love for one's fellow men. When I and my Father are one, why seek that One?

CHAPTER 3

The Koan[1]

By D. T. SUZUKI

Zen is a unique product of the Oriental mind and its uniqueness consists, as far as its practical aspect goes, in its methodical training of the mind in order to mature it to the state of *satori* when all its secrets are revealed. Zen may be called a form of mysticism, but it differs from all other forms of it in system, in discipline, and in final attainment. By this I mean principally the *koan* exercise and *zazen*.

Zazen, or its Sanskrit equivalent *dhyana*, means sitting cross-legged in quietude and in deep contemplation. The practice originated in India and spread all over the East. It has been going on through centuries now, and the modern followers of Zen still strictly observe it. In this respect *zazen* is the prevailing practical method of spiritual discipline in the East, but when it is used in connection with the *koan* it assumes a special feature and becomes the monopoly of Zen.

. . . .

. . . *Zazen* as practised by Zen devotees has not the same object in mind as is the case with Buddhists generally. In Zen, *dhyana* or *zazen* is used as the means of reaching the solution of the *koan*. Zen does not make *dhyana* an end in itself, for apart from the *koan* exercise, the practising of *zazen* is a secondary consideration. It is no doubt a necessary accompaniment to the mastery of Zen; even when the *koan* is understood, its deep spiritual truth will not be

---

[1] From Chapter VIII, *An Introduction to Zen Buddhism*, by D. T. Suzuki. Eastern Buddhist Society, Kyoto, 1934. Also published for the Buddhist Society of London, by Rider and Company, London, 1949.

driven home to the mind of the Zen student if he is not thoroughly trained in *zazen*. *Koan* and *zazen* are the two handmaids of Zen; the first is the eye and the second is the foot.

. . . .

Ko-an literally means "a public document" or "authoritative statute"—a term coming into vogue towards the end of the T'ang dynasty. It now denotes some anecdote of an ancient master, or a dialogue between a master and monks, or a statement or question put forward by a teacher, all of which are used as the means for opening one's mind to the truth of Zen. In the beginning, of course, there was no *koan* as we understand it now; it is a kind of artificial instrument devised out of the fullness of heart by later Zen masters, who by this means would force the evolution of Zen consciousness in the minds of their less endowed disciples.

. . . .

At the beginning, a Zen master was a kind of self-made man, he had no school education, he had not been sent to college to pass through a certain course of studies, but out of an inner impelling necessity which stirred up his spirit, he could not help going about and picking up whatever knowledge he needed. He was perfected by himself. Of course he had a teacher but the teacher did not help him in the way scholars nowadays are helped—helped too frequently, indeed, beyond the actual needs of the disciple, more than is really good for him. This lack of soft education made the ancient Zen master all the stronger and more full of virility. This was the reason why, in those early days of Zen, that is, during the T'ang dynasty, it was so active, so brilliant, so intense. . . .

Here . . . is one of the first *koans* given to latter-day students. When the Sixth Patriarch was asked by the monk Myo (Ming) what Zen was, he said: "When your mind is not dwelling on the dualism of good and evil, what is your original face before you were born?" (Show me this "face" and you get into the mystery of Zen. Who are you before Abraham was born?[2] When you have had a personal, intimate interview with this personage, you will better know who you are and who God is. The monk is here told to shake hands with this original man, or, if metaphysically put, with his own inner self.)

When this question was put to the monk Myo, he was already mentally ready to see into the truth of it. The questioning is merely on the surface, it is really an affirmation meant to open the mind of the listener. The Patriarch

---

[2] This is a reference to the cryptic saying of Christ: "Before Abraham was, I am." [N. W. R.]

noticed that Myo's mind was on the verge of unfolding itself to the truth of Zen. The monk had been groping in the dark long and earnestly; his mind had become mature, so mature indeed that it was like a ripe fruit which only required a slight shaking to cause it to drop on the ground; his mind only required a final touch by the hand of the master. The demand for "the original face" was the last finish necessary, and Myo's mind instantly opened and grasped the truth. But when this statement in the form of a question about "the original face" is given to a novice, who has had no previous discipline in Zen as Myo had, it is usually given with the intention to awaken the student's mind to the fact that what he has so far accepted as a commonplace fact or as a logical impossibility, is not necessarily so, and that his former way of looking at things was not always correct or helpful to his spiritual welfare. After this is realised, the student might dwell on the statement itself and endeavour to get at its truth if it has any. To force the student to assume this inquiring attitude is the aim of the *koan*. The student must then go on with his inquiring attitude until he comes to the edge of a mental precipice, as it were, where there are no other alternatives but to leap over. This giving up of his last hold on life will bring the student to a full view of "his original face," as desired by the statement of the Sixth Patriarch. Thus it can be seen that the *koan* is not handled now in precisely the same way that it was in those earlier days. As first proposed, it was the culmination, so to speak, of all that had been working in the mind of the monk Myo, whose elaboration herein received its final finish; instead of coming at the beginning of the Zen exercise, as it does now, the Sixth Patriarch's question came at the end of the race. But in modern days the *koan* is used as a starter; it gives an initial movement to the racing for Zen experience. More or less mechanical in the beginning, the movement acquires the tone needed for the maturing of Zen consciousness; the *koan* works as a leaven. When the sufficient conditions obtain, the mind unfolds itself into the full bloom of a *satori*. To use a *koan* thus instrumentally for the opening of the mind to its own secrets, is characteristic of modern Zen.

Hakuin used to produce one of his hands and demand of his disciples to hear the sound of it. Ordinarily a sound is heard only when two hands are clapped, and in that sense no possible sound can come from one hand alone. Hakuin wants, however, to strike at the root of our everyday experience, which is constructed on a so-called scientific or logical basis. This fundamental overthrowing is necessary in order to build up a new order of things on the basis of Zen experience. Hence this apparently most unnatural and therefore illogical demand made by Hakuin on his pupils. The former *koan* was about "the face," something to look at, while the latter is about "the sound," something that appeals to the sense of hearing; but the ultimate purport of both is the same; both are meant to open up the secret chamber of the mind, where the devotees can find numberless treasures stored. The sense of seeing or hearing has nothing to do with the essential meaning of the *koan;* as the Zen masters say, the *koan* is only a piece of brick used to knock at the gate, an index-finger pointing at the moon. It is only intended to synthesise or transcend—whichever expression you may choose—the dualism of the senses. So long as the mind is not free to perceive a sound produced by one hand, it is limited and is divided against itself. Instead of grasping the key to the secrets of creation, the mind is hopelessly buried in the relativity of things, and, therefore, in their superficiality. Until the mind is free from the fetters, the time never comes for it to view the whole world with any amount of satisfaction. The sound of one hand as a matter of fact reaches the highest heaven as well as the lowest hell, just as one's original face looks over the entire field of creation even to the end of time. Hakuin and the Sixth Patriarch stand on the same platform with their hands mutually joined.

To mention another instance. When Joshu was asked about the significance of Bodhidharma's coming east (which, proverbially, is the same as asking about the fundamental principal of Buddhism), he replied: "The cypress-tree in the courtyard."

"You are talking," said the monk, "of an objective symbol."

"No, I am not talking of an objective symbol."

"Then," asked the monk again, "what is the ultimate principle of Buddhism?"

"The cypress-tree in the courtyard," again replied Joshu.

This is also given to a beginner as a *koan*.

Abstractly speaking, these *koans* cannot be said to be altogether nonsensical even from a common-sense point of view, and if we want to reason about them there is perhaps room enough to do so. For instance, some may regard Hakuin's one hand as symbolising the universe or the unconditioned, and Joshu's cypress-tree as a concrete manifestation of the highest principle, through which the pantheistic tendency of Buddhism may be recognised. But to understand the *koan* thus intellectually is not Zen, nor is such metaphysical symbolism at all present here. Under no circumstances ought Zen to be confounded with philosophy; Zen has its own reason for standing for itself and

51

this fact must never be lost sight of; otherwise, the entire structure of Zen falls to pieces. The "cypress-tree" is forever a cypress-tree and has nothing to do with pantheism or any other ism. Joshu was not a philosopher even in its broadest and most popular sense; he was a Zen master through and through, and all that comes forth from his lips is an utterance directly ensuing from his spiritual experience. Therefore, apart from this much of "subjectivism," though really there are no such dualities in Zen as subject and object, thought and the world, the "cypress-tree" utterly loses its significance. If it is an intellectual or conceptual statement, we may endeavour to understand its meaning through the ratiocinative chain of ideas as contained in it, and we may come to imagine that we have finally solved the difficulty; but Zen masters will assure you that even then Zen is yet three thousand miles away from you, and the spirit of Joshu will be heard laughing at you from behind the screen, which you had after all failed to remove. The *koan* is intended to be nourished in those recesses of the mind where no logical analysis can ever reach. When the mind matures so that it becomes attuned to a similar frame to that of Joshu, the meaning of the "cypress-tree" will reveal itself. . . .

. . . .

The *koans*, therefore, as we have seen, are generally such as to shut up all possible avenues to rationalisation. After a few presentations of your views in the interview with the master, which is technically called *san-zen*, you are sure to come to the end of your resources, and this coming to a *cul-de-sac* is really the true starting point in the study of Zen. No one can enter into Zen without this experience. When this point is reached, the *koans* may be regarded as having accomplished half of the object for which they stand.

To speak conventionally—and I think it is easier for the general reader to see Zen thus presented—there are unknown recesses in our minds which lie beyond the threshold of the relatively-constructed consciousness. To designate them as "sub-consciousness" or "supra-consciousness" is not correct. The word "beyond" is used simply because it is a most convenient term to indicate their whereabouts. But as a matter of fact there is no "beyond," no "underneath," no "upon" in our consciousness. The mind is one indivisible whole and cannot be torn in pieces. The so-called *terra incognita* is the concession of Zen to our ordinary way of talking, because whatever field of consciousness is known to us is generally filled with conceptual riffraff, and to get rid of it, which is absolutely necessary for maturing Zen experience, the Zen psychologist sometimes points to the presence of some inaccessible region in our minds. Though in actuality there is no such region apart from our everyday consciousness, we talk of it as generally more easily comprehensible by us. When the *koan* breaks down all the hindrances to the ultimate truth, we all realise that there are after all no such things as "hidden recesses of mind" . . . .

The *koan* is neither a riddle nor a witty remark. It has a most definite objective, the arousing of doubt and pushing it to its furthest limits. A statement built upon a logical basis is approachable through its rationality; whatever doubt or difficulty we may have had about it dissolves itself by pursuing the natural current of ideas. All rivers are sure to pour into the ocean; but the *koan* is an iron wall standing in the way and threatening to overcome one's every intellectual effort to pass. When Joshu says, "the cypress-tree in the courtyard" or when Hakuin puts out his one hand, there is no logical way to get around it. You feel as if your march of thought had been suddenly cut short. You hesitate, you doubt, you are troubled and agitated, not knowing how to break through the wall which seems altogether impassable. When this climax is reached, your whole personality, your inmost will, your deepest nature, determined to bring the situation to an issue, throws itself with no thought of self or no-self, of this or that, directly and unreservedly against the iron wall of the *koan*. This throwing your entire being against the *koan* unexpectedly opens up a hitherto unknown region of the mind. Intellectually, this is the transcending of the limits of logical dualism, but at the same time it is a regeneration, the awakening of an inner sense which enables one to look into the actual working of things. For the first time, the meaning of the *koan* becomes clear and in the same way that one knows that ice is cold and freezing. The eye sees, the ear hears, to be sure, but it is the mind as a whole that has *satori;* it is an act of perception, no doubt, but it is a perception of the highest order. Here lies the value of the Zen discipline, as it gives birth to the unshakable conviction that there is something indeed going beyond mere intellection.

The wall of *koan* once broken through and the intellectual obstructions well cleared off, you come back, so to speak, to your everyday relatively-constructed consciousness. The one hand does not give out a sound until it is clapped by the other. The cypress-tree stands straight before the window; all human beings have the nose vertically set and the eyes horizontally arranged. Zen is now the most ordinary thing in the world. A field that we formerly supposed lay far beyond is now found to be the very field in which we walk, day in, day out. When we come out of *satori*, we see the familiar world with all its multitudinous objects and ideas together with their logicalness, and pronounce them "good."

• • • • • • • • •

One may say, "If Zen is really so far beyond the intellectual ken as you claim it to be, there ought not to be any system in it; in fact there could not be any, for the very conception of a system is intellectual. To be thoroughly consistent, Zen should remain a simple absolute experience excluding all that savours of process or system or discipline. The *koan* must be an excrescence, a superfluity, indeed a contradiction." Theoretically, or rather from the absolute point of view, this is quite correct; therefore, when Zen is asserted "straightforwardly" it recognizes no *koan* and knows of no roundabout way of proclaiming itself. Just a stick, a fan, or a word! Even when you say, "It is a stick," or "I hear a sound," or "I see the fist," Zen is no more there. It is like a flash of lightning, there is no room, no time in Zen even for a thought to be conceived. We speak of a *koan* or a system only when we come to the practical or conventional side of it. As has been said before, it is really a condescension, an apology, a compromise, that this present work has been written; much more the whole systematisation of Zen.

To outsiders, this "systematisation" appears to be no systematisation, for it is full of contradictions and even among the Zen masters themselves there is a great deal of discrepancy, which is quite disconcerting. What one asserts another flatly denies or makes a sarcastic remark about it, so that the uninitiated are at a loss what to make out of all these everlasting and hopeless entanglements. But the fact is that Zen really ought not to be considered from its surface; such terms as system, rationality, consistency, contradiction, or discordance belong to the surface of Zen; to understand Zen we are to turn up the whole piece of brocade and examine it from the other side, where we can trace at a glance all the intricacies of woof and warp. This reversing of the order is very much needed in Zen.

• • • • • • • • •

For the benefit of students who wish to know more about the *koans* which are given to Zen students for solution, a few of them are given here. When Kyosan received a mirror from Yisan, he brought it out before an assemblage of monks and said: "O monks, Yisan has sent here a mirror; shall it be called Yisan's or mine? If you call it mine, how is it that it comes from Yisan? If you call it Yisan's, how do you account for its being in my hands? If you can make a statement that hits the mark, the mirror will be retained; if you cannot, it will be broken in pieces." This he declared three times and as nobody came forward to make a statement the mirror was destroyed.

Tozan came to Ummon for instruction; the latter asked:

"Where do you come from?"

"From Sato."

"Where have you spent the summer?"

"At Hoji of Konan."

"When did you leave there?"

"On the twenty-fifth of the eighth month."

Ummon suddenly raised his voice and said: "I spare you thirty blows. You may now retire."

In the evening Tozan went to Ummon's room and asked what his fault was, so grave as to deserve thirty blows. Said the master, "Is this the way you wander all over the country? O you rice-bag!"

Yisan was having a nap, when Kyosan came in. Hearing the visitor, Yisan turned about towards the wall.

Said Kyosan: "I am your disciple, no formality is needed."

The master made a movement as if he were awakening from sleep, Kyosan started to leave the room, but the master called him back. Said Yisan, "I am going to tell you about my dream."

Kyosan leaned forward as if listening.

Yisan said, "You guess."

Kyosan went out and brought a basin filled with water and a towel. With the water the master washed his face but before he had resumed his seat another monk Kyogen came in. The master said: "We have been performing a miracle—and not a trivial one at that."

Kyogen replied: "I have been below and know all that has been going on between you."

"If so, tell me how it is," demanded the master.

Kyogen then brought him a cup of tea.

Yisan remarked, "O you two monks, what intelligent fellows you are! Your wisdom and miraculous deeds indeed surpass those of Sariputra and Maudgalyayana!"

Sekiso (Shih-shuang) died and his followers thought that the head-monk ought to succeed him. But Kyuho (Chiu-feng), who had been an attendant to the late master, said: "Wait, I have a question, and the successor ought to be able to answer it. The old master used to teach us thus: 'Stop all your hankerings; be like cold ashes and withered plants; keep the mouth tightly closed until mould grows about it; be like pure white linen, thoroughly immaculate; be as cold and dead as a censer in a deserted shrine.' How is this to be understood?"

"This," said the head-monk, "illustrates a state of absolute annihilation."

"There, he utterly fails to grasp the meaning."

"Do I? If so, have an incense stick lighted; if I do not really understtand the old master, I shall not be able to enter into a trance before the stick burns up."

So saying the head-monk fell into a state of unconsciousness from which he never arose. Stroking the back of his departed fellow-monk, Kyuho said: "As to getting into a trance you have shown a splendid example, but as to understanding the old master you have just the same significantly failed." This well illustrates the fact that Zen is entirely different from being absorbed in nothingness.

The number of *koans* is traditionally estimated at 1,700, which, however, is a very generous way of counting them. For all practical purposes, less than ten, or even less than five, or just one may be sufficient to open one's mind to the ultimate truth of Zen. A thoroughgoing enlightenment, however, is attained only through the most self-sacrificing application of the mind, supported by an inflexible faith in the finality of Zen. It is not to be attained by merely climbing up the gradation of the *koans* one after another as is usually practised by followers of the Rinzai school. The number really has nothing to do with it; the necessary requirements are faith and personal effort, without which Zen is mere babble. Those who regard Zen as speculation and abstraction will never obtain the depths of it, which can be sounded only through the highest will-power. There may be hundreds of *koans*, or there may be an infinite number of them as there are infinite numbers of objects filling up the universe, but it does not necessarily concern us. Only let one gain an all-viewing and entirely satisfying insight into the living actuality of things and the *koans* will take care of themselves.

This is where lurks the danger of the *koan* system. One is apt to consider it as everything in the study of Zen, forgetting the true object of Zen which is the unfolding of a man's inner life.

CHAPTER 4

Two from Twenty-five Koans[1]

REPOSE OF MIND

By SOKEI-AN

When Bodhidharma came to China the scholastic philosophy of Buddhism was at the height of its development. In southern China the Buddhist Emperor, Liang Wu-ti, was building many temples and monasteries and supporting many monks and nuns. His capital was Kenko (Chien K'ang), the present-day Nanking.

In northern China also Buddhism was active. Bearing their precious manuscripts, many teachers of Buddhism had already come by the northern route: over the Pamir plateau, through Chinese Turkestan, across the desert, and along the course of the Yellow River down to the city of Loyang, at the eastern bend of the Yellow River. Loyang was the capital of the country of Wei, and at that time was also a center of culture and of Buddhist activities.

Bodhidharma came by sea from southern India. He landed at Canton, and came up to Kenko (Nanking) where he met the Emperor Wu-ti, with whom he had a conversation about Buddhism. The Emperor said to Bodhidharma, "I am building many monasteries and supporting many monks. What merit shall I gain?"

Bodhidharma answered, "In a word, no merit!"

The Emperor failed to understand his words. Bodhidharma left the country, crossed the Yangtze River and went north to the country of Wei. This was

---

[1] From "Twenty-five Koans," in *Cat's Yawn*, by Sokei-an. First Zen Institute of America, New York, 1947.

a period of revolution. Furthermore, the court at Loyang was swarming with Hindu monks, and Bodhidharma found himself an unwelcome stranger there. He left the city of Loyang and went to the temple of Shorin, situated on Mount Su (Sung Shan).

Bodhidharma realized that scholastic and philosophical Buddhism had become dominant in China, and that the scholars of Buddhism had failed to grasp the reality of Buddhism. He was convinced that he must promulgate Buddhist Realism. This could not be conveyed in lectures, so he demonstrated it with his body.

Opposite Shorin Temple is a high cliff known as Shoshitsu Mountain. Bodhidharma took up his abode in a cave facing this cliff. For nine years he sat gazing at the face of this cliff and speaking no word to his visitors. The Chinese dubbed him the "Wall-gazing Brahmin." Day and night he sat meditating in the cross-legged posture.

. This meditation was not what is commonly conceived of as meditation, thinking of something far away. Bodhidharma was not intoxicated by the brew of human thoughts. His mind was pure as the empty ocean; it was realistic emptiness. The monks of the capital were engaged in translating sutras and in debating hair-splitting points of doctrine, elevating their minds with merely theoretical knowledge. The Buddhism which came from India at that time was like that, for the true Buddhism had died out in India a long time since. It was fortunate that Bodhidharma should have brought the true Buddhism to China; otherwise there would not be anything called Buddha-Mind among us today!

There was a famous scholar of Loyang, a student of Taoism and Confucianism, named Eka. He had heard of Bodhidharma, so he went to Shorinji to have an interview with him. Bodhidharma spoke no word to the visitor. So Eka went down the mountain.

Three years later he climbed the mountain again. It was mid-winter. Bodhidharma was meditating in the temple cave. Think of the strength of the monks of those days—what hardships they endured! Bodhidharma spoke no word, but remained in meditation.

Eka stood in the snow, waiting for Bodhidharma to speak. But Bodhidharma paid no attention to him: Eka was no more to him than a tree or a rock.

All night Eka stood in the snow. In the morning he was buried to his waist in the drifts, but still he stood there, intent upon asking Bodhidharma for the true teachings!

SENGAI

This is an illustration of a famous Zen poem taken from the *Questions and Answers in Zen*, by Fudaishi (d. 569 A.D.).

The calligraphy reads:

"He creeps along the log
  in fear and trembling,
He does not know that
  the bridge is flowing
  and the water is not."

These lines refer to the famous *gatha* of Fudaishi:

"Empty-handed I go, and behold the spade is in my hands;
I walk on foot, and yet on the back of an ox I am riding.
When I pass over the bridge, Lo, the water floweth not,
But the bridge doth flow."

Of these lines it has been said, "Those who desire to gain an insight into the truth of Zen, must first understand what this stanza really means."

Realizing the stranger's honest desire, in compassion Bodhidharma said to him, "Standing in the deep snow, what is it that you wish?"

Eka replied, "I beseech you, O Master, open your lips and bestow upon me your pure Dharma!"

The Master said, "So you are seeking the true Dharma! From ancient days monks have cast away their lives for true enlightenment. It is difficult to find. How dare you ask me to teach it to you!"

Eka drew his heavy dagger, cut off his left arm and presented it to the Master. "Thus I prove my sincerity!" he said.

This incident is described in the scriptures, but many students of the Zen school do not accept this cutting off the arm in the literal sense. "To cut off" is interpreted as casting aside all traditional methods for arriving at the final truth. Bodhidharma realized that Eka's mind was ready to accept his instruction and that he was capable of becoming a utensil of Dharma. Therefore he said to Eka, "Well then, what do you wish?"

Whereupon Eka spoke thus, "My mind has not yet found repose. I entreat you, Master, show me how I may attain repose of mind."

The Japanese word *anshin* is translated as "repose of mind," but its meaning is broader than that of the English words. *Shin* means "soul," "spirit" or "mind." To obtain absolute relaxation, to attain absolute freedom by the annihilation of every sort of agitation—this is *anshin*. *Anshin* is the foundation of life. Without it we cannot live one moment in joy. If we attain it we can live in repose under any circumstances.

Eka had been an earnest student of Confucianism and Taoism for many years, but he had not been able to find complete repose. He had visited many teachers, but something was not yet quite clear to him. There were still some doubts in the bottom of his mind. As long as you have that uneasiness, as an artist you cannot create, as a warrior you cannot fight, as a scholar you cannot teach, as a priest you cannot convince your fellow men. No matter how you act, if you have no repose of mind a true man will find you out. Eka was an honest student and admitted at once that he had some doubts.

The Master answered, "Lay your mind before me. I will repose your mind for you."

"Lay your mind before me"—in a word, "show me your mind." There is the Realist speaking! "You speak many things. I have heard many words. But show me THAT!"

There is a very expressive American slang phrase, "I come from Missouri—

you've got to show me!" In Zen we do not accept any speaking in terms.

Thus Bodhidharma said, "Show me your mind!"

Eka replied, "It is impossible for one to lay hold of one's mind."

The Master said, "I have already reposed your mind for you."

"I have already reposed your mind for you"—this is the koan. Of course the answer—how to handle this in the Zen school—is not written in any book, and a Zen monk will speak no more than this.

I have stirred up dust a plenty, and given legs to the snake that had no need of them. So I shall stir up no more dust.

THE CLATTER OF A BROKEN TILE

By SOKEI-AN

One day Chikan Zenji of Kyogen was mowing down the weeds around a ruined temple. When he threw away a bit of broken tile it clattered against a bamboo tree. All of a sudden he was enlightened. Whereat he extolled his attainment in this poem:

> "Upon the clatter of a broken tile
> All I had learned was at once forgotten.
> Amending my nature is needless;
> Pursuing the tasks of everday life
> I walk along the ancient path.
> I am not disheartened in the mindless void.
> Wheresoever I go I leave no footprint,
> For I am not within color or sound.
> Enlightened ones everywhere have said,
> 'Such as this is The Attainment.' "

KATTOSHU

Chikan Zenji of Kyogen was a native of Seishu (Ching Chou). Abhorring the layman's life he left his home, and since he was very honest in his desire to learn Buddhism he directed his steps toward I-san in Tanshu (Tan Chou), where he dwelt with the monks.

Having noticed that Chikan was capable of being a vessel of Dharma and hoping that his wisdom would be kindled and intensified, the Master of I-san said to him one day:

"I am not questioning you about your everyday learning or about your knowledge of the scriptures. But tell me, in a word, what were you when you were still in your mother's bosom and were ignorant of any direction, east or west, north or south? If you can answer this I shall bestow upon you my seal of acknowledgment as a token of the genuineness of your attainment."

This question of the Master of I-san was the first cause of Chikan's later enlightenment. Now, however, he stood disconcerted, trying his best to find some word with which to reply. He struggled with the question and made several answers, but the Master rejected them all. At last in despair he cried:

"I pray you, Osho, tell me some word about it!"

The Master said: "If I told you a word about it, that would be my understanding. Your answer must come from your own understanding. My giving you of my knowledge would avail you nothing."

Chikan returned from the Master's room and retreated within himself. Then, as you all know, he opened this book and opened that book. He searched through all the sutras, through the five thousand and forty-eight volumes of Buddhist canonical scriptures. But he never sought the answer in his own heart. I have those sutras in five thousand and forty-eight volumes there on my shelves, but nowadays no one monk can read them all in a lifetime.

At last Chikan sighed, "Pictured food cannot satisfy one's hunger. These scriptures are merely pictures of food." So he set fire to the canons and burned them.

"Hereafter I will learn no more Buddhism," he said. "I will be a monk who meditates all his life long. I will sustain myself by begging gruel and allow my mind to rest from toil."

Then he went sobbing down the mountain. Crossing the Yangtze River he wandered northward until he came one day to Nanyo (Nanyang) where the ruins of Chu Kokushi's old memorial pagoda and temple were still standing. Chu Kokushi (d. 775 A.D.) had been one of the disciples of the Sixth Patriarch. Chikan Zenji was a contemporary of Rinzai (d. 868 A.D.). So Chikan must have lived about two generations later than Chu Kokushi.

Knowing that Chu Kokushi—the teacher of the Emperor was called Kokushi or National Teacher—had attained his enlightenment without any teacher, Chikan decided to stay alone in this ruined temple. Today in India you will still come across these strange monks, at Buddhagaya for instance, sometimes sweeping the ground and sometimes meditating. Some are Japanese, some are Chinese. And in China you will see before the gateways of the temples monks sitting on the bare ground meditating day and night. This has been the attitude of the Buddhist monk from Sakyamuni's time until today. We know that enlightenment cannot be taught in schools.

Chikan worked very busily, as you know, cutting the weeds and sweeping the ground. He was not asleep in his meditation! In the everyday task of life he was going along the ancient path. This is the true way of practicing Zen. Then casually he threw away a piece of broken tile. It made a sound, KLANK! against a bamboo tree. Chikan's mind was suddenly opened. It was as if he had found moonlight in the hollow sea, was it not?

He went back to his hut and washed his body. Burning incense and bowing down in the direction of I-san, he paid homage to the Master through the distance, saying:

"O Osho, your great compassion was more than that of father and mother! If you had told me a word for my sake, this would not have happened to me to-day."

Then spontaneously he recited a poem. It is impossible to translate this old Tang Dynasty poetry word for word, but I shall try to describe in my commentary what I have failed to give in the translation.

> "Upon the clatter of a broken tile
> All I had learned was at once forgotten."

When Chikan attained realization all the knowledge he had previously learned became unimportant, just as the boat which takes you to the opposite shore becomes useless once you have reached there. The twelve divisions of the Buddhist scriptures are merely the vehicle which carries you to your own awareness. When you have attained this awareness you will forget your knowledge of Buddhism.

> "Amending my nature is needless;"

Neither one's own nature nor anything else that appears before one needs changing. Those who begin to practice meditation imagine they must shift their usual mental attitude. They fancy they must enter into some kind of trance, or must pass through all those stages of dhyana so often described in the sutras, especially in the passages dealing with Buddha's Nirvana. These elaborate descriptions are merely the criteria of our attainment in meditation. No matter how much we have learned, in no whit do we learn to change the nature of our mind: indeed it is impossible to change the nature of our mind. This mind is the mind we are seeking.

But people usually think that the state of Reality is to be found in the intangible chaos of the infinite. They run into the mountain cave and sitting there with closed eyes hibernate, imagining thus to attain the state of Sunyata—Emptiness. From ancient days many thinkers have held such a view. But Chikan said:

> "Pursuing the tasks of everyday life
> I walk along the ancient path.
> I am not disheartened in the mindless void."

It was thus, by active motion, that he manifested the old teachings. And moreover, though he had now entered the state of Emptiness and had taken up his abode there, he did not assume a negative attitude.

> "Wheresoever I go I leave no footprint,
> For I am not within color or sound."

You may think that you are moving around from morning to evening, but if you change your standpoint and then look at the whole world and yourself, you cannot say that you are moving. In the state of Emptiness there is nothing which can be called motion. You are not staying in any one particular place nor are you staying anywhere. Though all day long you are speaking, raising your eyebrows, standing, sitting, walking and lying, nevertheless in reality nothing has happened. As it is said in the old poem:

> "The shadow of the bamboo sweeps the stair
> All night long.
> Yet not a mote of dust is stirred.
> The moonbeams penetrate
> To the bottom of the pool,
> Yet in the water not a trace is left."

The last two lines of Chikan's poem I do not repeat, for they seem to me more likely to have been a commentator's memorandum which crept into the text. One who has reached this attainment does not need to pat himself on the back.

CHAPTER 5

The Zen Teaching of Huang Po on the Transmission of Mind[1]

Rendered into English by JOHN BLOFELD

The first part of this selection is taken from John Blofeld's introduction to his new rendering of this ninth-century Chinese Buddhist classic.   [N. W. R.]

All Buddhists take Gautama Buddha's Enlightenment as their starting point and endeavour to attain to that transcendental knowledge that will bring them face to face with Reality, thereby delivering them from rebirth into the space-time realm forever. Zen followers go further. They are not content to pursue Enlightenment through aeons of varied existences inevitably bound up with pain and ignorance, approaching with infinite slowness the Supreme Experience which Christian mystics have described as "union with the God-head." They believe in the possibility of attaining Full Enlightenment both here and now through determined efforts to rise beyond conceptual thought and to grasp that Intuitive Knowledge which is the central fact of Enlightenment. Furthermore, they insist that the experience is both sudden and complete. While the striving may require years, the reward manifests itself in a flash. But to attain this reward, the practice of virtue and dispassion is insufficient. It is necessary to rise above such relative concepts as good and evil, sought and found, Enlightened and unenlightened, and all the rest.

---

[1] From *The Zen Teaching of Huang Po on the Transmission of Mind*, Being the Teaching of the Zen Master Huang Po as recorded by the scholar P'ei Hsiu of the T'ang Dynasty. Rendered into English by John Blofeld (Chu Ch'an). Grove Press, New York, 1959.

To make this point clearer, let us consider some Christian ideas of God. God is regarded as the First Principle, uncaused and unbegat, which logically implies perfection; such a being cannot be discovered through the relativity of time and space. Then comes the concept "God is good" which, as Christian mystics have pointed out, detracts from His perfection; for to be good implies not being evil—a limitation which inevitably destroys the unity and wholeness inseparable from perfection. This, of course, is not intended to imply that "God is evil," or that "God is both good and evil." To a mystic, He is none of these things, for He transcends them all. Again, the idea of God as the creator of the universe suggests a dualism, a distinction between creator and created. This, if valid, places God on a lower level than perfection, for there can be neither unity nor wholeness where A excludes B or B excludes A.

Zen followers (who have much in common with mystics of other faiths) do not use the term "God," being wary of its dualistic and anthropomorphic implications. They prefer to talk of "the Absolute" or "the One Mind," for which they employ many synonyms according to the aspect to be emphasized in relation to something finite. Thus, the word "Buddha" is used as a synonym for the Absolute as well as in the sense of Gautama, the Enlightened One, for it is held that the two are identical. A Buddha's Enlightenment denotes an intuitive realization of his unity with the Absolute from which, after the death of his body, nothing remains to divide him even in appearance. Of the Absolute nothing whatever can be postulated; to say that it exists excludes non-existence; to say that it does not exist excludes existence. Furthermore, Zen followers hold that the Absolute, or union with the Absolute, is not something to be attained; one does not ENTER Nirvana, for entrance to a place one has never left is impossible. The experience commonly called "entering Nirvana" is, in fact, an intuitive realization of that Self-nature which is the true Nature of all things. The Absolute, or Reality, is regarded as having for sentient beings two aspects. The only aspect perceptible to the unenlightened is the one in which individual phenomena have a separate though purely transitory existence within the limits of space-time. The other aspect is space-less and timeless; moreover all opposites, all distinctions and "entities" of every kind, are here seen to be One. Yet neither is this second aspect, alone, the highest fruit of Enlightenment, as many contemplatives suppose; it is only when both aspects are perceived and reconciled that the beholder may be regarded as truly Enlightened. Yet, from that moment, he ceases to be the beholder, for he is conscious of no division between beholding and beheld.

This leads to further paradoxes, unless the use of words is abandoned altogether. It is incorrect to employ such mystical terminology as "I dwell in the Absolute," "The Absolute dwells in me," or "I am penetrated by the Absolute," etc.; for, when space is transcended, the concepts of whole and part are no longer valid; the part IS the whole—I AM the Absolute, except that I am no longer "I." What I behold then is my real Self, which is the true nature of all things; see-er and seen are one and the same, yet there is no seeing, just as the eye cannot behold itself.

The single aim of the true Zen follower is so to train his mind that all thought processes based on the dualism inseparable from "ordinary" life are transcended, their place being taken by that Intuitive Knowledge which, for the first time, reveals to a man what he really is. If All is One, then knowledge of a being's true self-nature—his original Self—is equally a knowledge of all-nature, the nature of everything in the universe. Those who have actually achieved this tremendous experience, whether as Christians, Buddhists or members of other faiths, are agreed as to the impossibility of communicating it in words. They may employ words to point the way to others, but, until the latter have achieved the experience for themselves, they can have but the merest glimmer of the truth—a poor intellectual concept of something lying infinitely beyond the highest point ever reached by the human intellect.

It will now be clear that Zen Masters do not employ paradoxes from a love of cheap mystification, though they do occasionally make humorous use of them when humour seems needed. Usually, it is the utter impossibility of describing the Supreme Experience which explains the paradoxical nature of their speech. To affirm or deny is to limit; to limit is to shut out the light of truth; but, as words of some sort must be used in order to set disciples on to the right path, there naturally arises a series of paradoxes—sometimes of paradox within paradox within paradox.

It should perhaps be added that Huang Po's frequent criticisms of those Buddhists who follow the more conventional path, cultivating knowledge, good works and a compassionate heart through successive stages of existence, are not intended to call into question the value to humanity of such excellent practices. As a Buddhist, Huang Po must certainly have regarded these things as necessary for our proper conduct in daily life; indeed, we are told by P'ei Hsiu that his way of life was exalted; but he was concerned lest concepts such as virtue should lead people into dualism, and lest they should hold Enlightenment to be a gradual process attainable by other means than intuitive insight.

Huang Po's Use of the Term "The One Mind"

The text indicates that Huang Po was not entirely satisfied with his choice of the word "Mind" to symbolize the inexpressible Reality beyond the reach of conceptual thought, for he more than once explains that the One Mind is not really MIND at all. But he had to use some term or other, and "Mind" had often been used by his predecessors. As Mind conveys intangibility, it no doubt seemed to him a good choice, especially as the use of this term helps to make it clear that the part of a man usually regarded as an individual entity inhabiting his body is, in fact, not his property at all, but common to him and to everybody and everything else. (It must be remembered that, in Chinese, "*hsin*" means not only "mind," but "heart" and, in some senses at least, "spirit" or "soul"—in short, the so-called REAL man, the inhabitant of the body-house.) If we prefer to substitute the word "Absolute," which Huang Po occasionally uses himself, we must take care not to read into the text any preconceived notions as to the nature of the Absolute. And, of course, "the One Mind" is no less misleading, unless we abandon all preconceived ideas, as Huang Po intended.

In an earlier translation of the first part of this book, I ventured to substitute "Universal Mind" for "the One Mind," hoping that the meaning would be clearer. However, various critics objected to this, and I have come to see that my term is liable to a different sort of misunderstanding; it is therefore no improvement on "the One Mind," which at least has the merit of being a literal translation.

Dhyāna-Practice

The book tells us very little about the practice of what, for want of a better translation, is often called meditation or contemplation. Unfortunately both these words are misleading as they imply some object of meditation or of contemplation; and, if objectlessness be stipulated, then they may well be taken to lead to a blank or sleeplike trance, which is not at all the goal of Zen. Huang Po seems to have assumed that his audience knew something about this practice—as most keen Buddhists do, of course. He gives few instructions as to how to "meditate," but he does tell us what to avoid. If, conceiving of the phenomenal world as illusion, we try to shut it out, we make a false distinction between the "real" and the "unreal." So we must not shut anything out, but try to reach the point where all distinctions are seen to be void, where nothing is seen as desirable or undesirable, existing or not existing. Yet this does not mean that we should make our minds blank, for then we should be no better than blocks of wood or lumps of stone; moreover, if we remained in this state, we should not be able to deal with the circumstances of daily life or be capable of observing the Zen precept: "When hungry, eat." Rather, we must cultivate dispassion, realizing that none of the attractive or unattractive attributes of things have any absolute existence.

Enlightenment, when it comes, will come in a flash. There can be no gradual, no partial, Enlightenment. The highly trained and zealous adept may be said to have prepared himself for Enlightenment, but by no means can he be regarded as partially Enlightened—just as a drop of water may get hotter and hotter and then, suddenly, boil; at no stage is it partly boiling, and, until the very moment of boiling, no qualitative change has occurred. In effect, however, we may go through three stages—two of non-Enlightenment and one of Enlightenment. To the great majority of people, the moon is the moon and the trees are the trees. The next stage (not really higher than the first) is to perceive that moon and trees are not at all what they seem to be, since "all is the One Mind." When this stage is achieved, we have the concept of a vast uniformity in which all distinctions are void; and, to some adepts, this concept may come as an actual perception, as "real" to them as were the moon and the trees before. It is said that, when Enlightenment really comes, the moon is again very much the moon and the trees exactly trees; but with a difference, for the Enlightened man is capable of perceiving both unity and multiplicity without the least contradiction between them!

· · · · · · · · ·

FROM: THE CHUN CHOU RECORD OF THE ZEN MASTER HUANG PO (TUAN CHI)

A collection of sermons and dialogues recorded by P'ei Hsiu while in the city of Chun Chou.

The Master said to me: All the Buddhas and all sentient beings are nothing but the One Mind, beside which nothing exists. This Mind, which is without beginning, is unborn[2] and indestructible. It is not green nor yellow, and has

---

[2] Unborn, not in the sense of eternity, for this allows contrast with its opposite; but unborn in the sense that it belongs to no categories admitting of alteration or antithesis.

neither form nor appearance. It does not belong to the categories of things which exist or do not exist, nor can it be thought of in terms of new or old. It is neither long nor short, big nor small, for it transcends all limits, measures, names, traces and comparisons. It is that which you see before you—begin to reason about it and you at once fall into error. It is like the boundless void which cannot be fathomed or measured. The One Mind alone is the Buddha, and there is no distinction between the Buddha and sentient things, but that sentient beings are attached to forms and so seek externally for Buddhahood. By their very seeking they lose it, for that is using the Buddha to seek for the Buddha and using mind to grasp Mind. Even though they do their utmost for a full aeon, they will not be able to attain it. They do not know that, if they put a stop to conceptual thought and forget their anxiety, the Buddha will appear before them, for this Mind is the Buddha and the Buddha is all living beings. It is not the less for being manifested in ordinary beings, nor is it greater for being manifested in the Buddhas.

. . . .

Q: From all you have just said, Mind is the Buddha; but it is not clear as to what sort of mind is meant by this "Mind which is the Buddha."

A: How many minds have you got?

Q: But is the Buddha the ordinary mind or the Enlightened mind?

A: Where on earth do you keep your "ordinary mind" and your "Enlightened mind?"

Q: In the teaching of the Three Vehicles it is stated that there are both. Why does Your Reverence deny it?

A: In the teaching of the Three Vehicles it is clearly explained that the ordinary and Enlightened minds are illusions. You don't understand. All this clinging to the idea of things existing is to mistake vacuity for the truth. How can such conceptions not be illusory? Being illusory, they hide Mind from you. If you would only rid yourselves of the concepts of ordinary and Enlightened, you would find that there is no other Buddha than the Buddha in your own Mind. When Bodhidharma came from the West, he just pointed out that the substance of which all men are composed is the Buddha. You people go on misunderstanding; you hold to concepts such as "ordinary" and "Enlightened," directing your thoughts outwards where they gallop about like horses! All this amounts to beclouding your own minds! So I tell you Mind is the Buddha. As soon as thought or sensation arises, you fall into dualism. Beginningless time and the present moment are the same. There is no this and no that. To understand this truth is called complete and unexcelled Enlightenment.

Q: Upon what Doctrine (*Dharma-principles*) does Your Reverence base these words?

A: Why seek a doctrine? As soon as you have a doctrine, you fall into dualistic thought.

Q: Just now you said that the beginningless past and the present are the same. What do you mean by that?

A: It is just because of your SEEKING that you make a difference between them. If you were to stop seeking, how could there be any difference between them?

Q: If they are not different, why did you employ separate terms for them?

A: If you hadn't mentioned ordinary and Enlightened, who would have bothered to say such things? Just as those categories have no real existence, so Mind is not really "mind." And, as both Mind and those categories are really illusions, wherever can you hope to find anything?

Q: Illusion can hide from us our own mind, but up to now you have not taught us how to get rid of illusion.

A: The arising and the elimination of illusion are both illusory. Illusion is not something rooted in Reality; it exists because of your dualistic thinking. If you will only cease to indulge in opposed concepts such as "ordinary" and "Enlightened," illusion will cease of itself. And then if you still want to destroy it wherever it may be, you will find that there is not a hairsbreadth left of anything on which to lay hold. This is the meaning of: "I will let go with both hands, for then I shall certainly discover the Buddha in my mind."

Q: If there is nothing on which to lay hold, how is the Dharma to be transmitted?

A: It is a transmission of Mind with Mind.

Q: If Mind is used for transmission, why do you say that Mind too does not exist?

A: Obtaining no Dharma whatever is called Mind transmission. The understanding of this Mind implies no Mind and no Dharma.

Q: If there is no Mind and no Dharma, what is meant by transmission?

A: You hear people speak of Mind transmission and then you talk of something to be received. So Bodhidharma said:

71

The nature of the Mind when understood,
No human speech can compass or disclose.
Enlightenment is naught to be attained,
And he that gains it does not say he knows.

If I were to make this clear to you, I doubt if you could stand up to it.
•   •   •   •   •   •   •   •   •

FROM: THE WAN LING RECORD OF THE ZEN MASTER HUANG PO (TUAN CHI)

A collection of dialogues, sermons and anecdotes recorded by P'ei Hsiu during his tenure of the prefecture of Wan Ling.

Q: If our own Mind IS the Buddha, how did Bodhidharma transmit his doctrine when he came from India?

A: When he came from India, he transmitted only Mind-Buddha. He just pointed to the truth that the minds of all of you have from the very first been identical with the Buddha, and in no way separate from each other. . . . Whoever has an instant understanding of this truth suddenly transcends the whole hierarchy of saints and adepts. . . . You have always been one with the Buddha, so do not pretend you can ATTAIN to this oneness by various practices.[3]

Q: If that is so, what Dharma do all the Buddhas teach when they manifest themselves in the world?

A: When all the Buddhas manifest themselves in the world, they proclaim nothing but the One Mind. Thus Gautama Buddha silently transmitted to Mahākāśyapa the doctrine that the One Mind, which is the substance of all things, is co-extensive with the Void and fills the entire world of phenomena. This is called the Law of All the Buddhas. Discuss it as you may, how can you even hope to approach the truth through words? Nor can it be perceived either subjectively or objectively. So full understanding can come to you only through an inexpressible mystery. The approach to it is called the Gateway of the Stillness beyond all Activity. If you wish to understand, know that a sudden comprehension comes when the mind has been purged of all the clutter of conceptual and discriminatory thought-activity. Those who seek the truth by

---

[3] We cannot BECOME what we have always been; we can only become intuitively aware of our original state, previously hidden from us by the clouds of maya.

means of intellect and learning only get further and further away from it. Not till your thoughts cease all their branching here and there, not till you abandon all thoughts of seeking for something, not till your mind is motionless as wood or stone, will you be on the right road to the Gate.[4]

---

[4] These words recall the admonitions of so many mystics—Buddhist, Christian, Hindu or Sufi—who have committed their experience to words. What Huang Po calls the total abandonment of HSIN—mind, thought, perceptions, concepts and the rest—implies the utter surrender of self insisted on by Sufi and Christian mystics. Indeed, in paragraph 28 he used the very words: "LET THE SELF PERISH UTTERLY." Such striking unanimity of expression by mystics widely separated in time and space can hardly be attributed to coincidence. No several persons entirely unacquainted with one another could produce such closely similar accounts of purely imaginary journeys. Hence one is led to suppose that what they describe is real. This seems to have been Aldous Huxley's view when he compiled that valuable work *The Perennial Philosophy*.

CHAPTER 6

Some Zen Stories

The following stories have their origins in various books of anecdotes about Zen life and training, including a thirteenth-century classic, *Shaseki-shu* (*Collection of Stone and Sand*), transcribed from the original Japanese by Nyogen Senzaki and Paul Reps. Under the title *101 Zen Stories*, an English version first appeared in America and Great Britain in 1939. In 1957 the stories were reissued as part of a book called *Zen Flesh, Zen Bones*,[1] a compilation of "Zen and pre-Zen material" by one of the two original transcribers, Paul Reps.

In his brief foreword to the 1957 edition, Reps said of "old Zen": "Here are fragments of its skin, flesh, bones, but not its marrow—never found in words." His comment referred to one of the famous stories about the original Zen patriarch, the Buddhist monk Bodhidharma, who first brought the "Great Teaching" from India to China in the sixth century. Bodhidharma had occasion to gather about him a few of his disciples in order to test their growth in understanding. Each of the four made his contribution to the question of "the nature of truth." To the first one's statement the Master replied, "You have my skin." To the second, "You have my flesh." To the third, "You have my bones." But when the fourth pupil, Eka, merely bowed and remained silent, Bodhidharma said, "You have my marrow." [N. W. R.]

---

1 Charles E. Tuttle Company, Rutland, Vermont—Tokyo, Japan, 1957.

THE MOON CANNOT BE STOLEN

Ryokan, a Zen master, lived the simplest kind of life in a little hut at the foot of a mountain. One evening a thief visited the hut only to discover there was nothing in it to steal.

Ryokan returned and caught him. "You may have come a long way to visit me," he told the prowler, "and you should not return empty-handed. Please take my clothes as a gift."

The thief was bewildered. He took the clothes and slunk away.

Ryokan sat naked, watching the moon. "Poor fellow," he mused, "I wish I could give him this beautiful moon."

A PARABLE

Buddha told a parable in a sutra:

A man traveling across a field encountered a tiger. He fled, the tiger after him. Coming to a precipice, he caught hold of the root of a wild vine and swung himself down over the edge. The tiger sniffed at him from above. Trembling, the man looked down to where, far below, another tiger was waiting to eat him. Only the vine sustained him.

Two mice, one white and one black, little by little started to gnaw away the vine. The man saw a luscious strawberry near him. Grasping the vine with one hand, he plucked the strawberry with the other. How sweet it tasted!

OBEDIENCE

The Master Bankei's talks were attended not only by Zen students but by persons of all ranks and sects. He never quoted sutras nor indulged in scholastic dissertations. Instead, his words were spoken directly from his heart to the hearts of his listeners.

His large audiences angered a priest of the Nichiren sect because the adherents had left to hear about Zen. The self-centered Nichiren priest came to the temple, determined to debate with Bankei.

"Hey, Zen teacher!" he called out. "Wait a minute. Whoever respects you will obey what you say, but a man like myself does not respect you. Can you make me obey you?"

"Come up beside me and I will show you," said Bankei.

Proudly the priest pushed his way through the crowd to the teacher.

Bankei smiled. "Come over to my left side."

The priest obeyed.

"No," said Bankei, "we may talk better if you are on the right side. Step over here."

The priest proudly stepped over to the right.

"You see," observed Bankei, "you are obeying me and I think you are a very gentle person. Now sit down and listen."

THE FIRST PRINCIPLE

When one goes to Obaku temple in Kyoto he sees carved over the gate the words "The First Principle." The letters are unusually large, and those who appreciate calligraphy always admire them as being a masterpiece. They were drawn by Kosen two hundred years ago.

When the master drew them he did so on paper, from which workmen made the larger carving in wood. As Kosen sketched the letters a bold pupil was with him who had made several gallons of ink for the calligraphy and who never failed to criticize his master's work.

"That is not good," he told Kosen after the first effort.

"How is that one?"

"Poor. Worse than before," pronounced the pupil.

Kosen patiently wrote one sheet after another until eighty-four First Principles had accumulated, still without the approval of the pupil.

Then, when the young man stepped outside for a few moments, Kosen thought: "Now is my chance to escape his keen eye," and he wrote hurriedly, with a mind free from distraction: "The First Principle."

"A masterpiece," pronounced the pupil.

THE SOUND OF ONE HAND

The Master of Kennin temple was Mokurai, Silent Thunder. He had a little protégé named Toyo who was only twelve years old. Toyo saw the older disciples visit the Master's room each morning and evening to receive instruction in sanzen or personal guidance in which they were given koans to stop mind-wandering.

Toyo wished to do sanzen also.

"Wait a while," said Mokurai, "you are too young."

But the child insisted, so the teacher finally consented.

In the evening little Toyo went at the proper time to the threshold of Mokurai's sanzen room. He struck the gong to announce his presence, bowed respectfully three times outside the door, and went to sit before the Master in respectful silence.

"You can hear the sound of the hands when they clap together," said Mokurai. "Now show me the sound of one hand."

Toyo bowed and went to his room to consider this problem. From his window he could hear the music of the geishas. "Ah, I have it!" he proclaimed.

The next evening, when his teacher asked him to illustrate the sound of one hand, Toyo began to play the music of the geishas.

"No, no," said Mokurai. "That will never do. That is not the sound of one hand. You've not got it at all."

Thinking that such music might interrupt, Toyo moved his abode to a quiet place. He meditated again. "What can the sound of one hand be?" He happened to hear some water dripping. "I have it," imagined Toyo.

When he next appeared before his teacher, Toyo imitated dripping water.

"What is that?" asked Mokurai. "That is the sound of dripping water, but not the sound of one hand. Try again."

In vain Toyo meditated to hear the sound of one hand. He heard the sighing of the wind. But the sound was rejected.

He heard the cry of an owl. This also was refused.

The sound of one hand was not the locusts.

For more than ten times Toyo visited Mokurai with different sounds. All were wrong. For almost a year he pondered what the sound of one hand might be.

At last little Toyo entered true meditation and transcended all sounds. "I could collect no more," he explained later, "so I reached the soundless sound."

Toyo had realized the sound of one hand.

NO WATER, NO MOON

When the Nun Chiyono studied Zen under Bukko of Engaku she was unable to attain the fruits of meditation for a long time.

At last one moonlit night she was carrying water in an old pail bound with bamboo. The bamboo broke and the bottom fell out of the pail, and at that moment Chiyono was set free!

In commemoration, she wrote a poem:

> In this way and that I tried to save the old pail
> Since the bamboo strip was weakening and about to break
> Until at last the bottom fell out.
> No more water in the pail!
> No more moon in the water!

CALLING CARD

Keichu, the great Zen teacher of the Meiji era, was the head of Tofuku, a cathedral in Kyoto. One day the governor of Kyoto called upon him for the first time.

His attendant presented the card of the governor, which read: Kitagaki, Governor of Kyoto.

"I have no business with such a fellow," said Keichu to his attendant. "Tell him to get out of here."

The attendant carried the card back with apologies. "That was my error," said the governor, and with a pencil he scratched out the words "Governor of Kyoto." "Ask your teacher again."

"Oh, is that Kitagaki?" exclaimed the teacher when he saw the card. "I want to see that fellow."

MOKUSEN'S HAND

Mokusen Hiki was living in a temple in the province of Tamba. One of his adherents complained of the stinginess of his wife.

Mokusen visited the adherent's wife and showed her his clenched fist before her face.

"What do you mean by that?" asked the surprised woman.

"Suppose my fist were always like that. What would you call it?" he asked.

"Deformed," replied the woman.

Then he opened his hand flat in her face and asked: "Suppose it were always like that. What then?"

"Another kind of deformity," said the wife.

"If you understand that much," finished Mokusen, "you are a good wife."
Then he left.

After his visit, this wife helped her husband to distribute as well as to save.

THE THIEF WHO BECAME A DISCIPLE

One evening as Shichiri Kojun was reciting sutras a thief with a sharp
sword entered, demanding either his money or his life.

Shichiri told him: "Do not disturb me. You can find the money in that
drawer." Then he resumed his recitation.

A little while afterwards he stopped and called:

"Don't take it all. I need some to pay taxes with tomorrow."

The intruder gathered up most of the money and started to leave. "Thank
a person when you receive a gift," Shichiri added. The man thanked him and
made off.

A few days afterwards the fellow was caught and confessed, among others,
the offence against Shichiri. When Shichiri was called as a witness he said:
"This man is no thief, at least as far as I am concerned. I gave him the money
and he thanked me for it."

After he had finished his prison term, the man went to Shichiri and became
his disciple.

RIGHT AND WRONG

When Bankei held his seclusion-weeks of meditation, pupils from many
parts of Japan came to attend. During one of these gatherings a pupil was
caught stealing. The matter was reported to Bankei with the request that the
culprit be expelled. Bankei ignored the case.

Later the pupil was caught in a similar act, and again Bankei disregarded
the matter. This angered the other pupils, who drew up a petition asking for
the dismissal of the thief, stating that otherwise they would leave in a body.

When Bankei had read the petition he called everyone before him. "You are
wise brothers," he told them. "You know what is right and what is not right.
You may go somewhere else to study if you wish, but this poor brother does
not even know right from wrong. Who will teach him if I do not? I am going
to keep him here even if all the rest of you leave."

A torrent of tears cleansed the face of the brother who had stolen. All
desire to steal had vanished.

RYONEN'S CLEAR REALIZATION

The Buddhist nun known as Ryonen was born in 1797. She was a grand-daughter of the famous Japanese warrior Shingen. Her poetical genius and alluring beauty were such that at seventeen she was serving the empress as one of the ladies of the court. Even at such a youthful age fame awaited her.

The beloved empress died suddenly and Ryonen's hopeful dreams vanished. She became acutely aware of the impermanency of life in this world. It was then that she desired to study Zen.

Her relatives disagreed, however, and practically forced her into marriage. With a promise that she might become a nun after she had borne three children, Ryonen assented. Before she was twenty-five she had accomplished this condition. Then her husband and relatives could no longer dissuade her from her desire. She shaved her head, took the name of Ryonen, which means to realize clearly, and started on her pilgrimage.

She came to the city of Edo and asked Tetsugyu to accept her as a disciple. At one glance the master rejected her because she was too beautiful.

Ryonen then went to another master, Hakuo. Hakuo refused her for the same reason, saying that her beauty would only make trouble.

Ryonen obtained a hot iron and placed it against her face. In a few moments her beauty had vanished forever.

THE GATES OF PARADISE

A soldier named Nobushige came to Hakuin, and asked: "Is there really a paradise and a hell?"

"Who are you?" inquired Hakuin.

"I am a samurai," the warrior replied.

"You, a soldier!" exclaimed Hakuin. "What kind of ruler would have you as his guard? Your face looks like that of a beggar."

Nobushige became so angry that he began to draw his sword, but Hakuin continued: "So you have a sword! Your weapon is probably much too dull to cut off my head."

As Nobushige drew his sword Hakuin remarked: "Here open the gates of hell!"

At these words the samurai, perceiving the master's discipline, sheathed his sword and bowed.

"Here open the gates of paradise," said Hakuin.

THE TUNNEL

Zenkai, the son of a samurai, journeyed to Edo and there became the retainer of a high official. He fell in love with the official's wife and was discovered. In self-defence, he slew the official. Then he ran away with the wife.

Both of them later became thieves. But the woman was so greedy that Zenkai grew disgusted. Finally, leaving her, he journeyed far away to the province of Buzen, where he became a wandering mendicant.

To atone for his past, Zenkai resolved to accomplish some good deed in his lifetime. Knowing of a dangerous road over a cliff that had caused the death . . . of many persons, he resolved to cut a tunnel through the mountain there.

Begging food in the daytime, Zenkai worked at night digging his tunnel. When thirty years had gone by, the tunnel was 2,280 feet long, 20 feet high, and 30 feet wide.

Two years before the work was completed, the son of the official he had slain, who was a skillful swordsman, found Zenkai out and came to kill him in revenge.

"I will give you my life willingly," said Zenkai. "Only let me finish this work. On the day it is completed, then you may kill me."

So the son awaited the day. Several months passed and Zenkai kept on digging. The son grew tired of doing nothing and began to help with the digging. After he had helped for more than a year, he came to admire Zenkai's strong will and character.

At last the tunnel was completed and the people could use it and travel in safety.

"Now cut off my head," said Zenkai. "My work is done."

"How can I cut off my own teacher's head?" asked the younger man with tears in his eyes.

IN THE HANDS OF DESTINY

A great Japanese warrior named Nobunaga decided to attack the enemy although he had only one-tenth the number of men the opposition commanded. He knew that he would win, but his soldiers were in doubt.

On the way he stopped at a Shinto shrine and told his men: "After I visit the shrine I will toss a coin. If heads comes, we will win; if tails, we will lose. Destiny holds us in her hand."

Nobunaga entered the shrine and offered a silent prayer. He came forth and tossed a coin. Heads appeared. His soldiers were so eager to fight that they won their battle easily.

"No one can change the hand of destiny," his attendant told him after the battle.

"Indeed not," said Nobunago, showing a coin which had been doubled, with heads facing either way.

THE SUBJUGATION OF A GHOST

A young wife fell sick and was about to die. "I love you so much," she told her husband, "I do not want to leave you. Do not go from me to any other woman. If you do, I will return as a ghost and cause you endless trouble."

Soon the wife passed away. The husband respected her last wish for the first three months, but then he met another woman and fell in love with her. They became engaged to be married.

Immediately after the engagement, a ghost appeared every night to the man, blaming him for not keeping his promise. The ghost was clever too. She told him exactly what had transpired between himself and his new sweetheart. Whenever he gave his fiancée a present, the ghost would describe it in detail. She would even repeat conversations, and it so annoyed the man that he could not sleep. Someone advised him to take his problem to a Zen master who lived close to the village. At length, in despair, the poor man went to him for help.

"Your former wife became a ghost and knows everything you do," commented the master. "Whatever you do or say, whatever you give your beloved, she knows. She must be a very wise ghost. Really you should admire such a ghost. The next time she appears, bargain with her. Tell her that she knows so much you can hide nothing from her, and that if she will answer you one question, you promise to break your engagement and remain single."

"What is the question I must ask her?" inquired the man.

The master replied: "Take a large handful of soy beans and ask her exactly how many beans you hold in your hand. If she cannot tell you, you will know she is only a figment of your imagination and will trouble you no longer."

The next night, when the ghost appeared the man flattered her and told her that she knew everything.

"Indeed," replied the ghost, "and I know you went to see that Zen master today."

"And since you know so much," demanded the man, "tell me how many beans I hold in this hand!"

There was no longer any ghost to answer the question.

ONE NOTE OF ZEN

After Kakua visited the emperor he disappeared and no one knew what became of him. He was the first Japanese to study Zen in China, but since he showed nothing of it, save one note, he is not remembered for having brought Zen into his country.

Kakua visited China and accepted the true teaching. He did not travel while he was there. Meditating constantly, he lived on a remote part of a mountain. Whenever people found him and asked him to preach he would say a few words and then move to another part of the mountain where he could be found less easily.

The emperor heard about Kakua when he returned to Japan and asked him to preach Zen for his edification and that of his subjects.

Kakua stood before the emperor in silence. He then produced a flute from the folds of his robe, and blew one short note. Bowing politely, he disappeared.

TEMPER

A Zen student came to Bankei and complained: "Master, I have an ungovernable temper. How can I cure it?"

"You have something very strange," replied Bankei. "Let me see what you have."

"Just now I cannot show it to you," replied the other.

"When can you show it to me?" asked Bankei.

"It arises unexpectedly," replied the student.

"Then," concluded Bankei, "it must not be your own true nature. If it were, you could show it to me at any time. When you were born you did not have it, and your parents did not give it to you. Think that over."

THE REAL MIRACLE

When Bankei was preaching at Ryumon temple, a Shinshu priest, who believed in salvation through the repetition of the name of the Buddha of Love, vas jealous of his large audience and wanted to debate with him.

Bankei was in the midst of a talk when the priest appeared, but the fellow made such a disturbance that Bankei stopped his discourse and asked about the noise.

"The founder of our sect," boasted the priest, "had such miraculous powers that he held a brush in his hand on one bank of the river, his attendant held up a paper on the other bank, and the teacher wrote the holy name of Amida through the air. Can you do such a wonderful thing?"

Bankei replied lightly: "Perhaps your fox can perform that trick, but that is not the manner of Zen. My miracle is that when I feel hungry I eat, and when I feel thirsty I drink."

THE LIVING BUDDHA AND THE TUBMAKER

Zen masters give personal guidance in a secluded room. No one enters while teacher and pupil are together.

Mokurai, the Zen master of Kennin temple in Kyoto, used to enjoy talking with merchants and newspapermen as well as with his pupils. A certain tub-maker was almost illiterate. He would ask foolish questions of Mokurai, have tea, and then go away.

One day while the tubmaker was there Mokurai wished to give personal guidance to a disciple, so he asked the tubmaker to wait in another room.

"I understand you are a living Buddha," the man protested. "Even the stone Buddhas in the temple never refuse the numerous persons who come together before them. Why then should I be excluded?"

Mokurai had to go outside to see his disciple.

TEACHING THE ULTIMATE

In early times in Japan, bamboo-and-paper lanterns were used with candles inside. A blind man, visiting a friend one night, was offered a lantern to carry home with him.

"I do not need a lantern," he said. "Darkness or light is all the same to me."

"I know you do not need a lantern to find your way," his friend replied, "but if you don't have one, someone else may run into you. So you must take it."

The blind man started off with the lantern and before he had walked very far someone ran squarely into him. "Look out where you are going!" he exclaimed to the stranger. "Can't you see this lantern?"

"Your candle has burned out, brother," replied the stranger.

BUDDHA'S ZEN

Buddha said: "I consider the positions of kings and rulers as that of dust motes. I observe treasures of gold and gems as so many bricks and pebbles. I look upon the finest silken robes as tattered rags. I see myriad worlds of the universe as small seeds of fruit, and the greatest lake in India as a drop of oil on my foot. I perceive the teachings of the world to be the illusion of magicians. I discern the highest conception of emancipation as a golden brocade in a dream, and view the holy path of the illuminated ones as flowers appearing in one's eyes. I see meditation as a pillar of a mountain. Nirvana as a nightmare of daytime. I look upon the judgment of right and wrong as the serpentine dance of a dragon, and the rise and fall of beliefs as but traces left by the four seasons."

III

ZEN AND
THE ARTS

In its own way, each one of the arts which Zen has inspired gives vivid expression to the sudden and instantaneous quality of its view of the world. The momentariness of sumi [ink] paintings and haiku [a verse form] and the total presence of mind required in cha-no-yu [tea ceremony] and kendo [swordsmanship] bring out the real reason why Zen has always called itself the way of instantaneous awakening.

—ALAN WATTS, *The Way of Zen*

III ZEN AND THE ARTS

1. Painting
   FOREWORD
   ZEN AND THE ART OF PAINTING
   D. T. Suzuki
   THE TAO OF PAINTING
   Mai-mai Sze

2. Gardens
   FOREWORD
   GARDENS
   Langdon Warner
   STONE GARDEN
   Will Petersen

3. Poetry
   FOREWORD
   HAIKU
   Alan Watts

4. Ceremonial Tea
   FOREWORD
   TEA
   Langdon Warner

5. Architecture
   THE TEA-ROOM
   Okakura Kakuzo

6. The No Drama
   FOREWORD
   SOTOBA KOMACHI
   Translated by Arthur Waley

CHAPTER 1

Painting

FOREWORD

On a day when he was to paint, he would seat himself by a bright window, put his desk in order, burn incense to his right and left, and place good brushes and excellent ink beside him; then he would wash his hands and rinse his ink-well, as if to receive an important guest, thereby calming his spirit and composing his thoughts. Not until then did he begin to paint. Does this not illustrate what he meant by not daring to face one's work thoughtlessly?[1]

Since according to the Zenist creed, the soul was identified with the universe, the harmony between these created a vast symbolism in which states of mind were expressed in landscape and landscapes were expressive of a state of mind.[2]

The acceptance of meditative disciplines as a normal part of human experience had a profound effect on the artists of China and Japan. The insight born of these disciplines inspired a sense of participation, of identification with all life, and it is this subtle spirit which infuses the great painting of the Far East.

But though the Zen-inspired artist recognized the kinship between his individual life and the life of all things, he did not fall into pantheism, as might have been expected, for he had come to apprehend deeply the truth that everything has its own and proper place in the continuity of the universe, and

---

[1] *An Essay on Landscape Painting*, by Kuo Hsi. E. P. Dutton & Company, Inc. New York, 1936.

[2] *The Civilizations of the East, Vol. IV, Japan*, by René de Grousset. Alfred A. Knopf, Inc., New York, 1934.

that he, as man, was but one of many forms participating in a great creative drama. He did not consider man as overlord and master of all he surveyed; his ego remained uninvolved. Without loss of human identity, or, at the other extreme, falling victim to sentimentality, he was thus able to find in nature clues through which to read and apprehend himself—"the winds of peaks are his lonely aspirations, and the torrents his liberated energies. Flowers, opening their secret hearts to the light and trembling to the breeze's touch, seem to be unfolding the mystery of his own human heart, the mystery of those intuitions and emotions which are too shy for speech. It is not one aspect or another of nature, one particular beauty or another; the pleasant sward and leafy glade are not chosen and the austere crags and caves, with the wild beasts that haunt them, left and avoided. It is not man's early surrounding, tamed to his desires, that inspires the artist; but the universe, in its wholeness and its freedom, has become his spiritual home."[3]

The Zen painters' profound communion with nature led to such admonitions as "become a bamboo . . . become a crane." In these suggestions, however, much more was implied than a mere heightening of the powers of exact observation. The crow on the wintry bough, the warbler swinging on a windy vine, the bamboo bent with snow, the forever-changing, forever-the-same waterfall or river, the waves that ceaselessly strike the shore—all these were part of the book of life, of that eternal "Isness" at which each man must really look if he hoped finally to be able to "see." Painting was a way of life.

The Zen painter acquired through practice and training a sureness of technique, an exactness of brush stroke comparable to the psycho-physical skills necessary for judo or swordsmanship. Once having taken up his brush, the artist using *sumi* ink on silk or paper could not put it down until he had finished, nor could he ever repaint. The material on which he worked was so absorbent that the flow of ink had to be free and continuous. Thus the artist's movements came to be compared to those of the dance, an expression of controlled spontaneity—spontaneity without caprice—which was, and still is, so much a part of the Zen attitude. (Here it probably came easy for the artist to grasp a certain similarity between *sumi* painting and life itself. Brush strokes once made were ineradicable, another intimation of that fateful law of cause and effect seen by Buddhists to govern all human activity.)

To Zen painters space was as real as solids—a surprisingly modern point of view. Space, though empty, was never vacant, for out of Emptiness or the

[3] *The Flight of the Dragon*, by Laurence Binyon, John Murray, Ltd., London, 1922.

Void came all life. Artists learned to suggest aliveness in unfilled surfaces and, in composition, to employ empty space in ways which are, from the point of view of conventional Western aesthetics, extremely daring. Thus, for instance, we see in a famous old painting a figure of a man with his back to us staring out across infinite distance, staff in hand, his robe blowing in the wind. Two-thirds of this painting is only an empty wash, yet as we look we too become the solitary traveler, and the space into which he stares on that windy autumn evening becomes as real as if we stood beside him on his lonely promontory. In art of this subtlety there are qualities that go further than naturalness or realism—though we might find such a masterpiece as this related to "reality" —if spelled with a capital R.

Something beyond the Western concept of beauty is present in Zen art. Indeed, Zen painters were never after beauty as such. The old master Ching Hao, who wrote a famous treatise, *Notes on Brushwork*, once replied tartly on this particular point to a young novice whom he met wandering in the Stone Drum Cliffs of the T'ai-hang Mountains.[4] During their exchange of views the young man, who to begin with felt he had little to learn from this seemingly uncouth rustic, remarked with glib assurance, "Painting is to make beautiful things, and the important point is to obtain their true likeness, is it not?" The old man answered, "It is not. Painting is to paint, to estimate the shapes of things and really obtain them, to estimate the beauty of things and reach it, to estimate the reality (significance) of things and grasp it. One should not take outward beauty for reality; he who does not understand this mystery will not obtain the truth, even though his pictures may contain likeness." When the puzzled but eager young man went on to question the difference between "likeness and truth," the old man replied, "Likeness can be obtained by shapes without spirit; but when truth is reached, spirit and substance are both fully expressed. He who tries to express spirit through ornamental beauty will make dead things." The young man left the mountain-dwelling sage convinced that painting could, and should, be practiced only by enlightened men.

[N. W. R.]

---

[4] *The Chinese on the Art of Painting*, Translations and Comments by Osvald Siren. Henri Vetch, Peiping, 1936.

ZEN AND THE ART OF PAINTING[1]

By D. T. SUZUKI

Among things which strongly characterize Japanese artistic talents we may mention the so-called "one-corner" style, which originated with Bayen (Ma Yüan, fl. 1175–1225), one of the greatest Southern Sung artists. The "one-corner" style is psychologically associated with the Japanese painters' "thrifty brush" tradition of retaining the least possible number of lines or strokes which go to represent forms on silk or paper. Both are very much in accord with the spirit of Zen. A simple fishing boat in the midst of the rippling waters is enough to awaken in the mind of the beholder a sense of the vastness of the sea and at the same time of peace and contentment—the Zen sense of the Alone. Apparently the boat floats helplessly. It is a primitive structure with no mechanical device for stability and for audacious steering over the turbulent waves, with no scientific apparatus for braving all kinds of weather— quite a contrast to the modern ocean liner. But this very helplessness is the virtue of the fishing canoe, in contrast with which we feel the incomprehensibility of the Absolute encompassing the boat and all the world. Again, a solitary bird on a dead branch, in which not a line, not a shade, is wasted, is enough to show us the loneliness of autumn, when days become shorter and nature begins to roll up once more its gorgeous display of luxurious summer vegetation.[2] It makes one feel somewhat pensive, but it gives one opportunity to withdraw the attention towards the inner life, which, given attention enough, spreads out its rich treasures ungrudgingly before the eyes.

Here we have an appreciation of transcendental aloofness in the midst of multiplicities—which is known as *wabi* in the dictionary of Japanese cultural terms. *Wabi* really means "poverty," or, negatively, "not to be in the fashionable society of the time." To be poor, that is, not to be dependent on things worldly—wealth, power, and reputation—and yet to feel inwardly the presence of something of the highest value, above time and social position: this is what essentially constitutes *wabi*. Stated in terms of practical everyday life, *wabi* is to be satisfied with a little hut, a room of two or three *tatami* (mats), like the log cabin of Thoreau, and with a dish of vegetables picked in the neighboring fields, and perhaps to be listening to the pattering of a gentle

[1] From "Zen and the Art of Painting," in *Zen and Japanese Culture*, by D. T. Suzuki. Bollingen Series LXIV. Pantheon Books, New York, 1959.

[2] For a picture of a similar nature, see my Zen Essays, III, facing p. 310. . . . Here the fishing boat as one of the most representative specimens is reproduced.

spring rainfall. While later I will say something more about *wabi*, let me state here that the cult of *wabi* has entered deeply into the cultural life of the Japanese people. It is in truth the worshiping of poverty—probably a most appropriate cult in a poor country like ours. Despite the modern Western luxuries and comforts of life which have invaded us, there is still an ineradicable longing in us for the cult of *wabi*. Even in the intellectual life, not richness of ideas, not brilliancy or solemnity in marshaling thoughts and building up a philosophical system, is sought; but just to stay quietly content with the mystical contemplation of Nature and to feel at home with the world is more inspiring to us, at least to some of us.

However "civilized," however much brought up in an artificially contrived environment, we all seem to have an innate longing for primitive simplicity, close to the natural state of living. Hence the city people's pleasure in summer camping in the woods or traveling in the desert or opening up an unbeaten track. We wish to go back once in a while to the bosom of Nature and feel her pulsation directly. Zen's habit of mind, to break through all forms of human artificiality and take firm hold of what lies behind them, has helped the Japanese not to forget the soil but to be always friendly with Nature and appreciate her unaffected simplicity. Zen has no taste for complexities that lie on the surface of life. Life itself is simple enough, but when it is surveyed by the analyzing intellect it presents unparalleled intricacies. With all the apparatus of science we have not yet fathomed the mysteries of life. But, once in its current, we seem to be able to understand it, with its apparently endless pluralities and entanglements. Very likely, the most characteristic thing in the temperament of the Eastern people is the ability to grasp life from within and not from without. And Zen has just struck it.

In painting especially, disregard of form results when too much attention or emphasis is given to the all-importance of the spirit. The "one-corner" style and the economy of brush strokes also help to effect aloofness from conventional rules. Where you would ordinarily expect a line or a mass or a balancing element, you miss it, and yet this very thing awakens in you an unexpected feeling of pleasure. In spite of shortcomings or deficiencies that no doubt are apparent, you do not feel them so; indeed, this imperfection itself becomes a form of perfection. Evidently, beauty does not necessarily spell perfection of form. This has been one of the favorite tricks of Japanese artists—to embody beauty in a form of imperfection or even of ugliness.

When this beauty of imperfection is accompanied by antiquity or primitive uncouthness, we have a glimpse of *sabi*, so prized by Japanese connoisseurs. Antiquity and primitiveness may not be an actuality. If an object of art suggests even superficially the feeling of a historical period, there is *sabi* in it. *Sabi* consists in rustic unpretentiousness or archaic imperfection, apparent simplicity or effortlessness in execution, and richness in historical associations (which, however, may not always be present); and, lastly, it contains inexplicable elements that raise the object in question to the rank of an artistic production. These elements are generally regarded as derived from the appreciation of Zen. The utensils used in the tearoom are mostly of this nature.

The artistic element that goes into the constitution of *sabi*, which literally means "loneliness" or "solitude," is poetically defined by a teamaster thus:

> As I come out
> To this fishing village,
> Late in the autumn day,
> No flowers in bloom I see
> Nor any tinted maple leaves.[3]

Aloneness indeed appeals to contemplation and does not lend itself to spectacular demonstration. It may look most miserable, insignificant, and pitiable, especially when it is put up against the Western or modern setting. To be left alone, with no streamers flying, no fireworks crackling, and this amidst a gorgeous display of infinitely varied forms and endlessly changing colors, is indeed no sight at all. Take one of those *sumiye* sketches, perhaps portraying Kanzan and Jittoku (Han-shan and Shih-tê),[4] hang it in a European or an American art gallery, and see what effect it will produce in the minds of the visitors. The idea of aloneness belongs to the East and is at home in the environment of its birth.

It is not only to the fishing village on the autumnal eve that aloneness gives form, but also to a patch of green in the early spring—which is in all likelihood even more expressive of the idea of *sabi* or *wabi*. For in the green patch, as we read in the following thirty-one-syllable verse, there is an indication of life impulse amidst the wintry desolation:

> To those who only pray for the cherries to bloom,

---

[3] Fujiwara Sadaiye (1162–1241).

[4] Zen poet recluses of the T'ang dynasty. A collection of their poems known as the *Kanzan Shi* (*Han-shan Shih*) or *Sanrai Shi* (*San-lai Shih*) or *Sanin Shi* (*San-yin shih*) is still in existence. The pair together, Kanzan and Jittoku, has been a favorite subject for Far Eastern painters. There is something in their transcendental air of freedom which attracts us even in these modern days. . . .

How I wish to show the spring
That gleams from a patch of green
In the midst of the snow-covered mountain-village![5]

This is given by one of the old teamasters as thoroughly expressive of *sabi*, which is one of the four principles governing the cult of tea, *cha-no-yu*. Here is just a feeble inception of life power as asserted in the form of a little green patch, but in it he who has an eye can readily discern the spring shooting out from underneath the forbidding snow. It may be said to be a mere suggestion that stirs his mind, but just the same it is life itself and not its feeble indication. To the artist, life is as much here as when the whole field is overlaid with verdure and flowers. One may call this the mystic sense of the artist.

Asymmetry is another feature that distinguishes Japanese art. The idea is doubtlessly derived from the "one-corner" style of Bayen. The plainest and boldest example is the plan of Buddhist architecture. The principal structures, such as the Tower Gate, the Dharma Hall, the Buddha Hall, and others, may be laid along one straight line; but structures of secondary or supplementary importance, sometimes even those of major importance, are not arranged symmetrically as wings along either side of the main line. They may be found irregularly scattered over the grounds in accordance with the topographical peculiarities. You will readily be convinced of this fact if you visit some of the Buddhist temples in the mountains, for example, the Iyeyasu shrine at Nikko. We can say that asymmetry is quite characteristic of Japanese architecture of this class.

This can be demonstrated *par excellence* in the construction of the tearoom and in the tools used in connection with it. Look at the ceiling, which may be constructed in at least three different styles, and at some of the utensils for serving tea, and again at the grouping and laying of the steppingstones or flagstones in the garden. We find so many illustrations of asymmetry, or, in a way, of imperfection, or of the "one-corner" style.

Some Japanese moralists try to explain this liking of the Japanese artists for things asymmetrically formed and counter to the conventional, or rather geometrical, rules of art by the theory that the people have been morally trained not to be obtrusive but always to efface themselves, and that this mental habit of self-annihilation manifests itself accordingly in art—for example, when the artist leaves the important central space unoccupied. But to my mind, this theory is not quite correct. Would it not be a more plausible

---

[5] Fujiwara Iyetaka (1158–1237).

explanation to say that the artistic genius of the Japanese people has been inspired by the Zen way of looking at individual things as perfect in themselves and at the same time as embodying the nature of totality which belongs to the One?

The doctrine of ascetic aestheticism is not so fundamental as that of Zen aestheticism. Art impulses are more primitive or more innate than those of morality. The appeal of art goes more directly into human nature. Morality is regulative, art is creative. One is an imposition from without, the other is an irrepressible expression from within. Zen finds its inevitable association with art but not with morality. Zen may remain unmoral but not without art. When the Japanese artists create objects imperfect from the point of view of form, they may even be willing to ascribe their art motive to the current notion of moral asceticism; but we need not give too much significance to their own interpretation or to that of the critics. Our consciousness is not, after all, a very reliable standard of judgment.

However this may be, asymmetry is certainly characteristic of Japanese art, which is one of the reasons informality or approachability also marks to a certain degree Japanese objects of art. Symmetry inspires a notion of grace, solemnity, and impressiveness, which is again the case with logical formalism or the piling up of abstract ideas. The Japanese are often thought not to be intellectual and philosophical, because their general culture is not thoroughly impregnated with intellectuality. This criticism, I think, results somewhat from the Japanese love of asymmetry. The intellectual primarily aspires to balance, while the Japanese are apt to ignore it and incline strongly towards imbalance.

Imbalance, asymmetry, the "one-corner," poverty, *sabi* or *wabi*, simplification, aloneness, and cognate ideas make up the most conspicuous and characteristic features of Japanese art and culture. All these emanate from one central perception of the truth of Zen, which is "the One in the Many and the Many in the One," or better, "the One remaining as one in the Many individually and collectively."

THE TAO OF PAINTING[1]

By MAI-MAI SZE

Painting in China was never separate from the *tao* of living. Its main focus was, and still is, the *Tao*, the Way, the Order of Nature or the way nature

---

[1]From *The Tao of Painting*, by Mai-mai Sze, Bollingen Series XLIX. Pantheon Books, New York, 1956. Reprinted in the Modern Library.

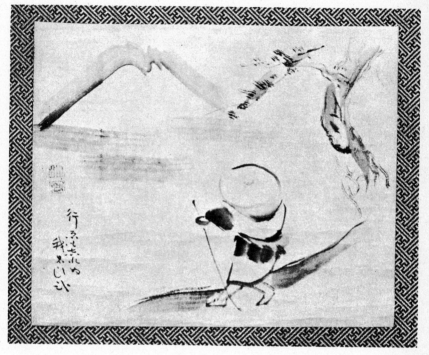

SENGAI

"The wind-blown
Smoke of Mount Fuji
Vanishing far away!
Who knows the destiny
Of my thought?"

works, which was alluded to not only in the classics but frequently in discussions of painting as the ideal—the harmony of Heaven and Earth that everything should express. In painting, this aim of the fusion of spirit, that which pertains to Heaven, and of matter, that which pertains to Earth, relates both to the artist's own development and to the work of art, for successful results require the exercise of insight as well as technical skill, the ability to render the inner character as well as its external form.

. . . .

Perhaps the most important factor in unifying and harmonizing all the elements of a picture is space. As that which contained everything in nature, the receptive, *yin* aspect of the *Tao* is emphasized. As space is filled with the *Ch'i*, the Spirit or Vital Force, it also has its *yang* aspect. It is this concept that makes the handling of space the most original contribution of Chinese painting and the most exhilarating aspect of the works themselves. While innumerable quotations could be cited from the Chinese literature of early periods, in particular the Taoist, to show how space was regarded as an equivalent of the *Tao*, it was mainly the influence of Zen Buddhism that led to the supreme statements about the *Tao* in the works of the Southern Sung painters, and in particular the landscapists. In the handling of vast space, their ink paintings are some of the greatest expressions of the human spirit. Where the Northern Sung painters excelled in height, in towering mountain peaks rich in detail, conveying an impression of the magnificence and multiplicity of nature, the Southern Sung painters merged the details in mists, obliterated them in space, and emphasized by depth of distances the silent majesty of nature and the mystery of the *Tao*. Both styles of painting lifted the spectator from the earth into liberating space. Both were virtually maps of the cosmos, for underlying philosophical ideas inspired these sublime views of nature. The great oceans on these maps were space, the perfect symbol of which was merely the blank silk or paper, and in many instances space was so represented in paintings. By the directness and purity of this device, the awareness of space was made more acute and its effects more profound. It should be added, however, that the effectiveness of blank spaces was achieved only through contrast with the vitality of the brushwork that rendered the forms it surrounded. Brushwork devoid of expressive power fails to contribute meaning to space and spoils the painting as an integrated statement of the unity and harmony of nature. A striking example of the fluctuations of the *Yin* and *Yang* is presented in the contrast between the eternalness of space depicted by the "absence of brush and ink" and the temporal, passing quality of that which was drawn and painted: the permanence of space and the transience of the substantial. To vary the *Yin-Yang* interpretation still further, space as it was rendered in the best of Chinese painting might be described as a spiritual solid.

The ideas about pictorial space are taken from the sources of Chinese thought. In Chapter XII of the *Chuang Tzü*, for instance, it is stated: "At the Great Beginning there was Non-Being. . . ." This Non-Being was described as "emptiness (*hsü* and *k'ung*)." And "the *Tao* abides in emptiness." By analogy, "to a mind that is still the whole universe surrenders." An amplification was given in the following passage: "Maintain the unity of your will. Do not listen with ears, but with the mind. Do not listen with the mind, but with the spirit (*ch'i*). The function of the ear ends with the hearing; that of the mind with symbols or ideas. But the spirit is an emptiness ready to receive all things." A Zen Buddhist term, descriptive of movement and space, expresses this state of receptivity as *k'ai wu* (open-awareness), to apprehend in the deepest and widest sense. By "stilling his heart," that is shedding the thoughts and emotions of his personal life, an individual could reflect in his heart-mind (*hsin*) or as a pool or a mirror, as the Taoists described it, the power (*Ch'i*) of the *Tao*, the harmony of Heaven and Earth. Hence the phrase "mirrorlike wisdom."

The stillness associated with emptiness of space and the *Tao* also is silence, which adds to the mystery of the *Tao* and stresses the reserve and meditative habits necessary for the painter to be receptive and able to express the *Tao*. Silence and emptiness of space possess vast powers of suggestion, stimulating the imagination and sharpening perception. And only through exercise of these highest faculties can the *Tao* be apprehended and expressed.

• • • • • • • • • •

In stilling the heart an individual can become one with the elements of nature, the great creative force of the *Tao*. This becoming one is the true meaning of wholeness. In painting, this goal is translated into the aim of the painter to identify himself with the object depicted, that is, to relate that in himself with that in all things which share the Oneness of the *Tao*.

CHAPTER 2

Gardens

FOREWORD

Japanese gardens, influenced like all the arts by the Zen aesthetic, differ radically from Western gardens with their profusion of flowers, their interest in color. In Japan the emphasis falls on other elements: sand, moss, stone lanterns, water—above all on unusual rocks which have often been brought at great expense from enormous distances, even as far away as Korea, for transplanting in private or public gardens. Japan is undoubtedly the only country in the world where certain rocks that are admired—one might even say worshiped—for their special forms, or their associative historic and cultural values, have attained the status of "national treasures."

Subtle suggestiveness and understatement pervade classic Japanese landscape gardening as they do poetry, painting, and the ceremonial taking of tea. Once again in garden design one sees the Zen qualities of simplification and evocation raised to the height of aesthetic principles.

One of the truest expressions of the Zen way with garden designing may be seen in the famous Kyoto garden of Ryoanji, an abstraction created with a rectangle of raked white sand and fifteen carefully selected rocks, arranged in five groups. There was a time in Japanese history when the first wave of European-American emulation swept the country, that this ancient Zen creation fell into temporary neglect, and, until comparatively recent times, traveling Westerners, chancing upon it, could only turn away in bewilderment for they possessed no clues to this unfamiliar stripped enclosure called a garden. Today—their eyes opened by abstract art—many Western visitors find at Ryoanji something deeply satisfying; subtle qualities that remain in their memories long after other more colorful Japanese scenes have faded.

When Christmas Humphreys first saw this garden he felt that it "best compared to unaccompanied Bach" and Fosco Maraini described it in *Meeting with Japan*[1] as—"a direct journey into the void from which all is born, an absurd chaste embrace of the mathematics of the heavenly spheres. . . . The Ryoanji garden was probably made in 1499, in other words four centuries before our own artists discovered the same language by a different route. Thus . . . the Japanese . . . tradition is our present, perhaps our future. . . . Little reflection is required to divine its true message; its stark simplicity, its asymmetrical equilibrium, stand for the meaning of ultimate things; they are not a pictorial representation of them. In Asia the artist's work is nearly always religious, because the life of the mind is not compartmentalized; life is itself religion. 'Picking up a blade of grass you make of it a lofty golden Buddha.' "

Will Petersen, a young American artist who now lives and teaches in Japan, devoted many hours in many weathers to the study of this fifteenth-century garden before writing the second piece in this section, which sheds a modern light on Ryoanji's consummate expression of the meaning of significant "emptiness."   [N. W. R.]

GARDENS[2]

By LANGDON WARNER

The fundamental thing about Japanese gardens, and what sets them apart from any other gardens of the civilized world, is usually lost sight of by Westerners. It is the fact that the art was definitely used in China and Japan to express the highest truths of religion and philosophy precisely as other civilizations have made use of the arts of literature and painting, of ritual dance and music. The Japanese tell us that the Chinese developed the garden art as a means of communicating high philosophical truths and, judging by their Sung dynasty paintings, it seems certain that they did. But since whatever the Sung

---

[1] Viking Press, New York, 1960.

[2] From *The Enduring Art of Japan*, by Langdon Warner. Harvard University Press, Cambridge, 1952. Reprinted by Grove Press, New York.

Chinese have done in the past assumes a halo of admired classicism and of nostalgic admiration to the Japanese, my guess is that there may have been less deliberate philosophic intention on the part of the classical Chinese garden designers than has been assumed. There remain, however, noble Chinese paintings from the twelfth to the seventeenth centuries that bear witness to a garden school—certainly a garden taste—of great subtlety and beauty. Of course, for splendid city and park and palace planning the Chinese had no superiors.

The Westerner is always attracted to the art of gardens in Japan not only by the obvious beauty of the accomplishment, but by vague hints that have reached him of the philosophical and emblematic content of that art. Our ignorance of this part of the subject is profound, and therefore we are in danger of indulging in sentimentality. Certain Japanese have been guilty of this same sin, but these have usually been writers about gardening, not gardeners.

The philosophic and symbolic content of the gardener's art is precisely that of any other important form of expression—neither less nor more. It is not the original cause of garden-making nor, generally, its purpose. Philosophy may well, however, come into play before the arrangement, selection, and elimination which are the art itself, and before horticulture, which is the craftsman's palette. One is tempted to dogmatize and say that philosophy about a garden is never permissible unless one has sweat to lay it out and labored over planting rocks, spreading the roots of young trees in pulverized soil, and leading ductile streams of water in their fit channels. But it would be just as true to say that no man should invoke the aid of a religious painting for worship until he had ground the pigments and himself laid them on the canvas.

This being so, it is proper to consider, so far as a Westerner may, something of the spiritual symbolism that has been expressed in the gardens laid out by Zen philosophers and has filtered down from them to the gardens made for and by laymen.

A Japanese mind, filled with half-memories of poems and paintings evoked by garden surroundings, will recognize through the power of association the yang-yin (male-female, light-dark, strong-weak) principles of pre-Confucian philosophy. And profound truths of many sorts, concerning even the essence of God, may be the result of thoughts thus deliberately evoked in a garden. Or again, if suggested by a not too farfetched likeness, a group of rocks can be recognized as the dragon and her cubs where they sport in the spray of the cataract. And, from knowledge of the dragon kind, one will be led to profitable thinking on the forces of nature, benign or dreadful, and on the origin of all things in mist and water.

Certain gardens have been designed primarily to call up such ideas, and it is important to record the fact that they have been in the past, and are today, successful. Further, these gardens are not mere curious documents, but have exerted a vital influence on the art of gardens in the East.

. . . The Westerner may gain much by a study of the art as it is practiced in Japan. For instance, observe the close wedding of the garden scheme with the dwelling, which the Japanese planner of gardens achieves by spending many days contemplating the site in various weathers and at all hours of the day. He makes small use of plans or sketches, but has a basket of pegs which he occasionally drives in the ground as he walks. Here and there he will set up a high bamboo pole to which have been lashed crosspieces that represent the spread of the branches of some tree he is to bring in. Thus he visualizes, by degrees, the whole area at his disposal, constantly returning to one or another part of the grounds to make sure that a vista is preserved or that a distant path is revealed. The scheme develops and shifts under his hand. And when men bring loads of rock and earth and trees with tightly balled roots, he hovers about to make sure that rocks are set to lie as the geologist would have them and that each tree's umbrage is to the sun. When his stream bed is done, its angles and its curves are those of nature, and the beaches are placed in those coves where running water would drop its load of gravel and of sand. So much is mere copying of nature's manner of working if you will, and in that sense it is like the work of the landscape painter when he contrives his own compositions. When all is done, with close regard to nature, step back into the open room of the house and sit with your tea, looking out. There water glints. But what its farthest stretch may be you do not know. The suggestion is that the stream flows on through pleasant country to an ocean miles away. The steppingstones that cross its narrowest place lead to a dip on the further bank beyond which the path accepts an invitation to climb and then hides in a thicket to come in view again further downstream where it skirts a little beach.

Thus the Zen practice is realized in the teasing charm of incompleteness—the suggestion that the onlooker finish his own idea according to his own imagination.

STONE GARDEN[1]

By WILL PETERSEN

Although it has been there for over four and a half centuries, it is only within the last few years that the stone garden of Ryōan-ji has become the object of much attention. Until recently, few persons were aware of its existence or had reason to be interested in it. Our concepts of art provided us with no means to approach it. Even those with a special interest in Japanese gardens let it lie in obscurity. It was, in fact, by our definitions not a garden at all. Devoid of "oriental" charm, without flowers, blossoming trees, stone lanterns, or delicate bridges arching over goldfish ponds, it had nothing to offer us but a few rocks scattered on an area strewn with sand. What was there to see?

Each age sees what it is prepared to discover. It is only after developments in our own traditions prepared us to see Ryōan-ji garden that we have come to respect it as a masterpiece. Whether regarded as a garden, or as sculpture or painting, we are now impressed by the perfection of its abstract relationships. Its reduction to essentials enables us to achieve a deeper understanding of principles underlying not only other gardens, but related forms of expression as well. The clean expanse of white sand evokes innumerable associations with the untouched white areas of *sumi* painting and calligraphy, *shoji* and floors laid with *tatami*, in more subtle fashion, with aspects of music, *haiku* poetry, and Nō dance. . . .

Although attributed to the famed artist Soami, the actual designer is unknown. It is relevant to mention, however, that in gardening, as well as in other arts of the time, Buddhist monks were the chief artists and leaders in aesthetic expression. With the introduction of Zen doctrines during the Kamakura era (1150–1310) the principles of religion were applied to the traditional rules of landscape garden composition. At this time several important treatises on gardening were written, based on prevailing religious-philosophical ideas. The application of religious principles became still stronger with the ascendency of Kyoto as the cultural capital of Japan, and reached a high point in the gardens of the Muromachi period. It was during this period, perhaps in 1499, that the garden of Ryōan-ji (a Buddhist temple of the Rinzai Zen sect) was laid out.

. . . Ryōan-ji garden has but a single vantage point. Enclosed on three sides by a low earthen wall, it can be viewed only from the veranda of the temple,

---

1 "Stone Garden," by Will Petersen. *Evergreen Review* (New York), Volume 1, Number 4.

extending along the fourth side. This single vantage point, together with the tranquility of the location in the hills outside of Kyoto, suggests the garden's purpose as an object of contemplation; not, however, as a comment on the transitoriness of life, a subject which occupied those of an earlier time. For, with no blossoms to fade and no leaves to wither and fall, the garden is not dependent on the impermanence of momentary beauty. Its beauty is that of the qualities of rock and sand, and of their abstract relationships. The garden, like all things, is not unchanging. But what significant changes do occur, occur not within the garden, but in the mind of the viewer and in his perception of the garden.

The vacant space of the garden, like silence, absorbs the mind, frees it of petty detail, and serves as a visual guide—a means for penetrating through the "realm of multitudes." . . .

Yet, while noting the vacant space, the rocks cannot be ignored. Like sand and its attributes, rocks constitute a basic element in the Japanese aesthetic; these, and other components, help create within the garden a complex of interwoven associations. It is possible to bring to this apparently simple garden the endless fine points of gardening, compounded with a wealth of religious, mythological or intellectual ideas and historical relevances accumulated over the centuries. Any discussion of the garden of Ryōan-ji is in peril if it fails to account for all of these. For example, it was customary to name stones individually after Buddhist figures and to assign them certain prescribed positions. In these compositions a triangular grouping, or a group of three stones, often referred to a Buddhist triad. Relationships of vertical and horizontal, round and flat rocks were based on philosophic, as well as aesthetic, considerations. Principles of *Yang-Yin* are also evident. There are echoes, too, of the Mt. Sumeru *world mountain* theme, common in earlier periods. Most commonly, however, the rocks of Ryōan-ji are said to depict rocks in a river or, on another scale, islands in the sea. More scholarly interpretations refer to the Zen parable of *tora-no-ko watashi* (Crossing of the Tiger Cubs), a title often given to the garden. Other interpretations liken the rocks to the sixteen *arhats*, another story in Zen.[2]

Most explanations of the garden are based primarily on the rocks—as forms, figures, objects or shapes. The sand is usually left unexplained. When explained, the sand, serving as vacant space, is referred to as a depiction of void. The question arises: if it is maintained that the garden is voidness

---

[2] All fifteen rocks cannot be seen at one time: perhaps suggesting that the senses cannot grasp all of reality from any one viewpoint.

In this sketch a flowering morning glory entwines a bamboo fence. The thirty-one syllable verse, known as a *tanka*, celebrates this flower, a favorite subject with Japanese poets since it blossoms so beautifully in the morning only to wither forever at nightfall. There are a number of translations of the accompanying poem. I have made my own translation, based on one of Dr. Suzuki's which seemed to me best to convey the true meaning.

"The morning dawns,
The night soon follows.
Life—transient as dew.
Yet the morning glory, unconcerned,
Goes on blooming, blooming,
Its short complete life."

(If this idea had been expressed in a *haiku*, it might have ended with the words "Yet the morning glory . . ." leaving the reader to fill in the thought.)

translated into sand, why would not a rectangle of sand alone express this concept? Why the rocks? And why their careful choice and arrangement, if we are to grasp a sense of emptiness?

It is at this point that we come to one of the basic paradoxes of Buddhist thought: Only through form can we realize emptiness. Emptiness is thus considered not as a concept reached by the analytical process of reasoning, but as a statement of intuition or perception: "a fact of experience as much as the straightness of a bamboo and the redness of a flower."[3]

From this "fact of experience" is derived the principle of *sumi* painting. The blank sheet of paper is perceived only as paper, and remains as paper. Only by filling the paper does it become empty. Much in the same way the sound of the frog plopping into the still pond creates the silence in Basho's well-known *haiku*. The sound gives form to the silence—the emptiness. In the Nō play it is through voice and instrument that we are aware of profound silence; elaborately colorful costumes create simplicity and bareness; and in the dance, movement creates stillness, and stillness becomes movement.

Emptiness, expressed as vacant space in visual art, silence in music, time and spatial ellipses in poetry or literature, or non-movement in dance, requires aesthetic form for its creation and comprehension. As stated above, the idea of emptiness is not a concept reached by analytical reasoning, but one that must be perceived in aesthetic terms. Aesthetic form is pre-requisite to conceptual perception. Thus, unless the frog leaps within a well-constructed poem the sound produces no silence. Unless the persimmons are completely realized, perfectly composed and executed, they will lie only on white paper— a charming vignette at best. Unless the Nō movements are faultless there will be awareness only of slow-movement, not of non-movement. And without the most careful choice and arrangement of rocks the sand of Ryōan-ji becomes incomprehensible.

The composition of rocks within each group, and of the rock groups with each other and with the surrounding space, is one of the supreme achievements of art.[4] Not one stone could be added, eliminated, or altered in position without destroying the composition and, consequently, its meaning.[5] Yet,

---

[3] *Zen Buddhism and Its Influence on Japanese Culture*, by D. T. Suzuki, page 32. Eastern Buddhist Society, Kyoto, 1938.

[4] For an excellent analysis of the composition see *The Art of Japanese Gardens*, by Loraine E. Kuck, pages 153–56. John Day Company, New York, 1940.

[5] This destruction of relationships is strikingly revealed in an old photograph (*Historical Gardens of Kyoto*, Kyoto, 1910) in which tufts of grass and moss are growing on the unkempt and unraked sand.

it may be asked: Why five groups? Why fifteen rocks? Would not one interesting group, or a single well-shaped rock, allow for an even greater expanse
of sand, and therefore heighten the perception of emptiness? Conceptually,
yes. Perceptually, no.

Perceptually, the single rock or rock group becomes the " center of interest"
and focuses the attention—holding it if, as sculpture, it is interesting; or
failing to hold it, if it is not. Free-standing sculpture demands or repels our
interest, but visually does not affect the space around it. Thought is concentrated and fixed on the form and its inevitable literary or emotional associations. If the surrounding space is considered, the tendency is in terms of
duality: of positive and negative.[6]

Two rock groups would set up two such focal points, creating a spatial
tension between them, but still unrelated to that space, which remains meaningless. Three groups form a common aesthetic and conceptual solution
which is almost universal. The establishment of asymmetry and variation
allows for varied and complex philosophic and aesthetic manipulation. This
triangular structure is an integral part of the Ryōan-ji garden composition.[7]
Limited to this solution, however, the emphasis remains upon the triad;
attention remains on the form. To go beyond the level of literal symbolism,
to penetrate deeper, to fully realize the vacant space, a further step must be
taken. To achieve the "perfect mutual solution" of form and vacant space,
the relationship must be such that the mind does not dwell on either form or
vacant space, but flows freely between both, and includes both. Thus, the
arrangement into five groups is a solution of subtlety and complexity, creating
infinite compositional shifts and visual movements, which prevent stoppage
or fixation and relate the rock and sand as an inseparable unit. Form is
arranged in vacant space in such a way that we perceive emptiness as form,
and form as emptiness.

The basic idea of emptiness, translated into aesthetic terms by various
perceptible means, does not mean, in philosophic terms, emptiness in the
sense that there was something before and nothing now. To illustrate, by
returning to visual expression, the emptiness of Ryōan-ji garden is not the
emptiness of Surrealist paintings like those of Dali, Tanguy, or de Chirico,
which evoke a mood, a planned response, and the yearning to be filled. In a

---

6 It is worth noting that the Zen Buddhists, emphasizing concepts of void, did not use
sculpture as a major expression.

7 An analysis of the garden's triangular compositions may be found in *Architecture of
Japan*, by Arthur Drexler, page 180. Museum of Modern Art, New York, 1955.

de Chirico we think of man, for man is suggested by various forms, shapes and objects identified with man. The emptiness is that of desertion. Man is implied, but is not present, and the resultant sensation is one of longing and loneliness. The vacant space of Ryōan-ji does not evoke a mood of loneliness; it is free of emotional associations. It arouses no thoughts of the absence of man, or of anything connected with human life; nor does it evoke the need to be filled.

In the paintings of Surrealists, space (actually a receding plane) extends endlessly away from the viewer (by means of lines of perspective) and does not return, but meets the equally endless space of sky at a far horizon. Tanguy's rocklike forms, depicted as distinct, separate forms, are set on the surface of this "endless empty space." The basis of the visual concept is the isolation of form in space, and of the separation of the two. By symbolic association: man lost in infinity.

This comparison may help us to understand the spatial concept of the stone garden, for it differs from the above both aesthetically and philosophically.

Aesthetically, or in terms of composition, the sand is strictly confined, with its four borders sharply delineated. (It may be argued that Tanguy's "endless space" is also sharply confined: by the horizon line at the top, and by the picture frame on the sides and at the bottom. However, the viewer is expected to assume that the space begins from the viewer, before the picture plane, and that it extends back beyond the horizon into infinity; the horizon does not mark the end, but merely serves as a device of perspective.) In viewing the garden, the eye is deliberately kept within the rectangle; there is no illusionary device to carry the vision beyond. In addition to being limited horizontally, the space is further controlled by the low earthen wall, which seems to create a shallow "box" and thereby limits the space vertically as well. The space of Ryōan-ji garden is not one of vastness [in the sense of dimension], but of introspection.

In this spatial structure, the rocks are not standing freely—set as isolated forms, independent and in opposition, or suggestive of lonely individuality—but are buried substantially in the ground. Some of the smaller rocks are, in fact, almost completely submerged, with their top surfaces barely above ground level. The proper burial of rocks is given great consideration in Japanese gardening, so that the effect is somewhat similar to icebergs, in which the revealed portion implies greater force and mass than is apparent. This also strengthens the relationship between rocks and sand. The rocks are not so much forms placed on the surface from above as bumps pushing up from below—bumps pushing into space.[8]

Closer to Ryōan-ji garden conceptions is the sculpture of Giacometti, whose thin skeletal figures rise from large solid blocks. The figures in themselves are not especially noteworthy; like the rocks, they exist to give form to the surrounding space. The space given form by Giacometti's figures is enormous. Yet, despite the affinity, the philosophic difference is evident in the conceptual dualism of form and vacant space. Giacometti's figure is man, lonely and isolated within "nothingness." It is the man of Existentialism *thrown into* the void: the concept of nothingness that stands apart, separate, and beside man—the nothingness of despair.

Restated: The *sunyata* of Buddhism is not the emptiness of absence, it is not a nothing existing beside a something, it is not a separate existence, nor does it mean extinction. It is always with individual objects, always co-existent with form, and where there is no form there is no emptiness. "Form is emptiness, and emptiness is form." Beneath these ideas is the Buddhist conception of an object or form as an event, and not as a thing or substance.[9]

In declaring that the garden represents islands in the sea, etc., as is most commonly done, is to be held by form. To say, on the other hand, in more abstract terms, that the sand represents void, is to ignore the rock. All of these are merely equations in which the garden represents x, the unknown. Regarded as a puzzle, the garden offers no solutions, but presents new questions to meet each answer.

If all great art operates on many levels all interpretations are valid—if we realize that all are inadequate. For all explanations are, in fact, no explanations. Iconography alone does not make art religious, although it may add to its ramifications, scope, and depth. It is admittedly useless and futile, as has been done in this paper, to speak of *sunyata*, emptiness, voidness—for as soon as we abstract from the garden as *art*, we lose it. All verbalizations are self-limiting and block perception. Ultimately the garden must be viewed as art, and viewed in silence. As a silent sermon it raises many questions, but

[8] During a recent visit it was noted that too much moss had been allowed to grow at the base of the rocks. Although subtle, the difference in the quantity and length of the moss was enough to upset the stone-sand relationships and to lessen the over-all impact of the garden. The moss had formed five bright green islands. The rocks no longer seemed to be coming up from the sand, but sat mountain-like upon the islands, which were almost "pretty" in appearance. The moss itself resembled lush forests in miniature.

[9] *The Essence of Buddhism*, by D. T. Suzuki, page 42. Buddhist Society of London, London, 1947.

asks for no answers. It calls to mind the flower held before his disciples by the silent Buddha, which brought forth no classification, description, analysis, or discussion, but only the comprehending smile of the clear-seeing.

Like all great art, the garden is perhaps a "visual *koan*." It remains in the mind, and, if it can be likened to anything, rather than "islands in the sea," it is the mind. It does not matter, therefore, of what materials the garden is composed. What is important is the mind that interprets the essentials. The garden exists within ourselves; what we see in the rectangular enclosure is, in short, what we are.

(NOTE: *The writer wishes to express his indebtedness to Mr.* SHINDO TSUJI, *Kyoto sculptor, for suggesting some of the views expressed in this paper.*)

CHAPTER 3

Poetry

FOREWORD

"Zen naturally finds its readiest expression in poetry rather than in philosophy because it has more affinity with feeling than with intellect; its poetic predilection is inevitable."[1]

One of the unique arts of Japan is the reading and writing of the stripped, evocative, seventeen-syllable poem called *haiku*—a form of literary expression which owes much of its spirit to Zen influence. The seeds of this ancient art—ancient at least in Western terms—were sown some seven hundred years ago, but its great blossoming came in the seventeenth century, and *haiku* writing has continued with marked vitality down to the present time.[2]

R. H. Blyth, who has devoted four rewarding volumes to the subject, considers *haiku* "the final flower of all Eastern culture." In a remark of Dr. Johnson's, "Nothing is little to him who feels it with great sensibility," he finds a proper "motto of all *haiku*," for this special poetic form concerns itself entirely with the simple, trivial, usually overlooked material of everyday life; with things which, however insignificant on the surface, are nonetheless "precious treasures and inexhaustible riches" to anyone who has learned not only to look but to see.

---

[1] *An Introduction to Zen Buddhism*, by D. T. Suzuki. Eastern Buddhist Society, Kyoto, 1934. Also published for the Buddhist Society of London by Rider and Company, London, 1949.

[2] Harold Henderson has said that in 1957 there were about fifty monthly magazines in Japan devoted to *haiku*. He estimated that these magazines and other publications—even "the counterpart of the *Wall Street Journal*"—published a yearly total of well over a million *haiku*.

An umbrella—one alone—
Passes by:
An evening of snow.

The white peony:
At the moon, one evening,
It crumbled and fell.

Because of the extreme economy of the established *haiku* form—alternate lines of 5, 7, 5 syllables in the original Japanese—the poet must gain his effects by very subtle means. Yet a successful *haiku* must, in spite of its brevity, not only evoke a mood but also manage to convey a picture vivid enough to stir the imagination of the reader or listener. Thus in the *haiku*, as in all other Zen-influenced arts, we find a certain demand laid on each participant. One is expected to "fill in," to continue where the artist, so to speak, leaves off.

Although in Blyth's opinion to properly read a single *haiku* requires years of "unconscious absorption" of Far Eastern culture, many Westerners have, without preparation, come on translations of these poems—Mr. Blyth's included—with an immediate sense of happy discovery. *Haiku's* artful simplicity can arouse and deepen awareness of the simple yet miraculous "is-ness" of everyday sights and sounds, for *haiku* is concerned with the Here and Now, with that necessity to "catch life as it flows" which is also so much a part of Zen philosophy.

Western poets usually tend to fill in details, to prepare their readers at some length for a poem's "high moment." Therein lies the basic difference between the approach of East and West to poetry, and yet when the high moment of a Western poem comes it is often very much in the mood and spirit of true *haiku*. Harold Gould Henderson in his *haiku* anthology[3] gives an illuminating example of this particular point of comparison. He quotes the climax of Edward Shanks's poem *Night Piece*:

So far . . . so low . . .
A drowsy thrush? A waking nightingale?
Silence. We do not know.

These lines, says Henderson, would pass the most meticulous tests for *haiku* were it not for the last four words, which are, by *haiku* standards, totally unnecessary. The word "silence" alone would have conveyed for a *haiku* poet all that was really required.

---

[3] *An Introduction to Haiku.* Doubleday, New York, 1958.

It is common knowledge that in passing from one language to another all poetry loses some of its original quality. This is particularly true with languages as unlike as English and Japanese. The "sound effects," the frequent use of onomatopoeia, the plays on words, the puns—these are scarcely transferable, yet when a too literal rendering of *haiku* is attempted we may get an example as ludicrous as that cited by Edward Seidensticker in his comments on Japanese translation difficulties:

> All I could say was "Oh, Oh!"
> At cherry-blossomed Yoshino.[4]

To rhyme a *haiku*, as Henderson often does in translation, is also a deviation from the Japanese convention, for since all Japanese words end in either a vowel or an "n," the use of rhyming in the original language would soon become, as Henderson says, "intolerably monotonous." He justifies his own use of rhyme in translation not only as a matter of personal taste, but also because rhyme in English can serve as a "substitute" for the "effect of definite form" given to Japanese versions by their strict alternation of five and seven syllables. Further, not to use rhyme (or assonance) in the English rendering is, says Henderson, to run the risk of producing translated *haiku* which may sound only like unfinished prose rather than poetry.

Although to understand this poetry at its most profound level necessitates some knowledge of the Japanese language[5]—so exquisite in nuance and so maddeningly oblique—Henderson's careful exposition of certain laws of *haiku* can greatly aid a Westerner's appreciation:

> In order to produce their effect, haiku writers make great use of what they call *renso*, or association of ideas, and this they do in several different ways. The older haiku-makers came to the conclusion that one experience common to all men was the change of weather with the different seasons, and so introduced into nearly all their poems what is known as a *ki*, or "season." This means that in nearly all their haiku there is some word or expression that indicates the time of year, and so forms a background for the picture that they are trying to bring up in the reader's mind.

---

[4] *Encounter*, August, 1958.

[5] Fosco Maraini's *Meeting with Japan* (Viking, New York, 1960) has a brief but illuminating discussion of the Japanese language, pages 246–257. For further elucidation see references in Donald Keene's *Living Japan* (Doubleday, New York), and G. B. Sansom's authoritative *Japan, a Short Cultural History* (Century Company, New York, 1931). To go deeper one must turn to books like P. Takenobu's *Kenkyushu's New Japanese-English Dictionary* (Tokyo), and S. Miyazaki's, *The Japanese Dictionary Explained in English* (Tokyo).

Such a *kigo* (season word) may be a definite naming of the season, like "summer heat" or "autumn wind," or a mere suggestion, like a reference to plum blossoms or to snow. The custom of using *kigo* has hardened into an almost inviolable rule, and most modern collections of haiku arrange their contents according to the seasons to which the poems refer.

It may be noted in passing that the use of *ki* is probably at the base of a charge that has been advanced that haiku are more concerned with nature than with human affairs. Such a statement is ridiculous. Haiku are more concerned with human emotions than with human acts, and natural phenomena are used to reflect human emotions, but that is all. The older and simpler forerunners of haiku may make the comparison in definite words, as in this, by Moritake (1452–1549):

> A morning-glory!
> And so—today!—may seem
> my own life-story.

meaning, of course, "I too may die today; and if I do . . ." But this was written before the haiku form had come into its own, and later poets preferred to get their effects by somewhat more subtle suggestion.

There are many other things suggested by *ki*, and just as morning-glories bring up thoughts of quickly fading beauty, so do the autumn winds suggest sadness, and plum blossoms the promise of perfect beauty to be attained by the later cherry blooms. It should be mentioned that the word "cuckoo" has not the same associations as with us. The song of the *hototogisu*, the little Japanese cuckoo, is usually heard at dusk. It is considered to be not only beautiful, but also slightly sad; other names for the *hototogisu* are "bird of the other world," "bird of disappointed love," etc.

As would naturally be expected, many haiku evoke associations by references to Buddhist beliefs, to social customs, and to episodes in Japanese history that every Japanese would know. Unfortunately these references would be as unintelligible to the Western reader as the connotations of Easter, Thanksgiving, or Guy Fawkes' Day would be to the average Japanese . . . .

Besides these, there is another form of association of ideas to which special attention must be drawn, as it is used in many haiku. This is a comparison of two or more ideas expressed in the poem itself, and it must always be looked for. In some haiku the comparison is obvious, as in this one, which is by the modern poet Kwaso:

> The tower high
> I climb; there, on that fir top
> sits a butterfly!

Here the point is in the contrast, while in Sodo's trinity of early summer:

> Green leaves to see,
> a mountain cuckoo, and the first
> bonito—all three!

115

the point is the piling up of the similar effects of three delightful things acting simultaneously on three different senses. (To a Japanese the first bonito is as much a delicacy as the first trout is to us.)

These two examples are quite simple and without any very deep meaning, but in other haiku the comparison of ideas may be so hidden that the author's intention will be realized only after repeated readings. It is interesting, though not important here, to note that the use of this particular form of association is probably due to the influence of Chinese classics, just as a Latin influence can be found in the inversions to which we are accustomed in our own poetry.

There is still another device which haiku-makers use to condense the expression of their thoughts. That is the omission of words which would be required in a grammatically formed sentence but which are not really needed to make the sense clear. It is a device which is extremely effective when used with discretion, but when second-rate writers use it to excess it may result in haiku that are more like puzzles than poems. The effect of haziness produced by over-condensation, however, should never be confused with the difficulty of understanding some of the great haiku, which may not give out their full meaning, even to those who are trained in the art of reading, until an explanation is given of the circumstances under which they were written. Really great haiku suggests so much that more words would lessen their meaning.

In addition to such general characteristics as have been discussed above, there are certain technical conventions which would have to be known to anyone who wishes to go back to the originals. Most important are the uses of the *kireji*, or "cut-words," like *kana*, which usually marks the end of a haiku, and *ya*, which divides a haiku into two parts that are to be equated or compared. Other conventions have grown up around the uses of *kigo*, the "season words." (In the absence of any other indication, a reference to deer means that the time is autumn, etc., etc.) Nearly all such conventions are used primarily to eliminate unnecessary words.

A few of Henderson's rhymed translations of famous *haiku* have been included here, with the original Japanese and the "as nearly as possible" English equivalents written alongside. Together these indicate not only the extraordinary economy and allusiveness of *haiku* but the formidable barriers facing a translator.

> The piercing chill I feel:
>   my dead wife's comb, in our bedroom,
>   under my heel . . .

Mi-ni-shimu   ya   bō-sai-no   kushi   neya   ni   fumu
Body-into-pierce : dead-wife's comb bedroom in tread-on

> As the spring rains fall,
>   soaking in them, on the roof,
>   is a child's rag ball.

Harusame ni   nuretsutsu   yane-no   te-mari   kana
Spring-rain in being-soaked roof's hand-ball kana

>   Blossoms on the pear—
>   and a woman in the moonlight
>   reads a letter there.

Nashi-no   hana   tsuki ni   fumi-yomu   onna   ari
Pear's   blossoms   moon by letter-reading woman there-is

—BUSON (1715–1783)

>   All the rains of June:
>   and one evening, secretly,
>   through the pines, the moon.

Samidare ya   aru   yo   hisokani matsu-no   tsuki
June-rains : certain night secretly pine-trees' moon

—RYOTA (1718–1787)

>   Get out of my road
>   and allow me to plant these
>   bamboos, Mr. Toad!

Soko   noite   take-ue-sase   yo   hiki-gaeru
That-place leaving allow-bamboo-planting!   toad

—CHORA (1729–1781)

>   Spring too, very soon!
>   They are setting the scene for it—
>   plum tree and moon.

Haru mo yaya keshiki totonou tsuki   to   ume
Spring also soon   scene   prepare   moon and plum

—BASHO (1643–1694)

>   A bush warbler comes:
>   all muddy are the feet he wipes
>   upon the blooming plums.

Uguisu ya doro-ashi nuguu ume-no-hana
Warbler : muddy-feet wipe plum-blossoms

>   A lovely thing to see:
>   through the paper window's hole,
>   the Galaxy.

Utsukushi ya   shōji-no   ana-no   Ama-no-gawa
Lovely   : sliding-door's hole's Heavenly-River

—ISSA (1762–1826)

117

In his invaluable book, *Japanese Literature*,[6] Donald Keene has written of the so-called linked verses, for which, so he tells us, the *haiku* served as a "poetic building block," *haiku* having originated as the opening verse of a series of linked-verse. These linked verses are in a way comparable to the scroll paintings of China and Japan which, when unrolled bit by bit, reveal landscapes or events through which the onlooker may travel at his own pace. Keene has translated from the famous seventeenth-century poet Basho's travel diary, *The Narrow Road of Oku*, the circumstances attendant on the writing of a series of these linked verses, and the story tells us a great deal about the quality of mind and spirit brought for centuries to the composition of poetry in Japan.

"As it was our plan to sail down the Mogami River, we waited at a place called Oishida for the weather to clear. The seeds of the old school of haikai had been scattered here, and the days of its flowering, unforgotten, still brought the sound of the northern flute to the solitary lives of the poets of Oishida. They said, 'We are groping ahead on the road of poetry, uncertain as to whether to follow the old or the new way, but here no one can guide us. Will you not help?' I was unable to refuse them, and joined in making a roll of linked verse. Of all the poetry-gatherings of my journey, this showed the most taste."

Here is what they wrote, beginning with the honored guest, Basho:

samidare wo	Gathering seawards
atsumete suzushi	The rains of May, coolly flows
Mogami-gawa	Mogami River.

BASHO

kishi ni hotaru wo	The little fishing boats tie
tsunagu funagai	Their firefly lights to the bank

ICHIEI

uribatake	The melon fields
izayou sora ni	Wait for the moon to shine from
kage machite	The hesitant sky.

SORA

sato wo mukai ni	Going off towards the village
kuwa no hosomichi	A path through the mulberry-trees.

SENSUI

6 Grove Press, New York, 1955.

Blyth in his lengthy study of *haiku*[7] has come up with a list of thirteen characteristics that he considers common to this poetic form: selflessness, loneliness, grateful acceptance, wordlessness, nonintellectuality, contradictoriness, humor, freedom, nonmorality, simplicity, materiality, love, courage.

A few examples will indicate the nature of his interpretations, and although they need not be taken as definitive, they are of interest here as another expression of the Zen *Weltanschauung*.

Selflessness. Blyth makes the point that it could equally well be considered Self-fullness—spelled, however, with a capital S, and implying "interpenetration with all things." The modern West might term it "loss of self."

> The butterfly having disappeared
> My spirit
> Came back to me.

Loneliness—by which is also implied "interpenetration with all things"—finds expression in a *haiku* about a mountain bird called the *kankodori* that lives far from the haunts of man and whose voice, somewhat resembling that of the wood pigeon, is heard always from a distance.

> Ah, *kankodori,*
> Deepen thou
> My loneliness.

Grateful acceptance.

> The grasses of the garden,—
> They fall
> And lie as they fall.

Wordlessness. In the *haiku*, words are used "not to express anything but rather to clear away something that seems to stand between us and the real things"—which are in truth not separate from ourselves at all.

> They spoke no word,
> The visitor, the host,
> And the white chrysanthemum.

Humor. (The *uguisu* is a Japanese bush warbler.)

> The *uguisu*
> Poops
> On the slender plum branch.

---

[7] *Haiku*, by R. H. Blyth: Volume 1, *Eastern Culture*. Hokuseido Press, Tokyo, 1949.

Freedom.

> Simply trust:
> Do not the petals flutter down,
> Just like that?

Simplicity.

> The Rose of Sharon
> By the roadside,
> Was eaten by the horse.

Materiality. Zen and *haiku* share an emphasis on "the material as against the so-called spiritual." In other words, *haiku* deals with *things*: snow, mice, scarecrows, children with runny noses, priests snoring, frogs croaking, the wind.

> Striking the fly
> I hit also
> A flowering plant.

Love. Here is meant love of the universe and all things in it, but a love without sentimentality, a quality which is not even to be read in the following.

> Mountain persimmons;
> The mother is eating
> The astringent parts.

Of *haiku* in general, Blyth has written:

"A haiku is not a poem, it is not literature; it is a hand beckoning, a door half-opened, a mirror wiped clean. It is a way of returning to nature, our moon nature, our cherry blossom nature, our falling leaf nature, in short to our Buddha nature. It is a way in which the cold winter rain, the swallows of evening, even the very day in its hotness, and the length of the night become truly alive, share in our humanity, speak their own silent and expressive language."[8]

Alan Watts, a perceptive contributor to Western understanding of Zen, has made his own recording of some translated *haiku*, with the original spoken in Japanese by Sumire Hasegawa Jacobs, daughter of the late noted Zen painter, Sabro Hasegawa. The text of this recording, which follows, sets forth with special clarity the relationship of Zen to *haiku*.   [N. W. R.]

---

[8] *Ibid.*

HAIKU[1]

By ALAN WATTS

> The sea darkens,
> The voices of the wild ducks
> Are faintly white.

> In the dark forest
> A berry drops.
> The sound of the water.

These are two complete poems from a kind of Japanese poetry known as haiku. To my mind this is beyond all doubt at once the simplest and the most sophisticated form of literature in the world, for the invariable mark of great artistry is its artlessness. It looks easy. It looks almost as if it were a work not of art but of nature.

When you are used to Western poetry the haiku comes as something of a shock. It seems to be no more than a fragment of poetry awakening anticipations which it does not fulfill.

> The stars on the pond.
> Again the winter shower
> Ruffles the water.

It seems to be a poem just begun but left unfinished. But with a little more familiarity you realize that haiku poetry excels in one of the rarest of the artistic virtues, the virtue of knowing when to stop; of knowing when enough has been said. And there are other respects in which this is the secret not only of art but of life itself. Haiku represents the ultimate refinement of a long tradition in Far Eastern literature which derived its inspiration from Zen Buddhism. . . . The unique quality of Zen Buddhism, and of all the arts which it has inspired, is a profoundly startling simplicity. There is a complete lack of the unessential and a marvelously refreshing directness.

. . . When one of the great Zen masters was asked, "What is the ultimate principle of Buddhism?" he answered, "A sesame bun." To the same sort of

---

[1] This is an edited transcript of a talk originally given over Station KPFA-FM in Berkeley, California. Subsequently it has been made available as one side of an LP record entitled "Haiku," manufactured by Musical Engineering Associates, Box 303, Sausalito, California, and sold by them at $5.95. The other side is a recitation of haiku in Japanese and English, with a musical background. Translations of haiku here quoted are by R. H. Blyth, from his four-volume *Haiku* (Hokuseido Press, Tokyo). ALAN WATTS.

The great poet Basho
(1644–1694) famed for his
haiku, took his pseudo-
nym from the Japanese
name for the banana tree.
The comic verse on the
scroll is based on the best
known of Basho's *haiku*,
of which there are many
translations, among them
this one:

"An old pond—
The sound of the water.
When a frog jumps in."

The meaning of Sengai's
wry verse is:

"If there were a pond
    hereabouts,
I would jump in
And let Basho hear the
    splash."

SENGAI

question another replied, "It is windy again this morning." Another handed the questioner a piece of cake. To look for some sort of deep symbolism in these replies is to miss the point completely, for they are the plainest and most complete answers to the great problems of philosophy and religion. For it is the chief intuition of Zen that the answer to the problem of life, or we might say to the problem of God, is so utterly obvious that one hardly needs even to look for it. According to Zen, the reason why our quest for some ultimate reality is so difficult is that we are looking in obscure places for what is out in the broad daylight. Our trouble is not that we haven't thought about it enough but that we have thought about it entirely too much. Once again, the art is one of knowing when to stop. As another Zen master said, "If you want to see into it, see into it directly, but when you begin to think about it it is altogether missed."

Zen answers profound questions with simple everyday facts: "It is windy again this morning." But watch out! This is not a kind of sentimental pantheism or nature mysticism. Still less is it a simple philistinism as if to say, "Stop asking silly questions and get on with your work." The difficulty of talking about Zen is that every attempt to explain it makes it more obscure. Somebody asked the Master Bokuju, "We have to dress and eat every day and how do we get out of all that?" In other words, "How does one put up with insufferable routine?" Bokuju answered, "We dress. We eat." The questioner said, "I don't understand." "If you don't understand," replied Bokuju, "put on your clothes and eat your food."

These answers may seem very prosaic, very matter-of-fact and dry, but haiku is the same insight, the same view of the ultimate reality in terms of poetry. Yet I must warn you again, do not look for symbolism or for a sort of practical materialism. The point is far more obvious than that. I think one of the easiest approaches to an appreciation of haiku is through the realization that a poetry of this kind lies buried in our own poetic literature, for there are quite a number of poems that are remembered only for a single line: "A rose red city, half as old as time," a line in which the poem attained for a single second to pure poetry, which is something as utterly indefinable as the meaning of Zen.

Blyth has made a considerable selection of haiku from English literature, conveniently saving me the trouble of searching around for examples:

> The tinkle of the thirsty rill
> Unheard all day, ascends again.

123

The weak-eyed bat, with short shrill shriek
Flits by on leathern wings.

Annihilating all that's made
To a green thought, in a green shade.

Some bird from out the brake
Starts into voice a moment
Then is still.

In shades the orange bright
Like golden lamps in a green night.

The wonder of these few lines is that in each instance they represent a moment of intense perception. Every one of us can recall a number of such moments in our lives, moments when we were aware of being alive in an unusually vivid way. I can recollect a glimpse of sunlit pigeons against a dark thundercloud. The sound of cowbells in a mountain silence on a hot afternoon. The noise of a distant waterfall in the dusk. The smell of burning leaves in the haze of an autumn day. A filigree of black branches against the cold blue of a winter sky. The moon hanging like a luminous fruit from a pine bough. And as I describe such moments I begin almost to speak in haiku. But I feel no desire to elaborate upon them, for the feeling is intense to the degree that I am not greedy with it, that I do not try to grasp it with my memory for more than a second or two.

Now this is part of the secret of Zen; that life reveals itself most plainly when you do not clutch at it either with your feelings or with your questing intellect. Touch and go! That is the whole art. That's why our eyes see best when they brush across things and do not stare in a fixed gaze. Everything kept goes stale. The reason is that whatever is momentous, living and moving is momentary. Minute by minute our experience moves along without return and we are in accord with it to the degree that we move with it as the mind follows music or as a leaf goes with the stream. Yet this is to say too much, for the moment we stop to philosophize about it, to make a system of it, we have missed a beat. The greatest of all the haiku poets, Basho, put it thus:

When the lightning flashes,
How admirable he who thinks not—
"Life is fleeting."

Though this is perhaps a poor haiku for the very reason that it begins to philosophize even though it philosophizes against philosophizing. But it only just begins—and this is the point. Being too much against philosophizing is just as much an arid intellectualism as being too much for it. Basho is to the point in the most famous of all haiku:

> The old pond.
> A frog jumps in.
> Plop!

These lines are said to represent the moment in which Basho's study of Zen came to its sudden fulfillment, when the mystery of the universe was solved in the plop of the falling frog.

This state of mind is technically called *mushin*, literally the state of no-mind. This is when we are simply aware of what is without distorting it by the complexities of self-consciousness as when, in efforts to get the very most out of life, we not only feel that we feel, but feel that we feel that we feel. The state of *mushin* is thus an extremely clear kind of unselfconsciousness where the poet is not divided from his subject, the knower from the known. If and when he speaks about his own feelings they are not seen as reactions but as an integral part of the experience which he records:

> The scarecrow in the distance.
> It walked with me
> As I walked.

> Sleet falling.
> Fathomless, infinite
> Loneliness.

> Winter desolation.
> In a world of one color
> The sound of the wind.

> The evening haze.
> Thinking of past things
> How far off they are.

The literary form of the haiku is even more rigid than that of the sonnet, which is perhaps the most formal style of English poetry. Not only must it be expressed in seventeen syllables but there are a number of traditional restrictions of the subject matter. Haiku must always be written in harmony with the current seasons of the year, and there is a strong tendency to adhere to certain customary themes; certain flowers, trees, insects, animals, festivals and landscape being the usual occasions of the poems. This makes a classified

125

anthology of haiku rather monotonous reading unless you jump about haphazardly from one part of the book to another. But strict limitations of form seem to be a condition of great artistry, an essential part of the very art being to see how much can be done with so little. Sometimes a haiku seems to represent a rather stilted and conventionally Japanese sort of scene as this from Shiki:

> A willow
> And two or three cows
> Waiting for the boat.

Or this, if I remember rightly, by Kobori-Enshiu:

> A cluster of summer trees
> A glimpse of the sea
> A pale evening moon.

Contrariwise there are times when the poet seems to outdo himself with ingenuity:

> A fallen leaf
> Returning to the branch?
> Butterfly.

Or this by Issa:

> A brushwood gate
> And for a lock
> This snail.

But the best haiku are those which arise from the tension between the rigidity of the form and the depth of the poetic feeling. Both Chinese and Japanese artists admire beyond everything a certain kind of restraint, an expression which hints rather than states, indicates rather than explains, suggests rather than describes; an art which leaves an enormous amount to the beholder's, or the listener's, imagination, instead of excluding his participation by a perfection of finished detail. Yet the listener is not expected to fill in the details literally but to share in the mood which the poem implies:

> Not a single stone
> To throw at the dog.
> The wintry moon.

> Leaves falling
> Lie one on another.
> The rain beats on the rain.

126

What is restrained is the temptation of every artist to show off, to leave his listener nothing to do but admire. But the haiku poet must, at great pains, acquire a certain primitivity and unfinishedness of expression which comes off only in a social context when the reader or listener is also in the know. It is a poetry where the reader is almost as important as the poet, where deep calls unto deep and the poem is successful to the degree that the reader shares the same poetic experience which, however, is never explicitly stated. This is not, though, as in the decadent period of Chinese poetry achieved by an extreme use of literary allusion intelligible only to an exclusive coterie of scholars. What the listener has to be in the know about is not literature but life, places, seasons, moods and, above all, the utterly indescribable insight of Zen Buddhism. This has been called an acute perception of the Thusness of things. Not their goodness or badness, beauty or ugliness, usefulness or uselessness nor even their abstract Isness or Being, but rather their very concrete Thinginess.

> Sticking on the mushroom
> The leaf
> Of some unknown tree.

> The tree frog
> Riding the banana leaf
> Sways and quivers.

> Walking in the winter rain
> The umbrella
> Pushes me back.

> Evening rain.
> The banana leaf
> Speaks of it first.

Haiku is, of course, in harmony with, and often accompanies, a style of Chinese and Japanese painting which similarly lifts just one corner of the view and leaves the rest to one's imagination, as when in black ink the artist merely suggests the barest hint of a bamboo swaying in the wind and leaves the rest of the paper blank. . . . And haiku is very frequently used as a type of accompanying verse to this sort of painting.

I believe that haiku had their origin in anthologies of short quotations from Chinese poems which the Zen Buddhists compiled for purposes of meditation. There is a large collection of such poems in the first volume of R. H.

Blyth's *Haiku* and they are taken from a book called the *Zenrin-kushu*. One of these puts the quality of Thusness a little more philosophically and therefore for us, perhaps a little more intelligibly when it says:

> If you do not believe,
> Look at September!
> Look at October!
> The yellow leaves falling, falling,
> To fill both mountain and river.

But again, and for the last time, let me say that you must not look here for any symbolism, any idea either of God revealed in the beauty of the autumn leaves or just autumn leaves with no God, or of the transiency of life, or of anything else. The mysterious and yet obvious Thusness of things is clear when you see it directly without asking questions.

Gensha, another old Zen master, was asked how to enter the path of Buddhism. He answered, "Do you hear that stream?" "Why yes." "There," he concluded, "is the way to enter." And the poet Gochiku put it quite properly in a haiku:

> The long night.
> The sound of the water
> Says what I think.

CHAPTER 4

Ceremonial Tea

FOREWORD

The roots of the Japanese art of ceremonial tea taking, *cha-no-yu*, go back many hundreds of years, back to China and Taoism. Legend has it that a devoted follower of the great Taoist philosopher, Lao-tzu, first offered a ritual cup of the "golden elixir" to his revered master at the gate of the Han Pass, sometime in the fifth century before the Christian era. Later records indicate that Zen monks were accustomed to gather before the image of Bodhidharma, the First Patriarch, to drink a special mixture of whipped green tea—a ritual that may well have been related to the mythical origins of the beverage. During Bodhidharma's nine unbroken years of meditation facing a blank wall (in his effort to reach supreme enlightenment), he found himself unable at last to keep his eyelids from closing with fatigue, and in despair one day he tore them off and threw them on the ground. Where the eyelids fell there sprang up a bush with shiny green leaves. Subsequently, disciples coming to sit at the great teacher's feet to learn from him the Perfect Wisdom, also found trouble with their eyelids during prolonged meditation. Finally they took to brewing the leaves of the bush that had grown from the First Patriarch's eyelids. This magic potion served to keep them wakeful. It was the first tea.

According to Okakura,[1] after the incursion of the barbarian Mongols, the Chinese abandoned ceremonial whipped tea and took to the more plebeian

---

[1] *The Book of Tea*, by Okakura Kakuzo. Dodd, Mead and Company, New York, 1906. Reprinted by the Charles E. Tuttle Company, Rutland, Vermont—Tokyo, Japan, 1956.

methods of steeping the leaves, and it was this method which reached Europe centuries later. The Japanese, however, who in 1281 successfully resisted the Mongol invaders, continued the practice of the "art of tea," thus demonstrating once again their genius at taking over, preserving, and in many instances improving on, the graces and ideals of their Chinese neighbors.

Tea drinking, accompanied by quiet conversation and the enjoyment of a suitable poem, a single fine example of brushwork, an inspired arrangement of flowers, the handling of a few unpretentious, carefully selected utensils, was in its beginning a pastime for Japanese philosophers and artists. During the turbulent sixteenth and seventeenth centuries it became popular with warriors and statesmen as well. Famous emperors, redoubtable generals, governors of provinces, set out to acquire the gentle refinements of tea. Seeking brief respite from their many troubles, they learned how, in the proper Zen spirit, to offer, or take, the soup-like whipped green liquid in some small rustic garden house, in an almost empty room designed as "the abode of vacancy." Here they could, for a brief hour, relax from the burden of their complicated daily lives. Along with their tea they might also hope to imbibe something of the Buddhist ideals of serenity, reverence, harmony and egolessness.

Although the great tea masters who became the acknowledged arbiters of taste in all fields of art were essentially an aristocracy, their influence nonetheless infused itself so strongly throughout the general culture that the Japanese language acquired the expression "*mucha*," or "It isn't tea"—a criticism not too unlike an Englishman's "It isn't cricket," as A. L. Sadler pointed out in his exhaustive study of the lore and laws of Teaism.[2] To this day in Japan, architecture, garden planning, flower arrangement, painting, the writing of poetry, all subtly but definably show their ancient relationship to the Zen-woven web of *cha-no-yu*.

Yet any atmosphere of stilted preciosity found around the tea ceremony as practiced today by no means expresses the tea cult's original ideals. A profound significance lay under the strict laws of serene and artless simplicity governing the art of tea, but these laws were not to be considered in any way unnatural or recondite. Matsudaira Fumai Harusato, Lord of the Province of Izumo and an accomplished tea man, had this to say on the subject:

"Teaism means contentment . . . to live contentedly and joyfully with bare

---

[2] *Cha-no-yu*, by A. L. Sadler. Kegan Paul, Trench, Trübner and Company, Ltd., London, 1930.

necessities is Teaism. . . . Those who keep their Teaism for the Tea-room are not properly educated in it. For what is a Tea-room but a shelter from the rain? Those who cannot practice *cha-no-yu* without requiring any other reason for enjoying it than the thing itself should give it up."

Rikyu, the master who taught the arts of tea to the all-powerful general Hideyoshi, also repudiated the notion that *cha-no-yu* harbored any special mystery. When questioned on the subject he said simply, "You place the charcoal so that the water boils properly and you make the tea to bring out the proper taste. You arrange the flowers as they appear when they are growing. In summer you suggest coolness and in winter cosiness. There is no other secret."

He then pressed home his points by reciting:

> Tea is nought but this,
> First you make the water boil,
> Then infuse the tea,
> Then you drink it properly,
> That is all you need to know.

When, however, following this explanation, the inquirer remarked in some disgust that he knew all that sort of thing already, the master replied with asperity, "Well, if there is anyone who knows it already I shall be very pleased to become his pupil."

And indeed there was much more to *cha-no-yu* than Rikyu would lead one to believe, for tea had become essentially "a way of life." Just how much was implied in the term "tea master" is suggested in a story Sadler tells about a master once invited by a wealthy man to come to his house for *cha-no-yu* on an early autumn day. While lingering with the three other guests in the *roji*, or waiting house, the master ventured to prophesy what verse among hundreds of choices they might expect to find hanging on this occasion in the alcove, or *tokonoma*. Upon entering the tea room they found that the prophecy had been correct. In the alcove hung a scroll on which was written certain famous verses of Eikei:

> What a lonely sight
> When the clover-grass grows long
> Round our dwelling place
> Not a trace of humankind
> Truly an autumnal scene.

When asked how he knew this particular verse would appear, the tea master replied that as they entered the part of the garden nearest the tea house, he had noticed fallen leaves and withered grasses. Their host had "just left the garden as it was and this lent it a most desolate and melancholy air so that immediately that verse came to mind and I imagined he would use it in the tokonoma today."

No less than one hundred rules for *cha-no-yu* were laid down in the sixteenth century. Many of these are concerned with the proper use of flowers, with how to scoop out tea, handle the hot water ladle, the charcoal, the caddies, the tea bowls—all to be done so as to create, with true Zen paradoxicality, a sense of artless naturalness. It is in the first few of these intricate rules, however, that we most clearly glimpse the Zen-inspired philosophy underlying the ritual.

"If any one wishes to enter the Way of Tea he must be his own teacher. It is only by careful observation that one learns.

"He is a fool who gives his opinion without suitable experience.

"No pains must be spared in helping anyone anxious to learn.

"One who is ashamed to show ignorance will never be any good.

"To become expert one needs first love, second dexterity, and then perseverance." [N. W. R.]

TEA[1]

By LANGDON WARNER

What one can say about the force exerted by the tea ceremony on so many facets of Japanese culture since the fifteenth century is far short of the truth. The mystery is that so restrained and rigorous an aesthetic has thoroughly flavored the life and tastes of a nation which could never have entirely comprehended such refinements, at least as a nation, and which includes its proper share of vulgarians and insensitive people.

There is danger in attributing to a whole nation some tendency the outsider finds charming in his contacts with a cultivated and enlightened few. Yet it must be recognized that generations of craftsmen have unquestionably produced architecture, pottery, textiles, and all the necessary endless furniture for living in a manner conforming to the reticent, demure taste of the Zen practitioners and of tea. This phenomenon must indicate something more

---

[1] From *The Enduring Art of Japan*, by Langdon Warner. Harvard University Press, Cambridge, 1952. Reprinted by Grove Press, New York.

than a blind ability on the part of the artisans to cater to a philosophy for which they lacked all sympathy or comprehension. I have been seated on the threshold of the shop of a simple craftsman and given tea made in an unglazed pot of common Chinese I-hsing ware. I did not realize till I took my leave that I had shared in a genuine tea ceremony. Even to some of the more formal details—the requisite number of sips, talk about the tea pot and its age and provenance, down to the *negoro* lacquer tray from which the color had been scrubbed by generations of use—we had conformed to the gentle rigors of Zen and tea.

The best understanding of the subject is to be found by the Westerner in Okakura's *Book of Tea*. There, in delicate English prose, is set down something of the spirit and the austerity of restraint which practice in the art of tea serving (for it is an art) engenders. I can but suggest the mood and the circumstances of the tea ceremony, for we have all been conscious of such a mood even if the circumstances are seldom deliberately practiced in the West and the atmosphere, with us, can hardly be consciously evoked.

Imagine, then, a Japanese gathering of four or five old cronies, imbued with the spirit of Zen philosophy, in a tiny room bare except for the gear of tea drinking—the hearth for charcoal set in the floor, the big iron kettle and the crane-wing hearth brush and a single picture in the niche with a flower arrangement set below.

The substance hidden under this simple shape is no esoteric Oriental affair, but something so common to humanity the world over that we all can grasp it. Origins and the history of the cult aside, it consists in a meeting of chosen spirits who have much to talk over. It is not accident that the national taste had made them predominantly interested in each others' art treasures and that the talk concerning these has directed the conversational channel now associated with tea. But I have heard the talk swing about to the local folklore and the archaeology of the neighborhood, to abstractions of philosophy, and to a disputed fact in history. And all the time the ceremony—if indeed it was that—has moved on its appointed course.

The instinct which has developed the tea ceremony exists universally, where a certain civility and leisure exist. Add that in Japan it has been the serious diversion for the best minds, that the philosophers have developed all the significance of using simple, even crude, utensils and have loved particularly those associated with past generations; then one begins to comprehend what the tea master may select for his garden and his gear.

His tearoom is a thatched cottage suggesting refined poverty and its setting may be a pine grove with vistas cut, the banks of a mountain brook where pure water for tea is at hand, or a garden set with shrubs and an occasional ancient pine. Just within sight of the low door, outside which entering guests will leave their shoes, is a bench for them to sit on till their number—four or five—is complete, and the signal comes that the host is ready.

Great care is lavished on this spot and all that is in view. From the bench, perhaps sheltered by a thatch, the path leads down to a stone water-basin beside the tea-house door. This path, long or short, is the tea master's garden. A thousand arts have been employed to make it suggest the wood or the mountain path or the temple close. It is most successful when one becomes convinced in traversing its few yards, that here, quite by chance, one has come across the dwelling of a retired gentleman, living remote and sufficient to himself. Here, one sees at once, will be found simple hospitality and good talk from some old man who has the wisdom that comes from being much alone. Such a person may be a retired minister of state, sick of the life of courts. He may be a simple country gentleman fallen on poverty and quite content. One looks forward to a talk with him and to handling the well-worn bamboo spoon that, years ago, he whittled to scoop out his tea. Here, best of all places, can be settled that vexed question of the ancient pottery kiln said to have been once the pride of the village in the valley. Surely some of its make will have been handed down in this man's family and he can set one right about the matter of the generations of the master craftsmen.

That path to the cottage door has demonstrated what a single garden can do, and you may ring the changes on it without limit and arrange your garden to suit any taste, from pleasant folly to a knowledge of the Absolute. It is no mystery that tea masters, with their Zen Buddhist cast of mind, should have made the most valuable contributions to the gardens of Japan.

It seems unkind and hardly necessary in this connection to add that serving tea, like other arts, has from time to time in the hands of lesser spirits become frozen into intolerable correctness. Three or four hours can seem like a lifetime if they are spent on one's knees in deadly terror of omitting one of the hundred ritual motions in handling the tea bowl or setting down the caddy or neglecting, in proper phrase, to compliment the host on his arrangement of flowers. Yet that is what a properly brought up young girl must frequently undergo during the process of learning what the Victorians called Deportment. Even the vocabulary and the phrases used, as well as their sequence in

drinking
a bowl of green tea
I stopped the war

the order of events, have been decreed by the professional instructors. At a professional's house one longs for the presence of some guest who, keeping insensibly within the unmarked boundaries of appropriate subjects, creates an atmosphere of human intercourse quite unrestrained except by a sensitive regard for other people.

There have been periods in Japanese history when teaism became the rage—and rage is perhaps of all things most contradictory to the mood of tea. Vulgarians, anxious to purchase a reputation for culture, outbid each other for famous tea bowls and tea caddies. Incapable of critical judgment of the objects, they paid outrageously for things already made famous through association with famous tea masters—a kind of snobbery not unfamiliar in the West and precisely that fostered by our book dealers to tempt collectors by means of association values.

There is a delightful Korean peasant rice bowl called the Ido, which has half a dozen brocaded bags, kimonos for the different seasons, and which lives in five boxes, each inscribed by one of its former owners. It was brought back from the Taikō's Korean campaign in the early seventeenth century by a famous general, fell into the discriminating hands of one of the most accomplished tea masters, was used more than once by the Shogun and finally, twenty years ago, was sold for one hundred and eighty-nine thousand yen, which, at that time, amounted to ninety-eight thousand five hundred American gold dollars.

There was at the same sale a three-inch pottery tea caddy of demure exterior and, like the Ido, without embellishment, that sold for the equivalent of sixty-four thousand five hundred American gold dollars, and a tea scoop whittled out of a bamboo splinter that fell, under the same furious bidding, for fifteen thousand dollars gold. No one of these objects had the slightest intrinsic worth beyond any five-and-ten-cent-store bowl or caddy or scoop. Without its records in the Burke's Peerage of such things, no one of them would have fetched a dollar or two.

While this Emperor of all tea bowls is in our minds, it is worth a moment's study to discover everything that real discrimination, shorn of association and snobbery, can do to give it value. Most important is the fact that it comes nearly as close as any man-made object can come to possessing the incomparable beauties of a natural object. Fire has had its unpredictable way with clay and dull, colorless glaze and no man has embellished it. The result, in this particular case, happens to be as lovely a thing as a mottled stone one brings in from the beach to the writing desk. There is infinite variety. Use, and much careful wiping and the stain of tea juice have insensibly given it patination as the waves gave the stone. If, in addition to what the eye sees, one admits its undeniable utility, nothing is left to explain its price in the twentieth century except the very human attribute of association with glorious names. The set of ivory false teeth made for George Washington by Paul Revere has indeed similar association for an American but may lack the other more endearing qualities. Who but a dealer can guess what some patriot might pay for them?

Among the scores, even hundreds, of stories told to illustrate the very real delicacy and discrimination that tea inculcates is one about Sen Rikyū, the famous tea master, seventeen generations before the present master of that name, who went with his son to call on a fellow practitioner of tea and to examine his garden. The son admired the moss-grown wooden gate that opened to the path toward the door of the thatched tea hut. But his father said: "I don't agree. That gate must have been brought from some distant mountain temple at obvious expense. A rough wicket made by the local farmer would give the place a really quiet and lonely look, and not offend us by bringing up thoughts of difficulty and expense. I doubt if we shall find here any very sensitive or interesting tea ceremony."

Thus, on the whole, the really significant thing about the cult and practice of tea is that, in spite of occasional perversion of its very principles, no other custom in Japan can illustrate so perfectly the sensitive side of Japanese nature and no other force, unless that of Zen Buddhism which is close to it, has been so powerful to inculcate simplicity, directness, and self-restraint— in short, discriminating taste.

CHAPTER 5

Architecture

THE TEA-ROOM[1]

By OKAKURA KAKUZO

To European architects brought up on the traditions of stone and brick construction, our Japanese method of building with wood and bamboo seems scarcely worthy to be ranked as architecture. It is but quite recently that a competent student of Western architecture has recognised and paid tribute to the remarkable perfection of our great temples.[2] Such being the case as regards our classic architecture, we could hardly expect the outsider to appreciate the subtle beauty of the tea-room, its principles of construction and decoration being entirely different from those of the West.

The tea-room (the Sukiya) does not pretend to be other than a mere cottage—a straw hut, as we call it. The original ideographs for Sukiya mean the Abode of Fancy. Latterly the various tea-masters substituted various Chinese characters according to their conception of the tea-room, and the term Sukiya may signify the Abode of Vacancy or the Abode of the Unsymmetrical. It is an Abode of Fancy inasmuch as it is an ephemeral structure

---

1 "The Tea-Room," from *The Book of Tea*, by Okakura Kakuzo. Dodd, Mead and Company, New York, 1906. Reprinted by the Charles E. Tuttle Company, Rutland, Vermont—Tokyo, Japan, 1956.

2 We refer to Ralph N. Cram's *Impressions of Japanese Architecture and the Allied Arts*. The Baker & Taylor Company, New York, 1905. [This note from the 1926 edition of Mr. Okakura's often-republished classic is of interest only because so much has been published on Japanese architecture in the years since the appearance of Mr. Cram's book in 1905. One of the most recent reflections cf a growing world-wide interest is the publication in English of a Japanese architectural journal, *Shinkenchiku*, now appearing monthly in New York under the name *The Japan Architect*. N. W. R.]

built to house a poetic impulse. It is an Abode of Vacancy inasmuch as it is devoid of ornamentation except for what may be placed in it to satisfy some aesthetic need of the moment. It is an Abode of the Unsymmetrical inasmuch as it is consecrated to the worship of the Imperfect, purposely leaving some thing unfinished for the play of the imagination to complete. The ideals of Teaism have since the sixteenth century influenced our architecture to such degree that the ordinary Japanese interior of the present day, on account of the extreme simplicity and chasteness of its scheme of decoration, appears to foreigners almost barren.

The first independent tea-room was the creation of Senno-Soyeki, commonly known by his later name of Rikiu, the greatest of all tea-masters, who, in the sixteenth century, under the patronage of Taiko-Hideyoshi, instituted and brought to a high state of perfection the formalities of the Tea-ceremony. The proportions of the tea-room had been previously determined by Jowo— a famous tea-master of the fifteenth century. The early tea-room consisted merely of a portion of the ordinary drawing-room partitioned off by screens for the purpose of the tea-gathering. The portion partitioned off was called the Kakoi (enclosure), a name still applied to those tea-rooms which are built into a house and are not independent constructions. The Sukiya consists of the tea-room proper, designed to accommodate not more than five persons, a number suggestive of the saying "more than the Graces and less than the Muses," an anteroom (midsuya) where the tea utensils are washed and arranged before being brought in, a portico (machiai) in which the guests wait until they receive the summons to enter the tea-room, and a garden path (the roji) which connects the machiai with the tea-room. The tea-room is unimpressive in appearance. It is smaller than the smallest of Japanese houses, while the materials used in its construction are intended to give the suggestion of refined poverty. Yet we must remember that all this is the result of profound artistic forethought, and that the details have been worked out with care perhaps even greater than that expended on the building of the richest palaces and temples. A good tea-room is more costly than an ordinary mansion, for the selection of its materials, as well as its workmanship, requires immense care and precision. Indeed, the carpenters employed by the tea-masters form a distinct and highly honoured class among artisans, their work being no less delicate than that of the makers of lacquer cabinets.

The tea-room is not only different from any production of Western architecture, but also contrasts strongly with the classical architecture of Japan

139

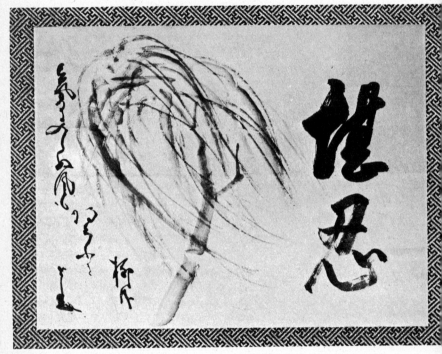

"Though there must be winds
That it does not like,—
Still the willow!"

itself. Our ancient noble edifices, whether secular or ecclesiastical, were not to be despised even as regards their mere size. The few that have been spared in the disastrous conflagrations of centuries are still capable of aweing us by the grandeur and richness of their decoration. Huge pillars of wood from two to three feet in diameter and from thirty to forty feet high, supported, by a complicated network of brackets, the enormous beams which groaned under the weight of the tile-covered slanting roofs. The material and mode of construction, though weak against fire, proved itself strong against earthquakes, and was well suited to the climatic conditions of the country. In the Golden Hall of Horiuji and the Pagoda of Yakushiji, we have noteworthy examples of the durability of our wooden architecture. These buildings have practically stood intact for nearly twelve centuries. The interior of the old temples and palaces was profusely decorated. In the Hoōdo temple at Uji, dating from the tenth century, we can still see the elaborate canopy and gilded baldachinos, many-coloured and inlaid with mirrors and mother-of-pearl, as well as remains of the paintings and sculpture which formerly covered the walls. Later, at Nikko and in the Nijo castle in Kyoto, we see structural beauty sacrificed to a wealth of ornamentation which in colour and exquisite detail equals the utmost gorgeousness of Arabian or Moorish effort.

The simplicity and purism of the tea-room resulted from emulation of the Zen monastery. A Zen monastery differs from those of other Buddhist sects inasmuch as it is meant only to be a dwelling place for the monks. Its chapel is not a place of worship or pilgrimage, but a college room where the students congregate for discussion and the practice of meditation. The room is bare except for a central alcove in which, behind the altar, is a statue of Bodhi Dharma, the founder of the sect, or of Sakyamuni attended by Kashiapa and Ananda, the two earliest Zen patriarchs. On the altar, flowers and incense are offered up in memory of the great contributions which these sages made to Zen. We have already said that it was the ritual instituted by the Zen monks of successively drinking tea out of a bowl before the image of Bodhi Dharma, which laid the foundations of the tea-ceremony. We might add here that the altar of the Zen chapel was the prototype of the Tokonoma,—the place of honour in a Japanese room where paintings and flowers are placed for the edification of the guests.

All our great tea-masters were students of Zen and attempted to introduce the spirit of Zennism into the actualities of life. Thus the room, like the other equipments of the tea-ceremony, reflects many of the Zen doctrines. The size

141

of the orthodox tea-room, which is four mats and a half, or ten feet square, is determined by a passage in the Sutra of Vikramadytia. In that interesting work, Vikramadytia welcomes the Saint Manjushiri and eighty-four thousand disciples of Buddha in a room of this size,—an allegory based on the theory of the non-existence of space to the truly enlightened. Again the roji, the garden path which leads from the machiai to the tea-room, signified the first stage of meditation,—the passage into self-illumination. The roji was intended to break connection with the outside world, and to produce a fresh sensation conducive to the full enjoyment of aestheticism in the tea-room itself. One who has trodden this garden path cannot fail to remember how his spirit, as he walked in the twilight of evergreens over the regular irregularities of the stepping stones, beneath which lay dried pine needles, and passed beside the moss-covered granite lanterns, became uplifted above ordinary thoughts. One may be in the midst of a city, and yet feel as if he were in the forest far away from the dust and din of civilisation. Great was the ingenuity displayed by the tea-masters in producing these effects of serenity and purity. The nature of the sensations to be aroused in passing through the roji differed with different tea-masters. Some, like Rikiu, aimed at utter loneliness, and claimed the secret of making a roji was contained in the ancient ditty:

> "I look beyond;
> Flowers are not,
> Nor tinted leaves.
> On the sea beach
> A solitary cottage stands
> In the waning light
> Of an autumn eve."

Others, like Kobori-Enshiu, sought for a different effect. Enshiu said the idea of the garden path was to be found in the following verses:

> "A cluster of summer trees,
> A bit of the sea,
> A pale evening moon."

It is not difficult to gather his meaning. He wished to create the attitude of a newly awakened soul still lingering amid shadowy dreams of the past, yet bathing in the sweet unconsciousness of a mellow spiritual light, and yearning for the freedom that lay in the expanse beyond.

Thus prepared the guest will silently approach the sanctuary, and, if a samurai, will leave his sword on the rack beneath the eaves, the tea-room

142

being preëminently the house of peace. Then he will bend low and creep into the room through a small door not more than three feet in height. This proceeding was incumbent on all guests,—high and low alike,—and was intended to inculcate humility. The order of precedence having been mutually agreed upon while resting in the machiai, the guests one by one will enter noiselessly and take their seats, first making obeisance to the picture or flower arrangement on the tokonoma. The host will not enter the room until all the guests have seated themselves and quiet reigns with nothing to break the silence save the note of the boiling water in the iron kettle. The kettle sings well, for pieces of iron are so arranged in the bottom as to produce a peculiar melody in which one may hear the echoes of a cataract muffled by clouds, of a distant sea breaking among the rocks, a rainstorm sweeping through a bamboo forest, or of the soughing of pines on some faraway hill.

Even in the daytime the light in the room is subdued, for the low eaves of the slanting roof admit but few of the sun's rays. Everything is sober in tint from the ceiling to the floor; the guests themselves have carefully chosen garments of unobtrusive colours. The mellowness of age is over all, everything suggestive of recent acquirement being tabooed save only the one note of contrast furnished by the bamboo dipper and the linen napkin, both immaculately white and new. However faded the tea-room and the tea-equipage may seem, everything is absolutely clean. Not a particle of dust will be found in the darkest corner, for if any exists the host is not a tea-master. One of the first requisites of a tea-master is the knowledge of how to sweep, clean, and wash, for there is an art in cleaning and dusting. A piece of antique metal work must not be attacked with the unscrupulous zeal of the Dutch house-wife. Dripping water from a flower vase need not be wiped away, for it may be suggestive of dew and coolness.

In this connection there is a story of Rikiu which well illustrates the ideas of cleanliness entertained by the tea-masters. Rikiu was watching his son Shoan as he swept and watered the garden path. "Not clean enough," said Rikiu, when Shoan had finished his task, and bade him try again. After a weary hour the son turned to Rikiu: "Father, there is nothing more to be done. The steps have been washed for the third time, the stone lanterns and the trees are well sprinkled with water, moss and lichens are shining with a fresh verdure; not a twig, not a leaf have I left on the ground." "Young fool," chided the tea-master, "that is not the way a garden path should be swept." Saying this, Rikiu stepped into the garden, shook a tree and scattered

143

over the garden gold and crimson leaves, scraps of the brocade of autumn! What Rikiu demanded was not cleanliness alone, but the beautiful and the natural also.

The name, Abode of Fancy, implies a structure created to meet some individual artistic requirement. The tea-room is made for the tea-master, not the tea-master for the tea-room. It is not intended for posterity and is therefore ephemeral. The idea that everyone should have a house of his own is based on an ancient custom of the Japanese race, Shinto superstition ordaining that every dwelling should be evacuated on the death of its chief occupant. Perhaps there may have been some unrealised sanitary reason for this practice. Another early custom was that a newly built house should be provided for each couple that married. It is on account of such customs that we find the Imperial capitals so frequently removed from one site to another in ancient days. The rebuilding, every twenty years, of Ise Temple, the supreme shrine of the Sun-Goddess, is an example of one of these ancient rites which still obtain at the present day. The observance of these customs was only possible with some such form of construction as that furnished by our system of wooden architecture, easily pulled down, easily built up. A more lasting style, employing brick and stone, would have rendered migrations impracticable, as indeed they became when the more stable and massive wooden construction of China was adopted by us after the Nara period.

With the predominance of Zen individualism in the fifteenth century, however, the old idea became imbued with a deeper significance as conceived in connection with the tea-room. Zennism, with the Buddhist theory of evanescence and its demands for the mastery of spirit over matter, recognised the house only as a temporary refuge for the body. The body itself was but as a hut in the wilderness, a flimsy shelter made by tying together the grasses that grew around,—when these ceased to be bound together they again became resolved into the original waste. In the tea-room fugitiveness is suggested in the thatched roof, frailty in the slender pillars, lightness in the bamboo support, apparent carelessness in the use of commonplace materials. The eternal is to be found only in the spirit which, embodied in these simple surroundings, beautifies them with the subtle light of its refinement.

That the tea-room should be built to suit some individual taste is an enforcement of the principle of vitality in art. Art, to be fully appreciated, must be true to contemporaneous life. It is not that we should ignore the claims of posterity, but that we should seek to enjoy the present more. It is not that we should disregard the creations of the past, but that we should try to assimilate them into our consciousness. Slavish conformity to traditions and formulas fetters the expression of individuality in architecture. We can but weep over those senseless imitations of European buildings which one beholds in modern Japan. We marvel why, among the most progressive Western nations, architecture should be so devoid of originality, so replete with repetitions of obsolete styles. Perhaps we are now passing through an age of democratisation in art, while awaiting the rise of some princely master who shall establish a new dynasty. Would that we loved the ancients more and copied them less! It has been said that the Greeks were great because they never drew from the antique.

The term, Abode of Vacancy, besides conveying the Taoist theory of the all-containing, involves the conception of a continued need of change in decorative motives. The tea-room is absolutely empty, except for what may be placed there temporarily to satisfy some aesthetic mood. Some special art object is brought in for the occasion, and everything else is selected and arranged to enhance the beauty of the principal theme. One cannot listen to different pieces of music at the same time, a real comprehension of the beautiful being possible only through concentration upon some central motive. Thus it will be seen that the system of decoration in our tea-rooms is opposed to that which obtains in the West, where the interior of a house is often converted into a museum. To a Japanese, accustomed to simplicity of ornamentation and frequent change of decorative method, a Western interior permanently filled with a vast array of pictures, statuary, and bric-à-brac gives the impression of mere vulgar display of riches. It calls for a mighty wealth of appreciation to enjoy the constant sight of even a masterpiece, and limitless indeed must be the capacity for artistic feeling in those who can exist day after day in the midst of such confusion of colour and form as is to be often seen in the homes of Europe and America.

The Abode of the Unsymmetrical suggests another phase of our decorative scheme. The absence of symmetry in Japanese art objects has been often commented on by Western critics. This, also, is a result of a working out through Zennism of Taoist ideals. Confucianism, with its deep-seated idea of dualism, and Northern Buddhism with its worship of a trinity, were in no way opposed to the expression of symmetry. As a matter of fact, if we study the ancient bronzes of China or the religious arts of the Tang dynasty and the Nara period, we shall recognise a constant striving after symmetry. The decoration of our classical interiors was decidedly regular in its arrangement. The Taoist and Zen conception of perfection, however, was different. The dynamic nature of their philosophy laid more stress upon the process through which perfection was sought than upon perfection itself. True beauty could be discovered only by one who mentally completed the incomplete. The virility of life and art lay in its possibilities for growth. In the tea-room it is left for each guest in imagination to complete the total effect in relation to himself. Since Zennism has become the prevailing mode of thought, the art of the extreme Orient has purposely avoided the symmetrical as expressing not only completion, but repetition. Uniformity of design was considered as fatal to the freshness of imagination. Thus, landscapes, birds, and flowers became the favourite subjects for depiction rather than the human figure, the latter being present in the person of the beholder himself. We are often too much in evidence as it is, and in spite of our vanity even self-regard is apt to become monotonous.

In the tea-room the fear of repetition is a constant presence. The various objects for the decoration of a room should be so selected that no colour or design shall be repeated. If you have a living flower, a painting of flowers is not allowable. If you are using a round kettle, the water pitcher should be angular. A cup with a black glaze should not be associated with a tea-caddy of black lacquer. In placing a vase on an incense burner on the tokonoma, care should be taken not to put it in the exact centre, lest it divide the space into equal halves. The pillar of the tokonoma should be of a different kind of wood from the other pillars, in order to break any suggestion of monotony in the room.

Here again the Japanese method of interior decoration differs from that of the Occident, where we see objects arrayed symmetrically on mantelpieces and elsewhere. In Western houses we are often confronted with what appears to us useless reiteration. We find it trying to talk to a man while his full-length portrait stares at us from behind his back. We wonder which is real, he of the picture or he who talks, and feel a curious conviction that one of them must be a fraud. Many a time have we sat at a festive board contemplating, with a secret shock to our digestion, the representation of abundance on the dining-room walls. Why these pictured victims of chase and sport, the elaborate carvings of fishes and fruit? Why the display of family plates, reminding us of those who have dined and are dead?

The simplicity of the tea-room and its freedom from vulgarity make it truly a sanctuary from the vexations of the outer world. There and there alone can one consecrate himself to undisturbed adoration of the beautiful. In the sixteenth century the tea-room afforded a welcome respite from labour to the fierce warriors and statesmen engaged in the unification and reconstruction of Japan. In the seventeenth century, after the strict formalism of the Tokugawa rule had been developed, it offered the only opportunity possible for the free communion of artistic spirits. Before a great work of art there was no distinction between daimyo, samurai, and commoner. Nowadays industrialism is making true refinement more and more difficult all the world over. Do we not need the tea-room more than ever?

The following photographs suggest something of the influence of Zen Buddhism on certain arts, skills, cults, disciplines, and "ways of life" which for centuries have been a part of Japan's unique culture. Zen has served both to mold the Japanese character and to act as an expression of it.

Two Zen priests of the Soto sect in traditional woven-bamboo hats. They are leaving on a pilgrimage from the main entrance of Eiheiji, a temple founded by the famous priest Dogen, a celebrated Zen master who lived from 1200 to 1253. Still considered one of his country's greatest philosophers, Dogen interested himself in the meaning of "time" or the "Eternal Now." From years of study in China he brought back a meditative technique known as "observing one's mind in tranquillity." Even at the moment of death he was able to remark, "I drop into the afterworld still living." *Japan Tourist Association*

Left Top: Rectangular view of the famed dry garden of Ryoanji. Created with deceptive simplicity from raked sand and the artful arrangement of fifteen rocks of varying size and shape, this fifteenth-century Zen garden appeals particularly to modern Westerners who enjoy "abstraction" in contemporary art forms. (See Section III, Zen and the Arts.) *Consulate General of Japan, N. Y.*

Left Bottom: Two priests with specially designed rakes restore the strict pattern of the white sand which takes the place of grass. *Consulate General of Japan, N. Y.*

Below: Close-up of a rock group, showing the whirling movement of the raked sand at its base, not unlike the eddying of water around rocks in a stream bed. Garden connoisseurs, however, warn against any formal symbolic interpretations of the design. Since this is an art of suggestion, there are as many ways to enjoy it as there are people to look at it. *Werner Bischof, Magnum Photos*

Below: Garden immediately adjoining the Shokintei tea house of the famous Katsura Imperial Villa in Kyoto, whose extensive grounds are generally considered the most beautiful in all Japan. The types and heights of trees and plants, the use of water, the stone lantern, the monolithic slab serving as a bridge, the textural complexity of the ground stones seen here are all characteristic of Japanese garden architecture. *Consulate General of Japan, N. Y.*

Right: An arrangement of rocks before an entrance, the top one containing water and a bamboo dipper for washing hands and rinsing mouth, done ceremoniously before entering a tearoom or a temple. The old "Secret Books" on Japanese gardens contain a vast lore about rocks, how to choose, transport, place, and even how to behave toward them. Since Buddhism teaches respect for the life in all things, it is not surprising to read: "A rock should be carefully considered before it is erected. Once it is put upright it should not be laid down, and vice versa. To do so might irritate the spirit of the rock." *Werner Bischof, Magnum Photos*

Left Top: Main gate of Ryosenan, a subtemple of Daitokuji in Kyoto and headquarters of the First Zen Institute of America in Japan. Here Western students may undertake the study and practice of traditional Rinzai Zen under trained Japanese masters.

Left bottom: Corner of a garden at Ryosenan, showing camellia tree, stone lantern, and carved rock.

Below: Interior view, looking south from the *shoin* (desk room) to the second room of the model Japanese house made in Nagoya in 1953, shipped from Japan in seven hundred crates, and reassembled in the garden of the Museum of Modern Art in New York City, to illustrate the "unique relevance" of traditional Japanese architecture to modern Western styles. Although representing an aristocrat's residence, typical of sixteenth- and seventeenth-century building in Japan, the interior's restraint, simplicity, and essential emptiness are noteworthy. In Japan today buildings of this kind often adjoin temples and serve as priests' residences. *Ezra Stoller*

Left: The ceremonial taking of tea, an art dating back to Japan's feudal era. Infinitely detailed rules of etiquette could have led to a tiresome cultism, if mastery of the art of tea did not imply connoisseurship in such related subjects as painting, calligraphy, flower arrangement, and poetry. *Consulate General of Japan, N. Y.*

Left bottom: Calligraphy, or the proper use of a writing brush, remains a major Japanese art, equal in importance with painting. Japanese artists traditionally kneel to paint, with silk or paper spread out before them. Many years of patient daily practice in acquiring flexibility of arm and wrist muscles precede the making of a master, whose pupils are often affectionately called "*deshi*," meaning younger brother, a name applied to the early disciples of the historic Buddha. *Japan Tourist Association*

Right top: The ancient art of swordsmanship not only requires physical skills but demands that the mind and senses be held in a constant harmonious state of "perfect fluidity." In Kendo, or the Way of the Sword, training aims at the Zen goal of transcending "the duality of life and death." The fencer must give himself over to that invisible "power" which becomes operative only when the holder of the sword understands how to become, and remain, "consciously unconscious" or "unconsciously conscious." *Courtesy of Kokusai Bunka Shinkokai, Tokyo*

Right bottom: Judo, which trains its practitioners to use "the instinctive wisdom of the body," is built on principles of highly attentive nonresistance and the elimination of habitual physical tensions born of fear and violence. *Japan Tourist Association*

Archery in Japan is practiced not merely for acquiring skill in marksmanship, or winning in competitions, but as a profound training in egolessness, to the end that finally "Bow, arrow, goal, and self" all become one. The black-costumed gentlemen are participants in a formal competition. The others are in a practice class. *Left photograph, Consulate General of Japan, N. Y.; right photographs, courtesy of Kokusai Bunka Shinkokai, Tokyo*

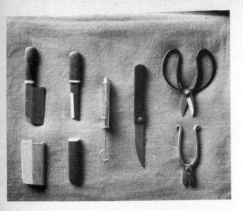

Below: A master of flower arrangement, one of the subtle arts which sprang originally from the feudal samurai and is now practiced by all classes of Japanese society. A master concerns himself not alone with teaching the prescribed laws and rules of the various schools. He seeks also to "draw the pupil's eye inwards," to create a deeper understanding of the "living totality" of the whole of nature. *Werner Bischof, Magnum Photos*

Above: Tools used in the art of formal flower arrangement.
Japan Tourist Association

Target, glove, arrow, and bow used in ceremonial archery. *Consulate General of Japan, N. Y.*

Contemporary tea bowl of traditional design in which irregularities of shape and texture are part of its distinction, and a tea whisk, made from a single piece of bamboo, always used to mix powdered green tea. *Museum of Modern Art, New York, N. Y.*

Below: Love of nature is deeply ingrained in the Japanese, who are able to worship the "divinity" of a great tree without yielding to either pantheism or anthropocentrism. *Frederick Hamilton*

Right Top: Set for a No drama showing the traditional dark green pine tree, symbolic of strength and longevity, painted on the backdrop. *Japan Travel Information Office, San Francisco*

Right Bottom: Masked actors in a scene from a classical No drama, an ancient form of Japanese theater which owes many of its unusual conventions to Zen ideology and philosophy. *Consulate General of Japan, N. Y.*

Puppetry in Japan. A complicated
art performed by a master mounted
on stilts with two black-robed, masked
assistants also manipulating the dolls in
full view of the audience while narrator-
singers, seated to one side, speak the
dialogue. Though not directly related
to Zen as is the No drama, the puppet
theater has been said to exemplify
certain Zen-like qualities expressed
also in swordsmanship and archery.
(See Section VI, Universal Zen.)
Frederick Hamilton

Below: A master of the puppet
theater, very old and almost blind. By
his understanding of the teaching of
"emptiness," and his identification
with the puppet, he is able to transcend
all the diffusion of activity on the stage
around him and to create not only
an artistic unity but a magic
illusion of "life." Like the swordsman
who transforms himself into his
opponent, the puppeteer becomes his
puppet without loss of his own identity.
Frederick Hamilton, Brander Matthews
Dramatic Museum, Columbia
University, New York, N. Y.

One of the traditions of the classic No drama is the wearing of masks by the principal characters, a convention that helps lend this highly stylized theater its unique effects of timeless mystery. Left to right: Mask of the demon Hannya, *Mitsui Collection, Tokyo;* of an old man, Okina, *Maeda Collection;* of a young girl, Ko-omote, *Tokyo National Museum;* of an old woman, Uba, *Hosho Collection, Tokyo;* of the fairy Shojo, *Nara National Museum;* and of the witch Yamauba, *Tokyo National Museum.*

In the West the fact that Zen's roots lie in Buddhism is occasionally overlooked or minimized. This is the Great Buddha of Kamakura, cast in 1252, an enormous bronze figure over forty feet high, with a face almost eight feet long. Seated in meditative posture, hands on lap, palms up and thumbs touching, eyes half closed, its countenance in repose, the image depicts that state of passionless calm which characterizes "enlightenment" in all Buddhist teaching. *Frederick Hamilton*

CHAPTER 6

The No Drama

FOREWORD

In the ancient and extraordinarily vital theater of Japan, with its unique history of continuity, three great forms of theatrical art have been maintained for centuries. There is the well-known Kabuki, or so-called popular theater; the old and distinguished Bunraku, which is puppetry of the highest order; and the esoteric and classic No. Kabuki and Bunraku date back to the seventeenth century; the repertory of the No belongs to the fourteenth and fifteenth centuries. It is the symbolic medieval No which has most effectively captured the imaginations of such eminent Western literary figures as Paul Claudel, Ezra Pound, William Butler Yeats, and Arthur Waley.

Anyone lending himself to the timeless experience of the No never forgets it, though he may be quite incapable of conveying to others an exact sense of its peculiar enchantment. The No explores time and space in ways unfamiliar to our Western aesthetic, and certainly far removed from our concepts of "theatricality." Even if one cannot follow the classical *utai*, or libretto, as devoted Japanese intellectuals and aesthetes do, the spell of the performance itself, independent of the story, remains. The eerie use of the human voice, in which normal breathing has been artfully suppressed; the occasional long-drawn, sad and solitary notes of a flute; the periodic sharp cries and catlike yowls from the chorus; the abrupt clack of sticks and the varied tonality of three kinds of drum; the gliding ghostly dances—bodies, fans, sleeves, cleaving space like ships caught in a sudden wind, or birds floating in gentle air;

167

the soft lift and half-turn of the principal actor's foot in its white *tabi*, the sudden summoning stomp on the bare resonant stage where every "property" has been abstracted to a mere symbol; the extravagant and lavish costumes; the unreal reality of the wooden masks worn by the participants; above all, the artful use of emptiness and silence, silence broken with the meaningful abruptness of the frog-into-the-pond plop of Basho's most famous *haiku*— these are a few of the traditional elements that help to create the special magic of No.

A fuller explanation of the externals of this classic dramatic form and a suggestion of its subjective implications have been well described and commented upon by Donald Keene in his scholarly book, *Japanese Literature*:

In many respects the *Nō* resembled the Greek drama. First of all, there was the combination of text, music and dance. Secondly, both theatres used a chorus, although in the *Nō* the chorus never takes any part in the action, confining itself to recitations for the principal dancer when he is in the midst of his dance. Again, the *Nō* uses masks, as did the Greek drama, but their use is restricted to the principal dancer and his companions, especially when they take the parts of women. Mask-carving has been considered an important art in Japan, and together with the gorgeous costumes, the masks add much to the visual beauty of the *Nō*. In contrast, the scenery is barely sketched, consisting usually of no more than an impressionistic rendering of the main outlines of the objects portrayed. The music, at least to a Western listener, is not of great distinction, very rarely rising to the level of melody, and most often little more than an accentuation of the declaimed or intoned word. A flute is played at important moments in the play, and there are several drums, some of which can serve to heighten the tension of the audience. The actual theatres in which the *Nō* plays are performed are small. Their most striking features are the *hashigakari*, a raised passage-way leading from the actors' dressing-room through the audience to the stage, and the square, polished-wood stage itself. The audience sits on three, or sometimes only two, sides of the stage, which is covered by a roof of its own like that of a temple. The actors make their entrances through the audience, but above them, and pronounce their first words before reaching the stage, an extremely effective way of introducing a character.

The performances in a *Nō* theatre last about six hours. Five *Nō* plays are presented in a programme, arranged as established in the sixteenth century. The first play is about the gods, the second about a warrior, the third about a woman, the fourth about a mad person, and the final play about devils, or sometimes a festive piece. Each of the plays in the *Nō* repertory is classified into one of these groups, and the purpose of having this fixed programme is to achieve the effect of an artistic whole, with an introduction, development and climax. The third, or woman-play, is the most popular, but to present a whole programme of such plays would mar the total effect as much, say, as having an Italian opera with five mad scenes sung by successive coloratura sopranos.

The tone of the *Nō* plays is serious, and often tragic. To relieve the atmosphere, the custom arose of having farces performed in between the *Nō* dramas of a programme, often parodies of the pieces that they follow. It might be imagined that the alternation of mood from the tragic tone of the *Nō* to a broad farce and then back again would prove too great a wrench for the sensibilities of the audience. This is not merely a case of comic relief in the manner of Shakespeare, for the farces last almost as long as the serious parts, and often specifically deride them. But the Japanese audiences have apparently enjoyed the very sharpness of the contrast between the two moods.

On the whole, however, the humour of the Japanese farces is not very interesting to us, and when a Western reader thinks of the *Nō* theatre, it will be of the tragedies. What are the qualities most to be admired in these works? There is first of all the poetry. This is written in alternating lines of 7 and 5 syllables, like most other Japanese verse, but in the plays attains heights otherwise unknown in the language. The short verses are sometimes miracles of suggestion and sharp imagery, but, at least for a Western reader, lack the sustained power of the greatest poetry. The *Nō* provides a superb framework for a dramatic poet. It is in some ways an enlarged equivalent of the tiny haiku, portraying only the moments of greatest intensity so as to suggest the rest of the drama. Like the *haiku* also, the *Nō* has two elements, the interval between the first and second appearance of the principal dancer serving the function of the break in the *haiku*, and the audience having to supply the link between the two. Sometimes there is also the intersection of the momentary and the timeless which may be noted in many *haiku*. Thus, for example, in the first part of the play *Kumasaka*, a travelling priest meets the ghost of the robber Kumasaka, who asks him to pray for the spirit of a person whom he will not name. Later that night the priest sees the robber as he was in former days, and the robber rehearses the circumstances of his death in an impassioned verse, ending:

"Oh, help me to be born to happiness."

> (*Kumasaka entreats the Priest with folded hands.*)

The cocks are crowing. A whiteness glimmers over the night. He has hidden under the shadow of the pine-trees of Akasaka,

> (*Kumasaka hides his face with his left sleeve.*)

Under the shadow of the pine-trees he has hidden himself away.[1]

In this play the meeting of the priest and robber is fortuitous, the happening of a moment, but the desperate struggle of the robber to escape from his past into the path of salvation goes on and on.

Behind these plays, as behind the *haiku*, were the teachings of Zen Buddhism,

---

[1] *The No Plays of Japan*, translated by Arthur Waley, page 101. George Allen and Unwin, London, 1921. Reprinted by Grove Press, New York.

whose greatest influence is probably found in the form of the *Nō* itself—the bareness of the lines of the drama, and the simplicity of the stage and sets. These teachings, which inspired so much of Japanese literature and art in the fourteenth and fifteenth centuries, probably came to the *Nō* largely with Kanami and Seami, who were closely associated with the court of the shoguns, which was deeply influenced by Zen masters. The use of Zen ideas takes various forms in the plays. In most of them the secondary character (the *waki*) is a priest, and sometimes he uses the language and ideas of Zen Buddhism. In the play *Sotoba Komachi* [which follows], one of the greatest, it is the poetess Komachi who voices the Zen doctrines, rather than the priests.[2]

[N. W. R.]

SOTOBA KOMACHI[1]

Translated by ARTHUR WALEY

With his introductory notes on the Komachi legend

The legend of Komachi is that she had many lovers when she was young, but was cruel and mocked at their pain. Among them was one, Shii no Shōshō, who came a long way to court her. She told him that she would not listen to him till he had come on a hundred nights from his house to hers and cut a hundred notches on the shaft-bench of his chariot. And so he came a hundred nights all but one, through rain, hail, snow, and wind. But on the last night he died.

Once, when she was growing old, the poet Yasuhide asked her to go with him to Mikawa. She answered with the poem:

> "I that am lonely,
> Like a reed root-cut,
> Should a stream entice me,
> Would go, I think."

When she grew quite old, both her friends and her wits forsook her. She wandered about in destitution, a tattered, crazy beggar-woman.

As is shown in this play, her madness was a "possession" by the spirit of the lover whom she had tormented. She was released from this "possession"

---

[2] *Japanese Literature*, by Donald Keene. Grove Press, New York, 1955.

[1] From *The Nō Plays of Japan, ibid.*

by virtue of a sacred *Stūpa*[2] or log carved into five parts, symbolic of the Five Elements, on which she sat down to rest.

In the disputation between Komachi and the priests, she upholds the doctrines of the Zen Sect, which uses neither scriptures nor idols: the priests defend the doctrines of the Shingon Sect, which promises salvation by the use of incantations and the worship of holy images.

There is no doubt about the authorship of this play. Seami (*Works*, p. 246) gives it as the work of his father, Kwanami Kiyotsugu. Kwanami wrote another play, *Shii no Shōshō*,[3] in which Shōshō is the principal character and Komachi the *tsure* or subordinate.

Seami also used the Komachi legend. In his *Sekidera Komachi* he tells how when she was very old the priests of *Sekidera* invited her to dance at the festival of Tanabata. She dances, and in rehearsing the splendours of her youth for a moment becomes young again.

SOTOBA KOMACHI

By KWANAMI

PERSONS: *A Priest of the Kōyasan. Ono No Komachi. Second Priest. Chorus.*

PRIEST. We who on shallow hills[4] have built our home
In the heart's deep recess seek solitude.

> (*Turning to the audience.*)

I am a priest of the Kōyasan. I am minded to go up to the Capital to visit
   the shrines and sanctuaries there.
The Buddha of the Past is gone.
And he that shall be Buddha has not yet come into the world.

SECOND PRIEST. In a dream-lull our lives are passed; all, all
That round us lies
Is visionary, void.
Yet got we by rare fortune at our birth
Man's shape, that is hard to get;
And dearer gift, was given us, harder to win,

[2] Sanskrit; Japanese, *sotoba*.
[3] Now generally called *Kayoi Komachi*.
[4] The Kōyasan is not so remote as most mountain temples.

The doctrine of Buddha, seed of our Salvation.
And me this only thought possessed,
How I might bring that seed to blossom, till at last
I drew this sombre cassock across my back.
And knowing now the lives before my birth,
No love I owe
To those that to this life engendered me,
Nor seek a care (have I not disavowed
Such hollow bonds?) from child by me begot.
A thousand leagues
Is little road
To the pilgrim's feet.
The fields his bed,
The hills his home
Till the travel's close.

PRIEST. We have come so fast that we have reached the pine-woods of
Abeno, in the country of Tsu. Let us rest in this place.

(*They sit down by the Waki's pillar.*)

KOMACHI. Like a root-cut reed,[5]
Should the tide entice,
I would come, I think; but now
No wave asks; no stream stirs.
Long ago I was full of pride;
Crowned with nodding tresses, halcyon locks,
I walked like a young willow delicately wafted
By the winds of Spring,
I spoke with the voice of a nightingale that has sipped the dew.
I was lovelier than the petals of the wild-rose open-stretched
In the hour before its fall.
But now I am grown loathsome even to sluts,
Poor girls of the people, and they and all men
Turn scornful from me.
Unhappy months and days pile up their score;
I am old; old by a hundred years.
In the City I fear men's eyes,

---

[5] See page 170.

And at dusk, lest they should cry "Is it she?"
Westward with the moon I creep
From the cloud-high City of the Hundred Towers.
No guard will question, none challenge
Pilgrim so wretched; yet must I be walking
Hid ever in shadow of the trees.
Past the Lovers' Tomb,
And the Hill of Autumn
To the River of Katsura, the boats, the moonlight.

> (*She shrinks back and covers her face, frightened of being known.*)

Who are those rowing in the boats?[6]
Oh, I am weary. I will sit on this tree-stump and rest awhile.

PRIEST. Come! The sun is sinking; we must hasten on our way. Look, look at that beggar there! It is a holy Stūpa that she is sitting on! I must tell her to come off it.

Now then, what is that you are sitting on? Is it not a holy Stūpa, the worshipful Body of Buddha? Come off it and rest in some other place.

KOMACHI. Buddha's worshipful body, you say? But I could see no writing on it, nor any figure carved. I thought it was only a tree-stump.

PRIEST. Even the little black tree on the hillside
When it has put its blossoms on
Cannot be hid;
And think you that this tree
Cut fivefold in the fashion of Buddha's holy form
Shall not make manifest its power?

KOMACHI. I too am a poor withered bough.
But there are flowers at my heart,[7]
Good enough, maybe, for an offering.
But why is this called Buddha's body?

PRIEST. Hear then! This Stūpa is the Body of the Diamond Lord.[8] It is the symbol of his incarnation.

---

6 Seami, writing c. 1430, says: "*Komachi* was once a long play. After the words 'Who are those,' etc., there used to be a long lyric passage" (*Works*, p. 240).

7 "Heart flowers," *kokoro no hana*, is a synonym for "poetry."

8 Vajrasettva, himself an emanation of Vairochana, the principal Buddha of the Shingon Sect.

KOMACHI. And in what elements did he choose to manifest his body?

PRIEST. Earth, water, wind, fire and space.

KOMACHI. Of these five man also is compounded. Where then is the difference?

PRIEST. The forms are the same, but not the virtue.

KOMACHI. And what is the virtue of the Stūpa?

PRIEST. "He that has looked once upon the Stūpa, shall escape for ever from the Three Paths of Evil."[9]

KOMACHI. "One thought can sow salvation in the heart."[10] Is that of less price?

SECOND PRIEST. If your heart has seen salvation, how comes it that you linger in the World?

KOMACHI. It is my body that lingers, for my heart left it long ago.

PRIEST. You have no heart at all, or you would have known the Body of Buddha.

KOMACHI. It was because I knew it that I came to see it!

SECOND PRIEST. And knowing what you know, you sprawled upon it without a word of prayer?

KOMACHI. It was on the ground already. What harm could it get by my resting on it?

PRIEST. It was an act of discord.[11]

KOMACHI. Sometimes from discord salvation springs.

SECOND PRIEST. From the malice of Daiba . . .[12]

KOMACHI. As from the mercy of Kwannon.[13]

---

9 From the Nirvāna Sūtra.

10 From the Avatamsaka Sūtra.

11 Lit. "discordant karma."

12 A wicked disciple who in the end attained to Illumination. Also called Datta; cp. *Kumasaka*, p. 95. [From the *Nō Plays of Japan*, op. cit. N. W. R.]

13 The Goddess of Mercy.

PRIEST. From the folly of Handoku . . .[14]

KOMACHI As from the wisdom of Monju.[15]

SECOND PRIEST. That which is called Evil

KOMACHI. Is Good.

PRIEST. That which is called Illusion

KOMACHI. Is Salvation.[16]

SECOND PRIEST. For Salvation

KOMACHI. Cannot be planted like a tree.

PRIEST. And the Heart's Mirror

KOMACHI. Hangs in the void.

CHORUS (*speaking for Komachi*). "Nothing is real.
  Between Buddha and Man
  Is no distinction, but a seeming of difference planned
  For the welfare of the humble, the ill-instructed,
  Whom he has vowed to save.
  Sin itself may be the ladder of salvation."
  So she spoke, eagerly; and the priests,
  "A saint, a saint is this decrepit, outcast soul."
  And bending their heads to the ground,
  Three times did homage before her.

KOMACHI. I now emboldened
  Recite a riddle, a jesting song.
  "Were I in Heaven
  The Stūpa were an ill seat;
  But here, in the world without,
  What harm is done?"[17]

CHORUS. The priests would have rebuked her;
  But they have found their match.

---

[14] A disciple so witless that he could not recite a single verse of Scripture.
[15] God of Wisdom.
[16] From the Nirvāna Sūtra.
[17] The riddle depends on a pun between *sotoba* and *soto wa*, "without," "outside."

PRIEST. Who are you? Pray tell us the name you had, and we will pray for you when you are dead.

KOMACHI. Shame covers me when I speak my name; but if you will pray for me, I will try to tell you. This is my name; write it down in your prayer-list: I am the ruins of Komachi, daughter of Ono no Yoshizane, Governor of the land of Dewa.

PRIESTS. Oh piteous, piteous! Is this
　Komachi that once
　Was a bright flower,
　Komachi the beautiful, whose dark brows
　Linked like young moons;
　Her face white-farded ever;
　Whose many, many damask robes
　Filled cedar-scented halls?

KOMACHI. I made verses in our speech
　And in the speech of the foreign Court.

CHORUS. The cup she held at the feast
　Like gentle moonlight dropped its glint on her sleeve.
　Oh how fell she from splendour,
　How came the white of winter
　To crown her head?
　Where are gone the lovely locks, double-twined,
　The coils of jet?
　Lank wisps, scant curls wither now
　On wilted flesh;
　And twin-arches, moth-brows tinged no more
　With the hue of far hills. "Oh cover, cover
　From the creeping light of dawn
　Silted seaweed locks that of a hundred years
　Lack now but one.
　Oh hide me from my shame."

(*Komachi hides her face.*)

CHORUS (*speaking for the Priest*). What is it you carry in the wallet strung at your neck?

SENGAI

This is Sengai's drawing of a No mask representing a female demon to which actors long ago gave the name "Hannya," from a Pali word meaning "wisdom." This is not, however, the wisdom of ordinary learning but the wisdom gained by "sloughing off all delusions." The characters *Maka hannya haramitta* express the idea of passing, by the exercise of this special wisdom, beyond all illusion and arriving at what is symbolically known as "the Other Shore."

KOMACHI. Death may come to-day—or hunger to-morrow.
  A few beans and a cake of millet;
  That is what I car ry in my bag.

CHORUS. And in the wallet on your back?

KOMACHI. A garment stained with dust and sweat.

CHORUS. And in the basket on your arm?

KOMACHI. Sagittaries white and black.

CHORUS. Tattered cloak,[18]

KOMACHI. Broken hat . . .

CHORUS. She cannot hide her face from our eyes;
  And how her limbs

KOMACHI. From rain and dew, hoar-frost and snow?

CHORUS (*speaking for Komachi while she mimes the actions they describe*).
  Not rags enough to wipe the tears from my eyes!
  Now, wandering along the roads
  I beg an alms of those that pass.
  And when they will not give,
  An evil rage, a very madness possesses me.
  My voice changes.
  Oh terrible!

KOMACHI (*thrusting her hat under the Priest's noses and shrieking at them menacingly*).
  Grr! You priests, give me something: give me something . . . Ah!

PRIEST. What do you want?

KOMACHI. Let me go to Komachi.[19]

PRIEST. But you told us you were Komachi. What folly is this you are talking?

---

[18] The words which follow suggest the plight of her lover Shōshō when he travelled to her house "a hundred nights all but one," to cut his notch on the bench.
[19] The spirit of her lover Shōshō has now entirely possessed her: this "possession-scene" lasts very much longer on the stage than the brief words would suggest.

KOMACHI. No, no. . . . Komachi was very beautiful.

Many letters came to her, many messages,—

Thick as raindrops out of a black summer sky.

But she sent no answer, not even an empty word.

And now in punishment she has grown old:

She has lived a hundred years—

I love her, oh I love her!

PRIEST. You love Komachi? Say then, whose spirit has possessed you?

KOMACHI. There were many who set their hearts on her,

But among them all

It was Shōshō who loved her best,

Shii no Shōshō of the Deep Grass.[20]

CHORUS (*speaking for Komachi, i.e. for the spirit of Shōshō*). The wheel goes

back; I live again through the cycle of my woes.

Again I travel to the shaft-bench.

The sun . . . what hour does he show?

Dusk. . . . Alone in the moonlight

I must go my way.

Though the watchmen of the barriers

Stand across my path,

They shall not stop me!

(*Attendants robe Komachi in the Court hat and travelling-clock of Shōshō.*)

Look, I go!

KOMACHI. Lifting the white skirts of my trailing dress,

CHORUS (*speaking for Komachi, while she, dressed as her lover, mimes the night-journey*).

Pulling down over my ears the tall, nodding hat,

Tying over my head the long sleeves of my hunting cloak,

Hidden from the eyes of men.

In moonlight, in darkness,

On rainy nights I travelled; on windy nights,

Under a shower of leaves; when the snow was deep,

KOMACHI. And when water dripped at the roof-eaves,—tok, tok. . . .

---

[20] Fukagusa, the name of his native place, means "deep grass."

CHORUS. Swiftly, swiftly coming and going, coming and going . . .
   One night, two nights, three nights,
   Ten nights (and this was harvest night). . . .
   I never saw her, yet I travelled;
   Faithful as the cock who marks each day the dawn,
   I carved my marks on the bench.
   I was to come a hundred times:
   There lacked but one. . . .

KOMACHI: (*feeling the death-agony of Shōshō*). My eyes dazzle. Oh the pain, the pain!

CHORUS. Oh the pain! and desperate.
   Before the last night had come,
   He died,—Shii no Shōshō the Captain.
(*Speaking for Komachi, who is now no longer possessed by Shōshō's spirit.*)
   Was it his spirit that possessed me,
   Was it his anger that broke my wits?
   If this be so, let me pray for the life hereafter,
   Where alone is comfort;
   Piling high the sands[21]
   Till I be burnished as gold.[22]
   See, I offer my flower[23] to Buddha,
   I hold it in both hands.
   Oh may He lead me into the Path of Truth,
   Into the Path of Truth.

---

[21] See *Hokkekyō*, II. 18.
[22] The colour of the saints in heaven.
[23] Her "heart-flower," i.e. poetic talent.

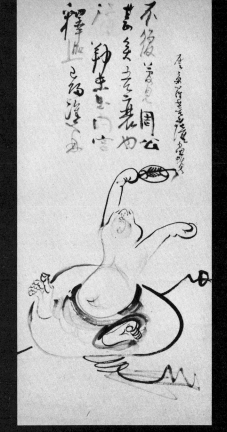

HUMOR IN ZEN

It has been suggested that the picture of Hotei (Pu-tai), the easy-going god of well-being, and the accompanying inscription represent the artist Sengai's own characteristic state of being. The verse, part of it a famous quotation from the *Analects of Confucius*, has been rendered by Dr. Suzuki in a free paraphrase presumably nearer the Zen spirit of the iconoclastic Sengai.

> "Sakyamuni Buddha is gone
> Maitreya Bodhisattva is not yet here
> It is they who keep us unnecessarily busy.
> What a fine refreshing nap I've had!
> No dreaming whatever like Confucius."

(Sakyamuni Buddha is the historic Buddha, the Indian founder of Buddhism. Maitreya Bodhisattva is the "Buddha of the Future.")

IV HUMOR IN ZEN

CHAPTER 1

Foreword

It would not be possible to present a Zen anthology without devoting a section to humor, for Zen's zany wit is part of the indefinable quality which sets it apart from other religious philosophies. In Zen, laughter is not merely permitted, it is insisted on. "It is possible to read the Bible without a smile, and the Koran without a chuckle. No one has died of laughing while reading the Buddhist sutras. But Zen writings abound in anecdotes that stimulate the diaphragm. Enlightenment is frequently accompanied by laughter of a transcendental kind which may further be described as a laughter of surprised approval."[1]

In Zen literature there are any number of stories like the following:

A monk came to a master for help in working on one of the classic questions in Zen dialectic, "What is the meaning of Bodhidharma's coming from the West?" The Master suggested that before proceeding with the problem the monk should make him a low salaam. As he was dutifully prostrating himself the master gave him a good swift kick. The unexpected kick resolved the murky irresolution in which the monk had been floundering for some time. When he felt the master's foot he "attained immediate enlightenment." Subsequently he said to everyone he met, "Since I received that kick from Ma Tsu, I haven't been able to stop laughing."[2]

Many Westerners have been first drawn to Zen by reading those apparently ridiculous, somehow irresistibly funny "conundrums" the *koans*, or irrational

---

[1] *Oriental Humor*, by R. H. Blyth. Hokuseido Press, Tokyo, 1959.

[2] Told in *The Practice of Zen*, by Chang Chen-chi. Harper and Brothers, New York, 1959.

scraps of dialogue between Zen teachers and novices like the following exchange between the Master Sekkyo and one of his monks:

Sekkyo (Shih-kung) asked one of his accomplished monks "Can you take hold of empty space?"
"Yes, sir," he replied.
"Show me how you do it."
The monk stretched out his arm and clutched at empty space.
Sekkyo said, "Is that the way? But after all you have not got anything."
"What then," asked the monk, "is your way?"
The master straightway took hold of the monk's nose and gave it a hard pull, which made the latter exclaim: "Oh, oh, how hard you pull at my nose. You are hurting me terribly!"
"That is the way to have hold of empty space," said the master.[3]

Such a story sends one's mind back to Lear's *Nonsense Verses* or Carroll's *Alice in Wonderland*, books whose enjoyment by readers of all ages seems in part to stem from the feeling that below an artless nonsensical surface there lurks hidden secret meaning. It is quite impossible to analyze the charm of these familiar books. One cannot, for instance, make clear the pleasure to be derived from reading the debate in *Alice* on the possibility of beheading the bodiless Cheshire cat. Everyone knows that in attempting to explain a joke the joke is utterly lost—and here a certain comparison can be made with Zen. Zen teachers are forever asserting that there is nothing that can be, or is to be, explained. Either you see or you don't—and that is that! Yet it is also true that part of the spell exerted by *The Gateless Gate, 101 Zen Stories*, and other collections of Zen anecdotes and "riddles" lies in the teasing feeling that one is *about* to see.

R. H. Blyth, who has contributed so much to Western appreciation of Zen, has said that when he first read Dr. Suzuki's series of *Essays in Zen Buddhism* he laughed aloud at every *koan*, yet was unable to explain why or at what. Indeed, he could almost say that the less he understood the more his risibility was stirred. This inability to analyze his amusement seemed unimportant to Blyth, for to him laughter is a breakthrough of "the intellectual barrier; at the moment of laughing something is understood; it needs no proof of itself; it is in no sense destructive or pessimistic or concerned with sin and punishment. Laughter is a state of being here and also everywhere, an

---

[3] *An Introduction to Zen Buddhism*, by D. T. Suzuki. Eastern Buddhist Society, Kyoto, 1934. Also published for the Buddhist Society of London by Rider and Company, London, 1949.

infinite and timeless expansion of one's nevertheless inalienable being. When we laugh we are free of all the oppression of our personality, or that of others, and even of God, who is indeed laughed away."

It may be expressions of just these qualities which account for the enduring popularity, down the centuries, of those two ragged, carefree, and holy Zen "lunatics," Kanzan and Jittoku[4]—so dear to Zen artists—who have nothing better to do than stand around grinning happily at falling leaves, or the new moon, or birds quarreling over a worm. Jittoku and Kanzan are free, free as the ragged scarecrows of the field which they resemble; and, as an old *haiku* of Dansui's reminds us,

> Even before His Majesty
> The scarecrow does not remove
> His plaited hat.

It is not without significance that Bodhidharma—or Daruma, as the Japanese call the esteemed and revered Patriarch who first brought the Great Teaching from India to the Sino-Japanese world—is represented among Japanese doll figures as a humorous little man with no legs and an inner abdominal balance which makes it impossible, if he has been pushed down, to keep him down. Zen teachers in Japan have been known to point out this resilient characteristic of the Daruma doll as a way of suggesting to top-heavy Westerners that consciousness may have another seat than the head alone, and that the maintenance of balance may not depend wholly on mental equipment or the power to reason.

Zen literature delights in dozens of stories similar to that of the eleventh-century master who got up to address a group seeking enlightenment and had only this to say: "Ha! ha! ha! What's all this? Go to the back of the hall and have some tea." He then got down and departed.

But one must never forget that, in Zen, illogical comments or nonsequitur replies to assigned problems have as their aim something beyond mere mystification. To sit around talking about Zen, arguing its points, philosophizing, conceptualizing—these are no part of the method of arousing an operational "awareness"—as several contributors to this volume have stressed. Making this point clear has allowed Zen masters the opportunity for some lively ripostes, and even for taking an occasional sly poke in the ribs at Zen's own expense. Such stories as "The Stone Mind" and "Fire-Poker Zen," from the

---

[4] In Chinese, Han-Shan and Shih-Te.

Shaseki-shu, aptly illustrate Zen's characteristic methods of driving home a point.

Hogen, a Chinese Zen teacher, lived alone in a small temple in the country. One day four traveling monks appeared and asked if they might make a fire in his yard to warm themselves.

While they were building the fire, Hogen heard them arguing about subjectivity and objectivity. He joined them and said: "There is a big stone. Do you consider it to be inside or outside your mind?"

One of the monks replied: "From the Buddhist viewpoint everything is an objectification of mind, so I would say that the stone is inside my mind."

"Your head must feel very heavy," observed Hogen, "if you are carrying around a stone like that in your mind."

Hakuin, one of the great Zen teachers of all time, used to tell his pupils about an old woman who ran a tea shop, and who had, in his opinion, a rare understanding of Zen. The skeptical pupils, unable to believe what he told them, kept going to the tea shop hoping to find out for themselves.

"Whenever the woman saw them coming she could tell at once whether they had come for tea or to look into her grasp of Zen. In the former case, she would serve them graciously. In the latter she would beckon to the pupils to come behind her screen. The instant they obeyed, she would strike them with a fire-poker. Nine out of ten of them could not escape her beating."

Zen has often exercised its existential humor at the expense of wordy theorizers and all those who "talked big" in abstract terms. A young student made a call upon a certain master and, anxious to show his advanced stage of attainment, remarked, "The mind, Buddha, and sentient beings, after all, do not exist. The true nature of phenomena is emptiness. There is no realization, no delusion, no sage, no mediocrity. There is no giving and nothing to be received." The master sat quietly listening for some time. Suddenly, without warning, he whacked the young man sharply with his bamboo pipe. The young man was outraged and plainly showed his anger. "If nothing exists," inquired the master, "where did this anger of yours come from?"

There is also an often-quoted injunction of a great *roshi* to "wash out one's mouth after using the name Buddha." In a not dissimilar vein, Christmas Humphreys tells a story of a certain master who remarked laconically to a pupil who had been talking at some length about Zen theory, "You have too much Zen." "But is it not natural for a student of Zen to talk about Zen?"

inquired the puzzled pupil. Put in another pupil, also addressing the master, "Why do you hate talking about Zen?" "Because," replied the master flatly, "it turns my stomach!"[5]

Wry irony on the themes of empty ritualistic behavior, the formalized side of Buddhist teachings, and exaggerated expressions of sanctity or piety also come in for their share of zestful ridicule. Take for example the story of the "Black-Nosed Buddha":

A nun who was searching for enlightenment made a statue of the Buddha and covered it with gold leaf. Wherever she went she carried this golden Buddha with her.

Years passed and, still carrying her Buddha, the nun came to live in a small temple in a country where there were many Buddhas, each one with its own particular shrine.

The nun wished to burn incense before her golden Buddha. Not liking the idea of the perfume straying to the others, she devised a funnel through which the smoke would ascend only to her statue. This blackened the nose of the golden Buddha, making it especially ugly.

A refreshing attitude toward monkish detachment is frequently expressed, as in an old Chinese story about a worthy elderly woman who had supported a monk for twenty years, having built him a little house in which to meditate and provided him with whatever food he needed. In time she began to wonder, quite humanly, what progress he was making in this ideal situation. Determined to find out, she hatched a little plot with the help of a willing young girl "rich in desire." The girl was to call upon the monk, ardently embrace him, confess an overpowering passion and ask his help. All she received from the monk, however, was the vaguely poetic statement that "an old tree grows on a cold rock in winter. Nowhere is there any warmth." When the girl returned with this report, the old woman fell into a rage. "To think I've been feeding that fellow for twenty years!" she cried. "How could he show so little consideration for your needs? He even made no attempt to help you understand your plight. Certainly he was not required to respond to your expression of desire, but at least he should have evidenced some understanding and compassion."

With that she went at once to the monk's dwelling, drove him forth, and burned the hut to the ground.

Then there is the better-known story of two monks who, on one of their

---

[5] *Zen Buddhism*, by Christmas Humphreys. William Heinemann, Ltd., London, 1949.

daily journeys with begging bowls, chanced upon a large puddle that blocked their way, and the way also of a well-dressed young lady. Perceiving the dilemma of the pretty young thing in her charming kimono, her clean *tabi* and *geta*, one of the monks, without second thought, picked up the girl, carried her across the puddle, deposited her safely on the dry farther side, and walked on his way. After a long silence the other monk felt obliged to speak of what had obviously been weighing heavily upon him. He reminded his brother that all association with women was strictly forbidden, yet he had just seen him lift a woman in his arms and carry her some distance. The first monk exclaimed in surprise, "Do you mean to tell me you're still carrying that girl? I put her down miles back."

Since Zen emphasizes One-ness and the essential non-difference between Being and Not-being, even the subject of death is permitted humorous overtones. Concern with worldly nonessentials in the face of the seeming "finality" of breathing one's last breath is a good subject for laughter, especially if supposedly enlightened Zen monks are involved.

"The usual posture for Zen monks to die in is sitting, that is, doing zazen, but the Third Patriarch, Seng Ts'an, died (in 606) standing with clasped hands. Chihhsien of Huanch'i, died 905 A.D., asked his attendants, "Who dies sitting?" They answered, "A monk." He said, "Who dies standing?" They said, "Enlightened monks." He then walked around seven steps with his hands hanging down, and died. When Teng Yinfeng was about to die in front of the Diamond Cave at Wutai, he said to the people around him, "I have seen monks die sitting and lying, but have any died standing?" "Yes, some," they replied. "How about upside down?" "Never seen such a thing!" Teng died standing on his head. His clothes also rose up close to his body. It was decided to carry him to the burning-ground, but he still stood there without moving. People from far and near gazed with astonishment at the scene. His younger sister, a nun, happened to be there, and grumbled at him, saying, "When you were alive you took no notice of laws and customs, and even now you're dead you are making a nuisance of yourself!" She then prodded her brother with her finger and he fell down with a bang. Then they went off to the crematorium."[6]

The point would seem to be that in the Zen view anything as natural, as *organic*, one might say, as death, falls properly within the realm of humor, the one universal solvent. In general, Zen humor reflects the quiet pleasure to be found in pulling out the rug from under any pomposity. [N. W. R.]

---

[6] *Oriental Humor*, by R. H. Blyth. Hokuseido Press, Tokyo, 1959.

CHAPTER 2

Monkey[1]

Translated by ARTHUR WALEY

A masterpiece of humorous allegory on the subject of the frailty and arrogance of human creatures was written in China in the sixteenth century and brilliantly translated some years ago by Arthur Waley under the title *Monkey*. This wise and rollicking picaresque tale—from whose original hundred chapters Mr. Waley chose thirty for presentation to an eternally grateful Western audience—manages with rare adroitness to mix the nonsensical and the meaningful as it describes the travels, feats, and failures of Monkey and his three pals, Pigsy, Sandy, and Tripitaka. One of the critics who greeted the novel's appearance in English with special appreciation described it as a "combination of Mickey Mouse, Davy Crockett and *Pilgrim's Progress*." Actually there is nothing comparable in Western literature to *Monkey's* singular mixture of the profound and the absurd, the spiritual and the worldly.

Of the four chief adventurers of this exuberant folk tale, Monkey has been said to symbolize "the restless instability of genius"; Pigsy, as his name well suggests, is expressive of "physical appetite, brute strength and a kind of cumbrous patience"; Sandy—stands for "sincerity" or "whole-heartedness"; and lastly, Tripitaka—a character built on an actual historic personage, the famous Chinese traveler of the seventh century, Hsuan Tsang—represents "the ordinary man, blundering anxiously through the difficulties of life." The

---

[1] From *Monkey*, translated from the Chinese by Arthur Waley. John Day Company, New York, 1943. Reprinted by Grove Press, New York.

basic subject of this immense classic, known in China as *Hsi Yu Ki*, was the almost incredible pilgrimage to India in pursuit of Buddhist knowledge made by Hsuan Tsang some nine centuries earlier.

In the following excerpt, Monkey, the lovable braggart and know-it-all, gets to Heaven and there has the kind of encounter with the Buddha that only China and Japan could laugh at without diminishing one whit their reverence for the Supreme Being of their faith. What is, in fact, being laughed at is only the overreaching cleverness of the human creature, so that nothing is thereby detracted from the Buddha's greatness or His all-embracing wisdom. [N. W. R.]

"I'll have a wager with you," said Buddha. "If you are really so clever, jump off the palm of my right hand. If you succeed, I'll tell the Jade Emperor to come and live with me in the Western Paradise, and you shall have his throne without more ado. But if you fail, you shall go back to earth and do penance there for many a kalpa[2] before you come back to me with your talk."

"This Buddha," Monkey thought to himself, "is a perfect fool. I can jump a hundred and eight thousand leagues, while his palm cannot be as much as eight inches across. How could I fail to jump clear of it?"

"You're sure you're in a position to do this for me?" he asked.

"Of course I am," said Buddha.

He stretched out his right hand, which looked about the size of a lotus leaf. Monkey put his cudgel behind his ear, and leapt with all his might. "That's all right," he said to himself. "I'm right off it now." He was whizzing so fast that he was almost invisible, and Buddha, watching him with the eye of wisdom, saw a mere whirligig shoot along.

Monkey came at last to five pink pillars, sticking up into the air. "This is the end of the World," said Monkey to himself. "All I have got to do is to go back to Buddha and claim my forfeit. The Throne is mine."

"Wait a minute," he said presently, "I'd better just leave a record of some kind, in case I have trouble with Buddha." He plucked a hair and blew on it with magic breath, crying, "Change!" It changed at once into a writing brush charged with heavy ink, and at the base of the central pillar he wrote, "The Great Sage Equal to Heaven reached this place." Then, to mark his disrespect, he relieved nature at the bottom of the first pillar, and somersaulted

---

[2] *Kalpa* is an Indian word for the duration of time which elapses between the origin and destruction of a world system. [N.W.R.]

back to where he had come from. Standing on Buddha's palm, he said, "Well, I've gone and come back. You can go and tell the Jade Emperor to hand over the palaces of Heaven."

"You stinking ape," said Buddha, "you've been on the palm of my hand all the time."

"You're quite mistaken," said Monkey. "I got to the end of the World, where I saw five flesh-coloured pillars sticking up into the sky. I wrote something on one of them. I'll take you there and show you, if you like."

"No need for that," said Buddha. "Just look down."

Monkey peered down with his fiery, steely eyes, and there at the base of the middle finger of Buddha's hand he saw written the words, "The Great Sage Equal to Heaven reached this place," and from the fork between the thumb and first finger came a smell of monkey's urine.

Three Old Chinese Zen Stories

In a predominantly pragmatic and serious book called *The Practice of Zen*,[1] recently published in America, its Tibetan-trained author, Chang Chen-chi, sets forth three old stories from Chinese Zen which illustrate with special aptness Zen's subtle, wry, even sometimes rough use of humor to ridicule fakery, or to deflate undue self-importance.

Of the last "typical anecdote" Chang Chen-chi remarks that it has particular pertinence for those who "blindly follow the hocus-pocus of Zen imitators." More than this, it illustrates "how Zen can become downright senseless folly in the hands of the wrong persons, a not uncommon case nowadays." [N. W. R.]

Su Tung Po, the celebrated poet of the Sung Dynasty, was a devout Buddhist. He had a very close friend named Fo Ying, a very brilliant Zen teacher. Fo Ying's temple was on the west bank of the Yang Tse River, while Su Tung Po's house stood on the east bank. One day Su Yung Po paid a visit to Fo Ying and, finding him absent, sat down in his study to await his return. Becoming bored with waiting, he began at length to scribble on a sheet of paper that he found lying on the desk, the last words being: "Su Tung Po, the great Buddhist who cannot be moved, even by the combined forces of the Eight Worldly Winds."[2] After waiting a while longer, Su Tung Po got tired

---

[1] Harper and Brothers, New York, 1959.

[2] Eight Worldly Winds is a term widely used by Buddhists to denote the eight worldly influences or interests that fan the passions and thus drive one on forever as a slave in [Sangsara]. They are: gain, loss; defamation, eulogy; praise, ridicule; sorrow, joy.

and left for home. When Fo Ying returned and saw Su Tung Po's composition on the desk, he added the following line: "Rubbish! What you have said is no better than breaking wind!" and sent it to Su Tung Po. When Su Tung Po read this outrageous comment, he was so furious that he at once took a boat, crossed the river, and hurried to the temple again. Catching hold of Fo Ying's arm, he cried: "What right have you to denounce me in such language? Am I not a devout Buddhist who cares only for the Dharma? Are you so blind after knowing me for so long?" Fo Ying looked at him quietly for a few seconds, then smiled and said slowly: "Su Tung Po, the great Buddhist who claims that the combined forces of the Eight Winds can hardly move him an inch, is now carried all the way to the other side of the Yang Tse River by a single puff of wind from the anus!"

• • • • • • • • •

Prime Minister Kuo Tze I of the Tang Dynasty was an outstanding statesman as well as a distinguished general. His success in both political and military service made him the most admired national hero of his day. But fame, power, wealth and success could not distract the prime minister from his keen interest in and devotion to Buddhism. Regarding himself as a plain, humble, and devoted Buddhist, he often visited his favorite Zen Master to study under him. He and the Zen Master seemed to get along very well. The fact that he held the position of prime minister, an exalted status in those days of old China, seemed to have no influence on their association. Apparently no noticeable trace of politeness on the Zen Master's part or of vain loftiness on the part of the minister existed in their relationship, which seemed to be the purely religious one of a revered Master and an obedient disciple. One day, however, when Kuo Tze I, as usual, paid a visit to the Zen Master, he asked the following question: "Your Reverence, how does Buddhism explain egotism?" The Zen Master's face suddenly turned blue, and in an extremely haughty and contemptuous manner he addressed the premier as follows: "What are you saying, you numbskull?" This unreasonable and unexpected defiance so hurt the feelings of the prime minister that a slight, sullen expression of anger began to show on his face. The Zen Master then smiled and said: "Your Excellency, this is egotism!"

• • • • • • • • •

A monk called himself the "Master of Silence." He was actually a fraud and had no genuine understanding. To sell his humbug Zen, he had two eloquent attendant monks to answer questions for him; but he himself never uttered a word, as if to show his inscrutable "Silent Zen." One day, during the absence of his two attendants, a pilgrim monk came to him and asked: "Master, what is the Buddha?" Not knowing what to do or to answer, in his confusion he could only look desperately around in all directions—east and west, here and there—for his missing mouthpieces. The pilgrim monk, apparently satisfied, then asked him: "What is the Dharma?" He could not answer this question either, so he first looked up at the ceiling and then down at the floor, calling for help from heaven and hell. Again the monk asked: "What is the Sangha?"[3] Now the "Master of Silence" could do nothing but close his eyes. Finally the monk asked: "What is blessing?" In desperation, the "Master of Silence" helplessly spread his hands to the questioner as a sign of surrender. But the pilgrim monk was very pleased and satisfied with this interview. He left the "Master" and set out again on his journey. On the road the pilgrim met the two attendant monks on their way home, and began telling them enthusiastically what an enlightened being this "Master of Silence" was. He said: "I asked him what Buddha is. He immediately turned his face to the east and then to the west, implying that human beings are always looking for Buddha here and there, but actually Buddha is not to be found either in the east or in the west. I then asked him what the Dharma is. In answer to this question he looked up and down, meaning that the truth of Dharma is a totality of equalness, there being no discrimination between high and low, while both purity and impurity can be found therein. In answering my question as to what the Sangha was, he simply closed his eyes and said nothing. That was a clue to the famous saying:

> If one can close his eyes and sleep soundly in the deep recesses of the
> cloudy mountains,
> He is then a great monk.

"Finally, in answering my last question, 'What is the blessing?' he stretched out his arms and showed both his hands to me. This implied that he was stretching out his helping hands to guide sentient beings with his blessings. Oh, what an enlightened Zen Master! How profound is his teaching!" When the attendant monks returned, the "Master of Silence" scolded them thus: "Where have you been all this time? A while ago I was embarrassed to death, and almost ruined, by an inquisitive pilgrim!"

---

[3] The Buddhist monastic order; the brotherhood of monks. [N. W. R.]

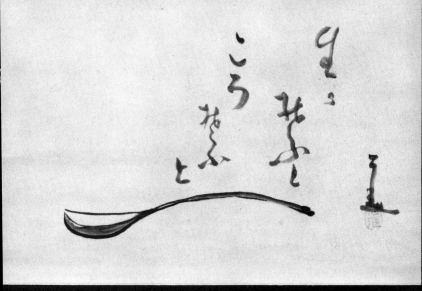

The characters above this sketch of an old-fashioned doctor's spoon read:

"Whether for life or whether for death."

This is part of an old and familiar Japanese saying that concludes with the words "depends on what's in the spoon."

V ZEN IN PSYCHOLOGY
AND EVERYDAY LIFE

CHAPTER 1

Psychoanalysis and Zen Buddhism[1]

By ERICH FROMM

The aim of Zen is enlightenment: the immediate, unreflected grasp of reality, without affective contamination and intellectualization, the realization of the relation of myself to the Universe. This new experience is a repetition of the pre-intellectual, immediate grasp of the child, but on a new level, that of the full development of man's reason, objectivity, individuality. While the child's experience, that of immediacy and oneness, lies *before* the experience of alienation and the subject-object split, the enlightenment experience lies after it.

The aim of psychoanalysis, as formulated by Freud, is that of making the unconscious conscious, of replacing Id by Ego. To be sure, the content of the unconscious to be discovered was limited to a small sector of the personality, to those instinctual drives which were alive in early childhood, but which were subject to amnesia. To lift these out of the state of repression was the aim of the analytic technique. Furthermore, the sector to be uncovered, quite aside from Freud's theoretical premises, was determined by the therapeutic need to cure a particular symptom. There was little interest in recovering unconsciousness outside of the sector related to the symptom formation. Slowly the introduction of the concept of the death instinct and eros and the development of the Ego aspects in recent years have brought about a certain broadening of the Freudian concepts of the contents of the unconscious. The non-

---

[1] From *Zen Buddhism and Psychoanalysis*, by Erich Fromm, D. T. Suzuki, and Richard De Martino. Harper and Brothers, New York, 1960.

Freudian schools greatly widened the sector of the unconscious to be uncovered. Most radically Jung, but also Adler, Rank, and the other more recent so-called neo-Freudian authors have contributed to this extension. But (with the exception of Jung), in spite of such a widening, the extent of the sector to be uncovered has remained determined by the therapeutic aim of curing this or that symptom; or this or that neurotic character trait. It has not encompassed the whole person.

However, if one follows the original aim of Freud, that of making the unconscious conscious, to its last consequences, one must free it from the limitations imposed on it by Freud's own instinctual orientation, and by the immediate task of curing symptoms. If one pursues the aim of the full recovery of the unconscious, then this task is not restricted to the instincts, nor to other limited sectors of experience, but to the total experience of the total man; then the aim becomes that of overcoming alienation, and of the subject-object split in perceiving the world; then the uncovering of the unconscious means the overcoming of affective contamination and cerebration; it means the de-repression, the abolition of the split within myself between the universal man and the social man; it means the disappearance of the polarity of conscious vs. unconscious; it means arriving at the state of the immediate grasp of reality, without distortion and without interference by intellectual reflection; it means overcoming of the craving to hold on to the ego, to worship it; it means giving up the illusion of an indestructible separate ego, which is to be enlarged and preserved, as the Egyptian pharaohs hoped to preserve themselves as mummies for eternity. To be conscious of the unconscious means to be open, responding, to *have* nothing and to *be*.

This aim of the full recovery of unconsciousness by consciousness is quite obviously much more radical than the general psychoanalytic aim. The reasons for this are easy to see. To achieve this total aim requires an effort far beyond the effort most persons in the West are willing to make. But quite aside from this question of effort, even the visualization of this aim is possible only under certain conditions. First of all, this radical aim can be envisaged only from the point of view of a certain philosophical position. There is no need to describe this position in detail. Suffice it to say that it is one in which not the negative aim of the absence of sickness, but the positive one of the presence of well-being is aimed at, and that well-being is conceived in terms of full union, the immediate and uncontaminated grasp of the world. This aim could not be better described than has been done by Suzuki in terms of "the art of living." One must keep in mind that any such concept as the art of living grows from the soil of a spiritual humanistic orientation, as it underlies the teaching of Buddha, of the prophets, of Jesus, of Meister Eckhart, or of men such as Blake, Walt Whitman, or Bucke. Unless it is seen in this context, the concept of "the art of living" loses all that is specific, and deteriorates into a concept that goes today under the name of "happiness." It must also not be forgotten that this orientation includes an ethical aim. While Zen transcends ethics, it includes the basic ethical aims of Buddhism, which are essentially the same as those of all humanistic teaching. The achievement of the aim of Zen, as Suzuki has made very clear, implies the overcoming of greed in all forms, whether it is the greed for possession, for fame, or for affection; it implies overcoming narcissistic self-glorification and the illusion of omnipotence. It implies, furthermore, the overcoming of the desire to submit to an authority who solves one's own problem of existence. The person who only wants to use the discovery of the unconscious to be cured of sickness will, of course, not even attempt to achieve the radical aim which lies in the overcoming of repressedness.

But it would be a mistake to believe that the radical aim of the de-repression has no connection with a therapeutic aim. Just as one has recognized that the cure of a symptom and the prevention of future symptom formations is not possible without the analysis and change of the character, one must also recognize that the change of this or that neurotic character trait is not possible without pursuing the more radical aim of a complete transformation of the person. It may very well be that the relatively disappointing results of character analysis (which have never been expressed more honestly than by Freud in his "Analysis, Terminable or Interminable?") are due precisely to the fact that the aims for the cure of the neurotic character were not radical enough; that well-being, freedom from anxiety and insecurity, can be achieved only if the limited aim is transcended, that is, if one realizes that the limited, therapeutic aim cannot be achieved as long as it remains limited and does not become part of a wider, humanistic frame of reference. Perhaps the limited aim can be achieved with more limited and less time-consuming methods, while the time and energy consumed in the long analytic process are used fruitfully only for the radical aim of "transformation" rather than the narrow one of "reform." This proposition might be strengthened by referring to a statement made above. Man, as long as he has not reached the creative relatedness of which *satori* is the fullest achievement, at best compensates for inherent potential depression by routine, idolatry, destructiveness, greed for property or fame, etc. When any of these compensations break down, his sanity is threatened. The cure of the potential insanity lies only in the change in attitude from split and alienation to the creative, immediate grasp of and response to the world. If psychoanalysis can help in this way, it can help to achieve true mental health; if it cannot, it will only help to improve compensatory mechanisms. To put it still differently: somebody may be "cured" of a symptom, but he cannot be "cured" of a character neurosis. Man is not a thing,[2] man is not a "case," and the analyst does not cure anybody by treating him as an object. Rather, the analyst can only help a man to wake up, in a process in which the analyst is engaged with the "patient" in the process of their understanding each other, which means experiencing oneness.

In stating all this, however, we must be prepared to be confronted with an objection. If, as I said above, the achievement of the full consciousness of the unconscious is as radical and difficult an aim as enlightenment, does it make any sense to discuss this radical aim as something which has any general application? Is it not purely speculative to raise seriously the question that only this radical aim can justify the hopes of psychoanalytic therapy?

If there were only the alternative between full enlightenment and nothing, then indeed this objection would be valid. But this is not so. In Zen there are many stages of enlightenment, of which *satori* is the ultimate and decisive step. But, as far as I understand, value is set on experiences which are steps in the direction of *satori*, although *satori* may never be reached. Dr. Suzuki once illustrated this point in the following way: If one candle is brought into an absolutely dark room, the darkness disappears, and there is light. But if ten or a hundred or a thousand candles are added, the room will become brighter and brighter. Yet the decisive change was brought about by the first candle which penetrated the darkness.[3]

What happens in the analytic process? A person senses for the first time that he is vain, that he is frightened, that he hates, while consciously he had believed himself to be modest, brave, and loving. The new insight may hurt him, but it opens a door; it permits him to stop projecting on others what he represses in himself. He proceeds; he experiences the infant, the child, the adolescent, the criminal, the insane, the saint, the artist, the male, *and* the

---

[2] Cf. my paper: "The Limitations and Dangers of Psychology," in *Religion and Culture*, ed. by W. Leibrecht. Harper and Brothers, New York, 1959, pp. 31ff.

[3] In a personal communication, as I remember.

female within himself; he gets more deeply in touch with humanity, with the universal man; he represses less, is freer, has less need to project, to cerebrate; then he may experience for the first time how he sees colors, how he sees a ball roll, how his ears are suddenly fully opened to music, when up to now he only listened *to* it; in sensing his oneness with others, he may have a first glimpse of the illusion that his separate individual ego is some*thing* to hold onto, to cultivate, to save; he will experience the futility of seeking the answer to life by *having* himself, rather than by being and becoming himself. All these are sudden, unexpected experiences with no intellectual content; yet afterwards the person feels freer, stronger, less anxious than he ever felt before.

So far we have spoken about *aims*, and I have proposed that if one carries Freud's principle of the transformation of unconsciousness into consciousness to its ultimate consequences, one approaches the concept of enlightenment. But as to *methods* of achieving this aim, psychoanalysis and Zen are, indeed, entirely different. The method of Zen is, one might say, that of a frontal attack on the alienated way of perception by means of the "sitting," the koan, and the authority of the master. Of course, all this is not a "technique" which can be isolated from the premise of Buddhist thinking, of the behavior and ethical values which are embodied in the master and in the atmosphere of the monastery. It must also be remembered that it is not a "five hour a week" concern, and that by the very fact of coming for instruction in Zen the student has made a most important decision, a decision which is an important part of what goes on afterwards.

The psychoanalytic method is entirely different from the Zen method. It trains consciousness to get hold of the unconscious in a different way. It directs attention to that perception which is distorted; it leads to a recognition of the fiction within oneself; it widens the range of human experience by lifting repressedness. The analytic method is psychological-empirical. It examines the psychic development of a person from childhood on and tries to recover earlier experiences in order to assist the person in experiencing of what is now repressed. It proceeds by uncovering illusions within oneself about the world, step by step, so that parataxic distortions and alienated intellectualizations diminish. By becoming less of a stranger to himself, the person who goes through this process becomes less estranged to the world; because he has opened up communication with the universe within himself, he has opened up communication with the universe outside. False consciousness disappears, and with it the polarity conscious-unconscious. A new realism dawns in which "the mountains are mountains again." The psychoanalytic method is of course only a method, a preparation; but so is the Zen method. By the very fact that it is a method it never guarantees the achievement of the goal. The factors which permit this achievement are deeply rooted in the individual personality, and for all practical purposes we know little of them.

I have suggested that the method of uncovering the unconscious, if carried to its ultimate consequences, may be a step toward enlightenment, provided it is taken within the philosophical context which is most radically and realistically expressed in Zen. But only a great deal of further experience in applying this method will show how far it can lead. The view expressed here implies only a possibility and thus has the character of a hypothesis which is to be tested.

But what can be said with more certainty is that the knowledge of Zen, and a concern with it, can have a most fertile and clarifying influence on the theory and technique of psychoanalysis. Zen, different as it is in its method from psychoanalysis, can sharpen the focus, throw new light on the nature of insight, and heighten the sense of what it is to see, what it is to be creative, what it is to overcome the affective contaminations and false intellectualizations which are the necessary result of experience based on the subject-object split.

In its very radicalism with respect to intellectualization, authority, and the delusion of the ego, in its emphasis on the aim of well-being, Zen thought will deepen and widen the horizon of the psychoanalyst and help him to arrive at a more radical concept of the grasp of reality as the ultimate aim of full, conscious awareness.

If further speculation on the relation between Zen and psychoanalysis is permissible, one might think of the possibility that psychoanalysis may be significant to the student of Zen. I can visualize it as a help in avoiding the danger of a false enlightenment (which is, of course, no enlightenment), one which is purely subjective, based on psychotic or hysterical phenomena, or on a self-induced state of trance. Analytic clarification might help the Zen student to avoid illusions, the absence of which is the very condition of enlightenment.

Whatever the use is that Zen may make of psychoanalysis, from the standpoint of a Western psychoanalyst I express my gratitude for this precious gift of the East, especially to Dr. Suzuki, who has succeeded in expressing it in such a way that none of its essence becomes lost in the attempt to translate Eastern into Western thinking, so that the Westerner, if he takes the trouble,

202

can arrive at an understanding of Zen, as far as it can be arrived at before the goal is reached. How could such understanding be possible, were it not for the fact that "Buddha nature is in all of us," that man and existence are universal categories, and that the immediate grasp of reality, waking up, and enlightenment, are universal experiences.

CHAPTER 2

Zen in Psychotherapy: The Virtue of Sitting[1]

By AKIHISA KONDO

Anxiety—and its attendant states of self-dissatisfaction, emptiness, meaninglessness—is not the discovery and exclusive possession of the twentieth century; it is as old as the human mind itself. For Dogen, founder of the Soto Sect of Zen Buddhism in Japan some 700 years ago, anxiety is a reflection of the uncertainty of human existence. When this anxiety is consciously and acutely felt, moreover, there commences the flow of the Bodhi spirit that leads to enlightenment. Anxiety, then, according to Dogen, is the driving force to enlightenment. Without it as a spur we are left to flounder in a shallow, insecure life, eternally caught in the vicious circle of ignorance. Anxiety when accepted, therefore, works as the striking of a match in the dark, giving us a revealing glimpse of our impasse and at the same time igniting our desire to break out of it.

For most people ordinary daily life is a streamlined façade of so-called happy living, a life filled with competitiveness, jealousy, possessiveness, arrogance, humiliation, hate, love, aggressiveness, success, failure, and whatnot. At every turn our psychic energy is distracted and squandered in pursuit of this or that aim. We are trapped in the endless, blind, vicious circle of these drives. And because we are busily pursuing them, we do not have time to listen to our inner voice.

This voice comes from the depths of our real self. It may take the form of

---

[1] "Zen in Psychotherapy: The Virtue of Sitting," by Akihisa Kondo. *Chicago Review*, Volume 12, Number 2, Summer 1958.

conscience, aesthetic feeling, creative thinking or activity, or just the warm, soft inner suggestion to return home. Whatever the form, it is the expression of something deep and basic, far beyond these forms. At the very moment when we hear and accept it we are actually affirming our real self. If we look deeper we find that listening to it is our unconscious act of faith—faith in our real self. Further, it is an unconscious act of our real self that leads us to have faith in it and to listen to its voice. However powerful and overwhelming our ignorant drives are, the Real Self is always working in and through us. But we do not have pure faith because our minds are too much preoccupied with other strong beliefs: in success, prestige, money, intellectual superiority. What we need is time and space so that, free from all interruptions and distractions, we can at least once a day collect our psychic energy and concentratedly bring it into direct contact with our inner, most powerful resources. In order to feel vividly this kind of pure faith we need to empty our mind, to liberate it from all false values, and to experience directly our real self in its wholeness.

Psychoanalysis in its recent development has clarified the nature of the blind drives which haunt us within the unconscious, and has exerted its efforts to helping people realize specifically by what drives they are driven. Horney called this kind of help a disillusioning process. She believed that when we become disillusioned of the idealized image of ourselves that handcuffs the development of our real self, our real self has a chance to grow. Her thinking in this regard is of course a great contribution to making clear how ignorant human beings are of themselves. She aimed at helping people realize and amply feel that the blind drives that are hindering them from listening to the voice of their real self ultimately come out of their idealized image that is illusory. From the Zen point of view, this is a fine step in discerning how grievously illusory are our ideas about ourselves and our life. Her approach, naturally, is analytical, and I am not in disagreement with her regarding its value—I myself find it very useful. However, the analytical approach is not the only one. Especially as regards coming closer to one's self, the Zen way is specific and positive. Let me point out what Zen suggests.

In Zen practice, although the need to discern the illusory nature of our concepts, ideas, and emotions is considered important, concentration on sitting is stressed. It is sitting with a single-mind. What does this mean? Those in the Zen temple will never make answer to one who wishes to know before experiencing it. What they say, if anything, is simply, "Just sit!" This is meaningful, because they know from their experience that one can know the meaning of sitting only by actually practicing sitting. The answer must come out of oneself, by one's own experience. Single-mindedness is just single-mindedness and leaves no room for interrogation. It is a sheer act of faith in oneself. It implies, therefore, total respect toward the real self. "What is real self?" is not to be intellectually understood, it is to be experienced. Zen regards sitting as the way in which to experience this Real Self. Enlightenment, the realization of the true self, comes out of the practice of sitting, out of the "sitting" state of mind, and this cannot be vicariously understood. This single-minded state, it must be pointed out, is not confined merely to static sitting, so called, but must carry over and be strengthened in all our dynamic activities.

Dogen's advice about sitting is substantially as follows: Avoid distracting contacts and activities. Don't eat too much or too little. Sit in a quiet place on a thick rug or mat, with a pillow under your seat and your legs crossed in half- or full-lotus position (or sit in a straight-back chair with your feet flat on the floor). Keeping the back straight, breathe naturally from the depths of the lower part of the abdomen. Don't think about good or bad, yes or no. Become concentrated but not in thoughts.

When we sit as he advises, all our psychic energy that has been scattered as a result of our pursuits and internal conflicts is collected into a unity again. Of course at first, since our mind has been accustomed to functioning distractedly, sitting is felt to be a constriction of our activities. We become impatient and irritable, build up conflicting ideas, and feel desperate. Zen practice has been called the strenuous way to enlightenment, and it requires considerable effort; therefore we shrink from it. But this point is the test of our determination. Will we follow our old easy futile way of life or enter upon the path to liberation? This is the crossroads. If we truly realize the futility, meaninglessness, and emptiness of our past way of life, our determination to seek emancipation will be stronger. In this connection I wish to point out the meaningfulness of Dogen's assertion that the consciousness of the Bodhi-Spirit as the propelling force for practicing Zen must be acutely experienced. If we continue to practice while fighting all kinds of temptations to escape, we come to experience a calmness that is charged with vitality. This comes about partly because our psychic energy is no more wasted in futile drives and partly because it has become unified. Nor is this all. Every part of our body and mind is filled with vitality. Actually we are not aware of mind apart from body or body apart from mind; only a total feeling of fullness exists. In this stage we are no longer separated from our sitting, so to speak. At this time, according to the school of Zen followed, some will concentrate on a *koan*, others will just practice sitting. Whatever the method, the result is the same: in place of the separatedness experienced before, more and more we enjoy oneness in ourselves. Our total being is strengthened as a consequence. We feel in ourselves tremendous stability, fullness, and harmony. We feel alive. So Dogen says, "Sitting is the gateway of truth to total liberation."

This is the virtue of sitting that is called the power of sitting. This power or virtue achieved through sitting is not restricted in its functioning to the time of sitting. Once it is achieved it mobilizes and expresses itself every moment, and is strengthened through its functioning at all times. This may be called the dynamic functioning of the state of mind developed in sitting. It is, of course, different from the state of so-called enlightenment. Nonetheless in the steady deepening and strengthening of the practice of sitting there is enlightenment ever fulfilling itself. Enlightenment, then, is the fruit of sitting practice and not its goal. Actually, from a strict Zen point of view, in the very single-mindedness of the sitting and in the very life in which it functions, the real self is expressing itself most strongly and naturally without any consciousness on the part of the individual himself necessarily. In this sense only can we say there is enlightenment. According to Dogen, "There is enlightenment in practice and practice in enlightenment." To be sure, there are different expressions of experiences corresponding to differences in personality. Yet when one lives in the fullness of this kind of sitting, seriously absorbed in the problem of his true self, it is not astonishing that he can suddenly become enlightened at any time, since his real self is always expressing itself and only his consciousness is unaware of it. Emyo sought instruction from the Sixth Patriarch, who answered, "All right, I will teach you. At the very moment when you do not think good or bad, right or wrong, what is your original face?" Emyo was suddenly enlightened.

As a student of Zen I have personally profited a great deal. But as a therapist of neurotic patients I am greatly indebted to Zen teaching for their recovery. Perhaps, therefore, the following brief observations relating to my therapeutic experience with patients will not be inappropriate.

In addition to interview sessions, I strongly recommend patients to practice sitting as Dogen suggests. Inevitably at first it is almost unbearable for them

Some complain of physical pains and strains. Some complain of irritability and the great difficulty of keeping a motionless posture. Others say they feel more depressed and lonesome. Still others complain that they are haunted by stabbing ideas and fantasies and frustrated by their inability to achieve a tranquil state of mind. And some see only meaninglessness in this kind of practice. These protests add up to one general complaint: the method is ineffective and only leads to an intensification of the symptoms. This is quite understandable. In the first place, since they are accustomed to resorting to measures that achieve a pseudo-solution of their problems, they have an established pattern of activity. Sitting alone prohibits them from following their accustomed way of life. They feel frustrated because they cannot follow their usual pattern of scattering their energy, which they take to be natural activity but which actually is an escape mechanism to avoid facing their problems. So they feel constriction. Secondly, when the dispersion of their energy in external activities is blocked, they have no other way to turn except inward. They now must see the inside of themselves. Again, in order to avoid facing their actual problems they start to juggle various ideas or fantasies. Nevertheless, especially for the shallow and aggressive patients, now comes the chance to experience themselves inwardly. Willynilly they see the problems they suffer from and hate to face. Because they hate to see the problem they hate the way they are brought to see it—that is why they think the method is ineffective. They feel their sufferings intensified because they have to see the problems causing their sufferings, the very problems from which they are trying to escape. In my interviews with the patient, of course I pay respectful attention to his complaints, as well as to the content of his ideas, fantasies, and emotional experiences, and I try to help him elucidate their meaning. But I suggest continuing to practice sitting, and advise him not to pay much attention to his ideas and fantasies, stressing only the importance of sitting itself. If the patient feels it difficult to sit more than fifteen minutes, I do not urge him to sit longer, but strongly advise him to sit regularly and devotedly every day. Usually patients concur in these instructions and begin to feel they can get along in their sitting. Not infrequently a patient reports that he does not know why, but he feels his irritability or anxiety considerably lessened. From the therapist's side it is very impressive that the patient, as he practices sitting steadily, begins to show, unconsciously, more intensive concentration in working on his problems in the therapeutic session. In other words, through the patient's practice of sitting his psychic energy has begun to become assembled, unified, and available for constructive work. I don't say that the patient after sitting for a period of time becomes enlightened. What I say is that he is helped considerably to become charged with more psychic energy and vitality. His dreams show a more constructive picture and his posture begins to show more stability. Often patients say, "When I sit I feel I am rooted and full of sap, where before I felt helplessly buffeted by every emotional wind or storm." Or "I feel as if there is a bubbling fountain within me. I don't feel tired or frustrated any more." It is noteworthy that in these self-expressions images of water or trees abound.

I believe, from my experience, that any teaching is ineffective fundamentally, whether it be psychoanalysis or psychotherapy or Zen, unless it helps a person feel, experience, and become confident of his fundamental resourcefulness, his real self, his Buddha-nature, his inborn freedom and security, his uniqueness and universality, from the inside of himself and by himself. Neurotic or normal, we are all human beings. As human beings we share the same fate. The neurotic's case is merely an extreme one. But as Buddhism teaches, basically we are all alike in our ignorance of ourselves and in our capability of becoming emancipated from such ignorance through self-realization. Buddhism from the very beginning of its long history clearly recognized the nature of human existence and sought to emancipate human beings from their suffering. Zen, however it may be understood, has this aim.

I have tried to show how Zen intends to bring us to self-realization through sitting. This is a practice leading to single-mindedness, first, by assembling our psychic energy into a unity, and second, by strengthening it through constant practice in our daily living, leading to a stage where we are fully charged with strong vitality and power, where we sit and act with stability and security—in other words, the stage of no-mindedness. It is always a matter of chance when the Self will come to its own realization in our consciousness. The enlightenment experience comes about through the ripening of sitting, just as a fruit or a flower appears as the natural result of the growth of the tree. The roots of such enlightenment have been nourished for a long time in the rich soil of sitting.

It is almost routine to talk about enlightenment. It is the ultimate in the practice of Zen and surely it is important. But how important is it to talk about enlightenment all the time when for those who are enlightened it is pointless and for those who are not, incomprehensible, and frequently a hindrance in that it agitates their already too greedy preoccupation with enlightenment? It is my belief that, enlightenment or not, sitting is strengthening. How much so is something one has to experience for himself.

Sozan, a Zen Master, visited Tozan, a Zen Master. Tozan asked, "Who are you?" Sozan answered, "Honjaku is my name." Tozan said, "Say something more to the point!" Sozan said, "I shan't speak further." Tozan asked, "Why not?" "I don't call myself Honjaku," answered Sozan.

After a number of interviews I asked a patient of mine who was very much concerned that she was an illegitimate child (and who had been sitting according to my instructions), "Who were you before you were an illegitimate child?" She looked puzzled for an instant, then suddenly burst into tears, crying out, "I am I! Oh, I am I!"

Where is the Real Self in these contradicting statements?

CHAPTER 3

On the General Sense of Zen Thought[1]

By HUBERT BENOIT

Man has always reflected upon his condition, has thought that he is not as he would like to be, has defined more or less accurately the faults of his manner of functioning, has made in fact his "auto-criticism." This work of criticism, sometimes rough-and-ready, attains at other times on the contrary, and in a number of directions, a very high degree of depth and subtlety. The undesirable aspects of the natural[2] man's inward functioning are often very accurately recognised and described.

With regard to this wealth of diagnosis one is struck by the poverty of therapeutic effect. The schools which have taught and which continue to teach the subject of Man, after having demonstrated what does not go right in the case of the natural man, and why that does not go right, necessarily come to the question "How are we to remedy this state of affairs?" And there begins the confusion and the poverty of doctrines. At this point nearly all the doctrines go astray, sometimes wildly, sometimes subtly, except the doctrine of Zen (and even here it is necessary to specify "some masters of Zen"). . . .

The essential error of all the false methods lies in the fact that the proposed remedy does not reach the root-cause of the natural man's misery. Critical analysis of man's condition does not go deep enough into the determining cause of his inner phenomena; it does not follow the links of this chain down

---

[1] From *The Supreme Doctrine, Psychological Studies in Zen Thought*, by Hubert Benoit. (Foreword by Aldous Huxley.) Pantheon Books, New York, 1955.

[2] The expression "the natural man" [as here used] describes man as he is before the condition known as satori.

211

to the original phenomenon. It stops too quickly at the symptoms. The searcher who does not see further than such and such a symptom, whose analytic thought, exhausted, stops there, evidently is not able to conceive a remedy for the whole situation except as a development, concerted and artificial, of another symptom radically opposed to the symptom that is incriminated. For example: a man arrives at the conclusion that his misery is the result of his manifestations of anger, conceit, sensuality, etc., and he will think that the cure should consist in applying himself to produce manifestations of gentleness, humility, asceticism, etc. Or perhaps another man, more intelligent than this one, will come to the conclusion that his misery is a result of his mental agitation, and he will think that the cure should consist in applying himself, by such and such exercises, to the task of tranquillising his mind. One such doctrine will say to us, "Your misery is due to the fact that you are always desiring something, to your attachment to what you possess," and this will result, according to the degree of intelligence of the master, in the advice to give away all your possessions, or to learn to detach yourself inwardly from the belongings that you continue to own outwardly. Another such doctrine will see the key to the man's misery in his lack of self-mastery, and will prescribe "Yoga" methods aimed at progressive training of the body, or of feelings, or of the attitude towards others, or of knowledge, or of attention.

All that is, from the Zen point of view, just animal-training and leads to one kind of servitude or another (with the illusory and exalting impression of attaining freedom). At the back of all that, there is the following simple-minded reasoning: "Things are going badly with me in such and such a way; very well, from now on I am going to do exactly the opposite." This way of regarding the problem, starting from a *form* that is judged to be bad, encloses the searcher within the limits of a domain that is *formal*, and, as a result, deprives him of all possibility of re-establishing his consciousness beyond all form; when I am enclosed within the limits of the plane of dualism no reversal of method will deliver me from the dualistic illusion and restore me to Unity. It is perfectly analogous to the problem of "Achilles and the Tortoise"; the manner of posing the problem encloses it within the very limits that it is necessary to overstep, and as a result, renders it insoluble.

The penetrating thought of Zen cuts through all our phenomena without stopping to consider their particularities. It knows that in reality nothing is wrong with us and that we suffer because we do not understand that everything works perfectly, because in consequence we believe falsely that all is not well and that it is necessary to put something right. To say that all the trouble derives from the fact that man has an illusory belief that he lacks something would be an absurd statement also, since the "lack" of which it speaks is unreal and because an illusory belief, for that reason unreal, could not be the cause of anything whatever. Besides, if I look carefully, I do not find positively in myself this belief that I lack something (how could there be positively present the illusory belief in an absence?); what I can state is that my inward phenomena behave as if this belief were there; but, if my phenomena behave in this manner, it is not on account of the presence of this belief, it is because the direct intellectual intuition that nothing is lacking sleeps in the depths of my consciousness, that this has not yet been awakened therein; it is there, for I lack nothing and certainly not that, but it is asleep and cannot manifest itself. All my apparent "trouble" derives from the sleep of my faith in the perfect Reality; I have, awakened in me, nothing but "beliefs" in what is communicated to me by my senses and my mind working on the dualistic plane (beliefs in the non-existence of a Perfect Reality that is One); and these beliefs are illusory formations, without reality, consequences of the sleep of my faith. I am a "man of little faith," more exactly without any faith, or, still better, of sleeping faith, who does not believe in anything he does not see on the formal plane. (This idea of faith, present but asleep, enables us to understand the need that we experience, for our deliverance, of a Master to awaken us, of a teaching, of a revelation; for sleep connotes precisely the deprivation of that which can awaken.)

In short everything appears to be wrong in me because the fundamental idea that everything is perfectly, eternally and totally positive, is asleep in the centre of my being, because it is not awakened, living and active therein. There at last we touch upon the first painful phenomenon, that from which all the rest of our painful phenomena derive. The sleep of our faith in the Perfect Reality that is One (outside which nothing "is") is the primary phenomenon from which the whole of the entangled chain depends; it is the causal phenomenon; and no therapy of illusory human suffering can be effective if it be applied anywhere but there.

To the question "What must I do to free myself?" Zen replies: "There is nothing you need do since you have never been enslaved and since there is nothing in reality from which you can free yourself." This reply can be misunderstood and may seem discouraging because it contains an ambiguity

213

一棹両橈
六泥入水
吾老文與聟
何をもして管見
船をふ

SENGAI

This painting is called "Teaching in a Boat." It portrays the legendary "Boatman," a great master of the Tang period in China who always received aspirants and seekers in his boat. One day an official visited him and the following dialogue took place:

Official: "How're you doing, Sir?"
Master, raising his oar: "Get it?"
Official: "No."
Master: "If I slap the quiet water with an oar, my chance of hitting a fish with golden scales is slim."

Knowing that this story would be familiar to anyone who looked at this painting, Sengai has written above the picture:

"Blow upon blow, he knocks him in,
And is splashed himself with the mud and water.
But though the other may think he knows what's what,
How far he is indeed from the heart of the boatman!"

inherent in the word "do." Where the natural man is concerned the action required resolves itself dualistically, into conception and action, and it is to the action, to the execution of his conception that the man applies the word "do." In this sense Zen is right, there is nothing for us to "do"; everything will settle itself spontaneously and harmoniously as regards our "doing" precisely when we cease to set ourselves to modify it in any manner and when we strive only to awaken our sleeping faith, that is to say when we strive to conceive the primordial idea that we have to conceive. This complete idea, spherical as it were and immobile, evidently does not lead to any particular action, it has no special dynamism, it is this central purity of Non-Action through which will pass, untroubled, the spontaneous dynamism of real natural life. Also one can and one should say that to awaken and to nourish this conception is not "doing" anything in the sense that this word must necessarily have for the natural man, and even that this awakening in the domain of thought is revealed in daily life by a reduction (tending towards cessation) of all the useless operations to which man subjects himself in connexion with his inner phenomena. . . .

. . . There is no "path" towards deliverance, and that is evident since we have never really been in servitude and we continue not to be so; there is nowhere to "go," there is nothing to "do." Man has nothing directly to do in order to experience his liberty. . . . What he has to do is indirect and negative; what he has to understand, by means of work, is the deceptive illusion of all the "paths" that he can seek out for himself and try to follow. When his persevering efforts shall have brought him the perfectly clear understanding that *all* that he can "do" to free himself is useless, when he has definitely stripped of its value the very idea of all imaginable "paths," then "satori" will burst forth, a real vision that there is no "path" because there is nowhere to go, because, from all eternity, he was at the unique and fundamental centre of everything.

So the "deliverance," so-called, which is the disappearance of the illusion of being in servitude, succeeds, chronologically, an inner operation but is not in reality caused by it. This inward formal operation cannot be the cause of that which precedes all form and consequently precedes *it*; it is only the instrument through which the First Cause operates.

In fact the famous narrow gate does not exist in the strict sense of the word, any more than the path onto which it might open; unless one might wish so to call the understanding that there is no path, that there is no gate, that there

215

is nowhere to go because there is no need to go anywhere. That is the great secret, and at the same time the great indication, that the Zen masters reveal to us.

Practicing Zen Through Observing One's Mind in Tranquility[1] — The Non-Koan Way in Zen

By CHANG CHEN-CHI

. . . Let us comment on the technique of "observing one's mind in tranquility"—the original and more "orthodox" Zen practice which has been neglected for so long in the overwhelming attention given to koan exercises.

The Zen practice of the Tsao Tung [Soto] School can be summed up in these two words: "serene reflection" (Chinese: *mo chao*). This is clearly shown in the poem from the "Notes on Serene-Reflection," by the famous Zen Master, Hung Chih, of the Tsao Tung School:

> Silently and serenely one forgets all words;
> Clearly and vividly *That* appears before him.
> When one realizes it, it is vast and without edges;
> In its Essence, one is clearly aware.
> Singularly reflecting is this bright awareness,
> Full of wonder is this pure reflection.
> Dew and the moon,
> Stars and streams,
> Snow on pine trees,
> And clouds hovering on the mountain peaks—
> From darkness, they all become glowingly bright;
> From obscurity, they all turn to resplendent light.

---

[1] From "Practicing Zen Through Observing One's Mind in Tranquility," in *The Practice of Zen*, by Chang Chen-chi. Harper and Brothers, New York, 1959.

Infinite wonder permeates this serenity;
In this Reflection all intentional efforts vanish.
Serenity is the final word [of all teachings];
Reflection is the response to all [manifestations].
Devoid of any effort,
This response is natural and spontaneous.
Disharmony will arise
If in reflection there is no serenity;
All will become wasteful and secondary
If in serenity there is no reflection.
The Truth of serene-reflection
Is perfect and complete.
Oh look! The hundred rivers flow
In tumbling torrents
To the great ocean!

Without some explanations and comments on this poem, the meaning of "serene-reflection" may still be enigmatic to many readers. The Chinese word, *mo*, means "silent" or "serene"; *chao* means "to reflect" or "to observe." *Mo chao* may thus be translated as "serene-reflection" or "serene-observation." But both the "serene" and the "reflection" have special meanings here and should not be understood in their common connotations. The meaning of "serene" goes much deeper than mere "calmness" or "quietude"; it implies transcendency over all words and thoughts, denoting a state of "beyond," of pervasive peace. The meaning of "reflection" likewise goes much deeper than its ordinary sense of "contemplation of a problem or an idea." It has no savor of mental activity or of contemplative thought, but is a mirror-like clear awareness, ever illuminating and bright in its pure self-experience. To speak even more concisely, "serene" means the tranquility of no-thought (Chinese: *wu nien*), and "reflection" means vivid and clear awareness. Therefore, serene-reflection is *clear awareness in the tranquility of no-thought*. This is what the *Diamond Sutra* meant by "not dwelling on any object, yet the mind arises."

The great problem here is, how can one put his mind *into* such a state? To do so requires verbal instruction and special training at the hands of a teacher. The "wisdom eye" of the disciple must first be opened, otherwise he will never know how to bring his mind to the state of serene-reflection. If one knows how to practice this meditation, he has already accomplished something in Zen. The uninitiated never know how to do this work. This serene-reflection meditation of the Tsao Tung sect, therefore, is not an ordinary exercise of quietism or stillness. It is the meditation of Zen, of *Prajnaparamita*. Careful study of the preceding poem will show that the intuitive and transcendental "Zen elements" are unmistakably there.[2]

The best way to learn this meditation is to train under a competent Zen Master. If, however, you are unable to find one, you should try to work through the following "Ten Suggestions"—the quintessential instructions on Zen practice that the author has learned through great difficulties and long years of Zen study. It is his sincerest hope that they will be valued, cherished, and practiced by some serious Zen students in the West.

Ten Suggestions on Zen Practice:

1. Look inwardly at your state of mind before any thought arises.

2. When any thought does arise, cut it right off and bring your mind back to the work.

3. Try to look at the mind all the time.

4. Try to remember this "looking-sensation" in daily activities.

5. Try to put your mind into a state as though you had just been shocked.

6. Meditate as frequently as possible.

7. Practice with your Zen friends the circle-running exercise (as found in the "Discourses of Master Hsu Yun").[3]

8. In the midst of the most tumultuous activities, stop and look at the mind for a moment.

9. Meditate for brief periods with the eyes wide-open.

10. Read and reread as often as possible the *Prajnaparamita Sutras*, such as the *Diamond* and *Heart Sutras*, the *Prajna of Eight Thousand Verses*, the *Mahaprajnaparamita Sutra*, etc.

Hard work on these ten suggestions should enable anyone to find out for himself what "serene-reflection" means.

---

[2] "There exists a great dearth of documentation for the practical instructions which must have been given by the Tsao Tung Masters. One of the reasons that may have contributed to this shortage of written material is the "secret tradition" of the Tsao Tung sect, which discourages its followers from putting verbal instructions down in writing. Thus time has erased all traces of many such oral teachings." From page 43, *The Practice of Zen.* [N. W. R.]

[3] ". . . . [Then] after a long silence, the Master cried: "Go!" Immediately all the disciples, responding to his call, followed him, running in a large circle. After they had run for a number of rounds, a supervising monk made the "stopping signal" by suddenly whacking the board on a table, making a loud slapping noise. Instantly all the runners stopped and stood still. After a pause they all sat down on their seats in the cross-legged posture. Then the entire hall became deadly quiet; not the slightest sound could be heard, as though they were in some deep mountain fastness. This silent meditation lasted for more than an hour. Then everyone rose from his seat and the circling exercise started again. After running a few more rounds, all suddenly stopped once more when they heard the slapping board make the signal." From "Discourses of Master Hsu Yun," page 50, *The Practice of Zen.* [N. W. R.]

CHAPTER 5

Zen Buddhism and Everyday Life

By ROBERT LINSSEN[1]

Most writers agree on the fact that Zen is not to be understood but to be lived; and far from being incompatible with the requirements of everyday life, Zen confers on it its own full revealing value. There are no actions which we should consider as "ordinary" in contrast to others which we regard as "exceptional" or extraordinary. Zen asks us to bring to bear the intensity of an extraordinary attention in the midst of all so-called "ordinary" circumstances. Reality is where we are from moment to moment. *The determining factor of our realization depends on the mental attitude in which we approach external and internal circumstances and phenomena.* The quality or kind of happening is secondary. Each incident of daily life, each perception of the concrete world, can be an occasion for "Satori."

We may recall the thought of a Zen Master who insisted on the fact that "Infinite is in the finite of each instant. . . ."

Any action which bears the imprint of the avidity of the "I-process," its instinct for possession and domination, is a negative and incomplete action. It can only engender slavery, misery and conflict both for the individual and the community.

An eminently positive and constructive action is that in which the fullness of life is expressed at the very instant of its emergence. It is sufficient unto itself. It requires nothing and awaits nothing. It is just such a discrete, silent and

---

[1] From Chapter XXI, "Zen Buddhism and Everyday Life," in *Living Zen*, by Robert Linssen. George Allen and Unwin, Ltd., London, 1958.

anonymous process which sustains the whole Universe, from the infinitely small world of the atom to the distant nebulae of the infinitely great.

We can seize it within ourselves in the full power of its plenitude from the moment the tensions of avidity cease.

Our difficulty lies in the fact that the tensions of our avidities are generally situated in the deep zones of our unconscious. We often think that we are relaxed and perfectly present to the present, when in fact a host of tensions and secret aspirations remain buried in the innermost recesses of our mind. Therefore our actions are never fully lived, for they perpetually bear the imprint of a secret call and of a subtle anticipation. . . .

• • • • • • • • •

Zen substitutes an atmosphere of relaxation, serenity and simplicity for the tensions created by our strivings to "become," to possess and to dominate.

. . . The moment we are aware of the falseness of such an attitude we "let go," and the suffering inherent in our inner tensions is succeeded by the felicity and relaxation of *Being*.

True detachment is not the result of spiritual discipline.

If we simply reject, by an act of will, things and beings for which we feel attachment, we are merely evading the problem, for the Sage would ask us immediately: 'Who is rejecting this or that?'

. . . The man who has realized Satori has not decided to be detached, but, being intensely aware of the infinite riches of his nature, he can no longer be attached to anything. He can no longer feel desire or attachment because his awakening has revealed to him that *he is at the heart of the beings and things of the whole universe, at the heart of that which is most precious and irreplaceable in these beings and things. In other words, affective detachment is not a means, it is a consequence.*

The Zen masters teach us that one should not train oneself in meditation or detachment. They only formulate one requirement: that of a vigilance, an attention, a wide-awakeness of every moment, because the flame of life lies in the heart of each passing second.

Humanity could be compared to two and a half thousand million greyhounds rushing in pursuit of a mechanical hare on a vast race-track. These "human greyhounds" are taut, over-tense, avid and violent, but Zen tries to teach them that what they think is a real hare is only a mechanical hoax. The moment man fully realizes what is implied by this truth he "lets go," and the

221

bitterness of his struggles and violence are succeeded by relaxation, peace, harmony and love.

The consequences of such a release are immense, not only for the physical, nervous and mental health of man as an individual, but also for humanity as a whole.

Such are the essential bases of effective non-violence, compassion and kindliness as taught by Buddhism in general and Zen in particular. . . .

We all know that in most animals fear paralyses their instinctive reflexes. That which is true for animals applies also to man from certain points of view. Most of the mistakes we make, as well as our indiscretions and blunders, arise directly or indirectly from our fear and greed.

When the mind has "let go" and is free from the "tensions" of becoming, the body and the nervous system both undergo an extremely beneficial transformation. Recent progress in psychosomatics has shown the important modifications occurring in the degree of alkalinity of the blood and in divers hormonal secretions as a result of our emotional states.

Relaxation of the body along with relaxation and silence of the mind can be coupled with the highest lucidity, both mental and physical.

What strikes us when we observe authentically integrated beings, or men who have "realized" themselves, is the astonishing adequacy to circumstances which they reveal at all times, and the extraordinary agility with which they can at certain moments take action themselves in order to avert a danger threatening others. There is a striking difference between this attitude and that revealed in Hindu Samadhis, for in most of the latter the acuity of inner contemplation tends to disassociate the mystic from the external universe and to make him oblivious to the world.

. . . .

Amongst the direct consequences of effective experience of Zen, we should mention progressive simplification of existence.

The discovery of our true nature, or even approach to the inexhaustible riches which it conceals, delivers us from most of our needs such as possessions, worldly vanities and thirst for varied enjoyments.

In so far as we are capable of discovering the hidden treasure which lies in our own depths, as in the depths of all things, the external values tend to lose their attraction. By this we should not jump hastily to conclusions regarding the anti-social character of the integrated man or of the man who is on the way to such a state.

An anti-social man is one whose fundamental egoism only engenders passions, violence, possessiveness, jealousy, domination and continual demands.

When we are "dying" to ourselves these various sources of misery, conflict and suffering dry up automatically.

Again we should point out that *the simplification of needs is not a means but a consequence.*

How far should this be applied? What are the minimum or maximum needs appropriate to each person? No one can define them or draw up a system around them. That is where we should exercise our judgment, these problems force us to the "Use of the Great Body" of which the Zen Masters speak; and this Use depends for each one of us on the place and circumstances. If we were to codify the laws concerning it they might soon become a great bondage for us.

. . . .

True youth is much more psychological than physical.

We can see people who biologically are young, but who psychologically are characterized by a lack of inner life which is akin to death.

In so far as we are freed from the "force of habit" we accede to the creative dynamism of an intense inner life. The controlling factors of psychological ageing are routine, sterile repetition of identical habits and the accentuation of divers forms of egoism.

When the illusion of the "I-process" is unmasked all our desires, mental routines and memory-automatisms disappear. We are renewed from instant to instant. Each day is veritable re-birth to us, for every morning we awaken freed from the grip of the innumerable yesterdays of our existence. We begin again at zero, and we leave behind all danger of mental fossilization. We are freed from our fundamental fear by virtue of which we were clinging to our inner certainties and carefully protected routines of thought. The atmosphere of anxiety of the past, with its unjustified fears, gives way to the infinitely serene confidence of Reality Itself.

CHAPTER 6

The Awakening of a New Consciousness in Zen[1]

By D. T. SUZUKI

My position in regard to "the awakening of a new consciousness," summarily stated, is as follows:

The phrasing, "the awakening of a new consciousness" as it appears in the title of this paper, is not a happy one, because what is awakened in the Zen experience is not a "new" consciousness, but an "old" one which has been dormant ever since our loss of "innocence," to use the Biblical term. The awakening is really the re-discovery or the excavation of a long-lost treasure.[2]

There is in every one of us, though varied in depth and strength, an eternal longing for "something" which transcends a world of inequalities. This is a somewhat vague statement containing expressions not altogether happy. "To

---

[1] From "The Awakening of a New Consciousness in Zen," *Eranos Jahrbuch*, Band XXIII, 1954. Rhein-Verlag, Zurich.

[2] Cf. "The Ten Oxherding Pictures," IX, entitled "Returning to the Origin, Back to the Source." In the *Lankavatara Sutra*, reference is also made to visiting one's native town where every road is familiar. "A new consciousness" is not at all new. Hakuin (1685-1768) refers to Ganto, an ancient master of the T'ang dynasty, while Kosen (1816-1892) brings out Confucius as a witness to his *satori* experience. In Zen literature we often come across such expressions as "Back at home and quietly sitting," "Like seeing one's family in a strange town," etc.

The term "new" may be permissible from the point of view of psychology. But Zen is mainly metaphysical, and it deals with a total personality and not parts of it. Rinzai talks about "the whole being in action" (*zentai sayu*). This is the reason why in Zen beating, slapping, kicking, and other bodily activities are in evidence. Concrete experiences are valued more than mere conceptualisation. Language comes secondary. In Zen, consciousness in its ordinary scientific sense, has no use; the whole being must come forward. The whole elephant is needed and not its parts as studied by the blind. This will be clearer later on.

transcend" suggests "going beyond," "being away from," that is, a separation, a dualism. I have, however, no desire to hint that the "something" stands away from the world in which we find ourselves. And then "inequalities" may sound too political. When I chose the term I had in mind the Buddhist word *asama* which contrasts with *sama*, "equal" or "same." We may replace it by such words as "differentiation" or "individualisation" or "conditionality." I just want to point out the fact that as soon as we recognise this world to be subject to constant changes we somehow begin to feel dissatisfied with it and desire something which is permanent, free, above sorrow, and of eternal value.

This longing is essentially religious and each religion has its own way of designating it according to its tradition. Christians may call it longing for the Kingdom of Heaven or renouncing the world for the sake of divine love or praying to be saved from eternal damnation. Buddhists may call it seeking for emancipation or freedom. Indians may understand it as wishing to discover the real self.

Whatever expressions they may use, they all show a certain feeling of discontent with the situation·in which they find themselves. They may not yet know exactly how to formulate this feeling and conceptually represent it either to themselves or to others.

I specified this obscure feeling as a longing for something. In this, it may be said, I have already a preconceived idea by assuming the existence of a something for which there is a longing on our part. Instead of saying this, it might have been better to identify the feeling of dissatisfaction with such modern feelings as fear or anxiety or a sense of insecurity. But the naming is not so important. As long as the mind is upset and cannot enjoy any state of equilibrium or perfect equanimity, this is a sense of insecurity or discontent. We feel as if we were in the air and trying to find a place for landing.

Two ways are open: outward and inward. The outward one may be called intellectual and objective, but the inward one cannot be called subjective or affective or conative. The "inward" is misleading, though it is difficult to designate it in any other way. For all designations are on the plane of intellection. But as we must name it somehow, let us be content for a while to call it "inward" in contrast to "outward."

Let me give you this caution here: as long as the inward way is to be understood in opposition to the outward way—though to do otherwise is impossible because of the human inability to go beyond language as the means of communication—the inward way after all turns to be an outward way. The really inward way is when no contrast exists between the inward and the outward. This is a logical contradiction. But the full meaning of it will I hope become clearer when I finish this paper.

The essential characteristic of the outward way consists in its never-ending procession, either forward or backward, but mostly in a circular movement, and always retaining the opposition of two terms, subject and object. There is thus no finality in the outward way, hence the sense of insecurity, though security does not necessarily mean "standing still," "not moving anywhere," or "attached to something."

The inward way is the reverse of the outward way. Instead of going out endlessly and dissipating and exhausting itself, the mind turns inwardly to see what is there behind all this endless procession of things. It does not stop the movement in order to examine what is there. If it does, the movement ceases to be a movement; it turns into something else. This is what the intellect does while the inward way refuses to do so. As soon as there is any kind of bifurcation, the outward way consists in taking things as they are, in catching them in their is-ness or suchness. I would not say, "in their oneness" or "in their wholeness." These are the terms belonging to the outward way. Even to say "is-ness" or "suchness" or "thusness" or in Japanese "*sono-mama*" or in Chinese "*chi-mo*," is not, strictly speaking, the inward way. "To be" is an abstract term. It is much better to lift a finger and say nothing *about* it. The inward way in its orthodoxy generally avoids appealing to language, though it never shuns it.

The inward way occasionally uses the term "one" or "all," but in this case "one" means "one that is never one," and "all" means "all that is never all." The "one" will be "a one ever becoming one" and never a closed-up "one." The "all" will be "an all ever becoming all" and never a closed-up "all." This means that in the inward way the one is an absolute one, that one is all and all is one, and further that when "the ten thousand things" are reduced to an absolute oneness which is an absolute nothingness, we have the inward way of perfecting itself.

Buddhism, especially Zen Buddhism as it developed in China, is rich in expressions belonging to the inward way. In fact, it is Zen that has effected, for the first time, a deep excavation into the mine of the inward way. To illustrate my point read the following—I give just one instance:

Suigan at the end of the summer session made this declaration: "I have been talking, east and west, all this summer for my Brotherhood. See if my eyebrows are still growing."[3]

One of his disciples said, "How finely they are growing!"

Another said, "One who commits a theft feels uneasy in his heart."

A third one without saying anything simply uttered "Kwan!"[4]

It goes without saying that all these utterances of the disciples as well as of the master give us a glimpse into the scene revealed only to the inward way. They are all expressions directly bursting out of an abyss of absolute nothingness.

Now we come to the psycho-metaphysical aspect of the inward way. Buddhists call this "abyss of absolute nothingness" *kokoro* in Japanese. *Kokoro* is *hsin* in Chinese and in Sanskrit *citta*, or *sarvasattvacitta* to use the term in Aśvaghosha's *Awakening of Faith*. *Kokoro* is originally a psychological term, meaning "heart," "soul," "spirit," "mind," "thought"; it later came to denote the kernel or essence of a thing, becoming synonymous metaphysically with "substance" and ethically "sincerity," "verity," "faithfulness," etc. It is thus difficult to give one English equivalent for *kokoro*.

Out of this *kokoro* all things are produced and all things ultimately go back to it. But this must not be understood in relation to time. The *kokoro* and all things are one and yet not one; they are two and yet not two. A monk asked Chao-chou (Joshu in Japanese), "I am told that the ten thousand things all return to the One, but where does the One return to?"

Chao-chou answered, "When I was in Ching-chou, I had a robe made which weighed seven *chin*." This *mondo*[5] demonstrates eloquently the difference between the outward way and the inward way. If this sort of question is asked of the philosopher he will go on writing one book after another. But

---

[3] An old Indian tradition states that if a man utters an untruth all his facial hair such as beard and eyebrows will fall off. Suigan has spent his summer talking about things that can never be talked about, hence his allusion to his eyebrows still growing.

[4] Language deals with concepts and therefore what cannot be conceptualised is beyond the reach of language. When language is forced, it gets crooked, which means that it becomes illogical, paradoxical, and unintelligible from the viewpoint of ordinary usage of language or by the conventional way of thinking. For instance, the waters are to flow and the bridge is to stay over them. When this is reversed the world of senses goes topsy-turvy. The flowers bloom on the ground and not on rock. Therefore, when a Zen master declares, "I plant the flowers on rock," this must sound crazy. This crookedness all issues from language being used in the way not meant for it. Zen wants to be direct and to act without a medium of any kind. Hence "Katz!" or "Kwan!" Just an ejaculation with no "sense" attached to it. Nor is it a symbol, it is the thing itself. The person is acting and not appealing to concepts. This is intelligible only from the inward way of seeing reality.

[5] "Question and answer."

the Zen master who thoroughly knows the inward way does not stop to think and instantly gives his answer which is final, with no going-on-and-on.

. . . The *kokoro* is thoroughly purged of all sorts of intellection, it is an abyss of absolute nothingness. And yet there is something moving in the midst of the *kokoro*. From the point of view of the outward way, this will be incomprehensible, because how could "absolute nothingness" be made to "move" at all? That such a thing should actually take place is a mystery. Some may call it "the mystery of being." As if from the unfathomable depths of an abyss, the *kokoro* is stirred. The *kokoro* wants to know itself. . . .

In Western terminology, the *kokoro* may be regarded as corresponding to God or Godhead. God also wants to know himself; he did not or could not remain himself eternally absorbed in meditation. Somehow he came out of his is-ness and uttered a *mantram*, "Let there be light!" and lo, the whole world leaped out into existence. From where? Nowhere! Out of nothing! Out of the Godhead! And the world is God and God is the world, and God exclaims, "It is good!"

According to Aśvaghosha, "In the midst of the *kokoro*, a *nen* is spontaneously awakened." A *nen* (*nien* in Chinese, *cittakshāna* in Sanskrit) is a moment of consciousness coming to itself; it is, one might say, a consciousness rising from the unconscious, though with a certain reservation. The Sanskrit, *ekacittakshāna*, literally means "one-mind-(or thought) moment." It is "a thought-instant" or "a consciousness-unit" which constitutes consciousness like a second or a minute which is a unit-measure for time. "Spontaneously" (*kotsunen* in Japanese) describes the way a *cittakshāna* rises in the *kokoro*. God uttered his fiat just as spontaneously. When the *kokoro* is said to have raised a thought to know itself, there was no conscious intentionality in it; it just happened so—that is, spontaneously.

But what we must remember in this connection is that when we say "no intentionality" we are apt to understand it in the outward way along the intellectual line and may find it difficult to reconcile it with the idea of human consciousness. It takes a long series of discussions to make this point clear, and as it does not directly concern us here, let it pass with this remark that with God as with the *kokoro* freedom and necessity are one.

When Buddhists make reference to God, God must not be taken in the Biblical sense. When I talk about God's giving an order to light, which is recorded in Genesis, I allude to it with the desire that our Christian readers may come to a better understanding of the Buddhist idea of the inward way. What follows, therefore, is to be understood in this spirit.

The Biblical God is recorded as having given his Name to Moses at Mount Sinai as "I am that I am." I do not of course know much about Christian or Jewish theology, but this "name," whatever the original Hebrew meaning of the word may be, seems to me of such significance that we must not put it aside as not essential to the interpretation of God-idea in the development of Christian thought. The Biblical God is always intensely personal and concretely intimate, and how did he ever come to declare himself under such a highly metaphysical designation as he did to Moses? "A highly metaphysical designation," however, is from the outward way of looking at things, while from the inward way "I am that I am" is just as "spontaneous" as the fish swimming about in the mountain stream or the fowl of the air flying across the sky. God's is-ness is my is-ness and also the cat's is-ness sleeping on her mistress' lap. This is reflected in Christ's declaration that "I am before Abraham was." In this is-ness, which is not to be assumed under the category of metaphysical abstractions, I feel like recognising the fundamental oneness of all the religious experiences.

The spontaneity of is-ness, to go back to the first part of this paper, is what is revealed in the "eternal longing" for something which has vanished from the domain of the outward way of intellectualisation. The *kokoro's* wishing to know itself, or God's demanding to see "light" is, humanly expressed, no other than our longing to transcend this world of particulars. While in the world, we find ourselves too engrossed in the business of "knowing" which started when we left the garden of "innocence." We all now want "to know," "to think," "to choose," "to decide," "to be responsible," etc., with everything that follows from exercising what we call "freedom."

"Freedom" is really the term to be found in the inward way only and not in the outward way. But somehow a confusion has come into our mind and we find ourselves madly running after things which can never be attained in the domain of the outward way. The feeling of insecurity then grows out of this mad pursuit, because we are no more able to be in "the spontaneity of is-ness."

We can now see that "The awakening of a new consciousness" is not quite a happy expression. The longing is for something we have lost and not for an unknown quantity of which we have not the remotest possible idea. In

229

fact, there is no unknown quantity in the world into which we have come to pass our time. The longing of any sort implies our previous knowledge of it, though we may be altogether ignorant of its presence in our consciousness. The longing of the kind to which I have been referring is a shadow of the original *kokoro* cast in the track of the inward way. The real object can never be taken hold of until we come back to the abode which we inadvertently quitted. "The awakening of a new consciousness" is therefore the finding ourselves back in our original abode where we lived even before our birth. This experience of home-coming and therefore of the feeling of perfect security is evinced everywhere in religious literature.

The feeling of perfect security means the security of freedom and the securing of freedom is no other than "the awakening of a new consciousness." Ordinarily, we talk of freedom too readily, mostly in the political sense, and also in the moral sense. But as long as we remain in the outward way of seeing things, we can never understand what freedom is. All forms of freedom we generally talk of are far from being freedom in its deepest sense. Most people are sadly mistaken in this respect.

That the awakening of a new consciousness is in fact being restored to one's original abode goes in Christianity with the idea of God's fatherhood. The father's "mansion" can be no other than my own home where I was born and brought up till I became willful and left it on my own account. But really, however willful I may be, I can never leave my original abode behind and wander from it. I am always where I was born and I can never be anywhere else. It is only my imagination or illusion that I was led to believe that I was not in it. To become conscious of this fact is to awaken a new consciousness so called. There is nothing "new" in this, it is only the recovery of what I thought I had lost; in the meantime I have been in possession of it; I have been in it, I have been carrying it all the time; no, I am it and it is I.

· · · · · · · · ·

In Zen the idea of restoration or re-cognition may be gleaned from Yeno's reference to "the original (or primal) face" which he wanted his disciples to see. This "face" is what we have even prior to our birth. In other words, this is the face of "innocence" which we have before our eating of the fruit from the tree of knowledge. "The tree of knowledge" is the outward way of intellection. When it begins to operate, "innocence" which is the inward way hides itself and becomes invisible. Most people take the "innocence" in a moral sense, but I would interpret it symbolically. "Innocence" corresponds to Aśvaghosha's "Original (or primal) Enlightenment" in which we were or are. It has never been lost even when "knowledge" is in full operation, because without it our existence has no significance whatever and "knowledge" itself of any kind would be altogether impossible. In this sense, "the inward way" is at once inward and outward. When it is separated and considered in opposition to "the outward way" it ceases to be itself.

Incidentally, Zen is often criticised as not having any direct contact with the world of particulars, but the critics forget the fact that Zen has never gone out of this world and therefore that the question of contact has no sense here.

Aśvaghosha's great work on the Mahayana is entitled *The Awakening of Faith*, but Zen generally does not use the term. The reason is that faith implies a division and Zen is emphatic in denying it in any sense. But if it (faith) is used in its absolute sense—which is in accordance with the inward way of seeing things—faith may be regarded as another name for *satori* and is no other than the awakening of "a new consciousness" though, as I have repeatedly said, there is really nothing "new" in Zen. Whatever this may be, "the awakening of a new consciousness" is the awakening of faith in Aśvaghosha's sense, that is, in its absolute sense. Then, faith corresponds to becoming aware of "Original Enlightenment" in which we are all the time. Faith is coming back to ourselves, to our own is-ness, and has nothing to do with the so-called objective existence of God. Christians and other theists seem to be unnecessarily busy in trying to prove God as objectively existing before they believe in him. But from the Zen point of view the objectivity of God is an idle question. I would say that those who are so engrossed in the question of this sort have really no God whatever, that is, subjectively as well as objectively. As soon as they have faith, they have God. Faith is God and God is faith. To wait for an objective proof is the proof—the most decisive one—that they have no God yet. Faith comes first and then God. It is not God who gives us faith, but faith that gives us God. Have faith and it will create God. Faith is God coming to his own knowledge.[6]

---

[6] Cannot I say that Christians wanted Christ and so they have him? And also that they still wanted his mother Maria and therefore they have her? Being Christ's mother, she could not stay with us on earth, so she was made to go up to Heaven. Where Heaven is, is immaterial. In our religious experience, what we in our logical way think to be the law of causation is reversed, the effect comes first and then the cause. Instead of the cause proceeding to the effect, the effect precedes the cause.

When a Shin Buddhist was asked, "Can Amida really save us?" he answered, "You are not yet saved!" Christians may have the same way of expressing their faith. They would tell us to have faith first and all other things will follow. Is it not a somewhat futile attempt on the part of the Christian theologian to try to prove the historicity of Christ and then to

When the Zen man has a *satori*, the whole universe comes along with it; or we may reverse this and say that with *satori* the whole universe sinks into nothingness. In one sense, *satori* is leaping out of an abyss of absolute nothingness, and in another sense it is going down into the abyss itself. *Satori* is, therefore, at once a total annihilation and a new creation.

A monk asked a Zen master, "Does 'this' go away with the universe when the latter is totally consumed by fire at the end of the kalpa?" The master answered, "Yes." When the same question was proposed to another master, he said, "No." From the inward way, "Yes" and "No" are one; destruction and construction are one.

The awakening of a new consciousness is the awakening of faith, and the awakening of faith is the creating of a new universe with infinite possibilities.[7] It is a new universe, yes, but in reality an old, old universe, where beings, sentient and non-sentient, have been dreaming their dreams, each in his way, ever since "Let there be light" came to work out its destiny. Here the Biblical time has no meaning.

. . . .

Before concluding, . . . there is one important thing which is needed in the study of modern Zen. By this I mean the koan system, which has opened a new way to Zen but which as we know is also doing a great deal of harm to it unless we are careful about its handling. As is the case of language, all human creations tend to produce good and bad indiscriminately. The innovation of the koan system or koan methodology which was needed for the propagation and preservation of a special spiritual discipline called Zen has created a new psychological study which I am sure will interest students of

---

proceed to tell us that for this reason we must believe in him? The same thing can be said of the crucifixion and the resurrection.

One may ask: If it is faith that is needed first, why so many different expressions of it? One faith goes out to Christ, another to Krishna, and still another to Amida, and so on. Why these variations? And why the fighting among them as we actually see in history?

I do not know if my interpretation of the phenomena is sufficient, but a tentative one is that faith, as soon as it goes out to express itself, is liable to be conditioned by all accidental things it finds around it, such as history, individual temperaments, geographical formations, biological peculiarities, etc. As regards the fighting among them, this will grow less and less as we get better acquainted with all these conditioning accidents. And this is one of our aims in the study of religion in all its differentiations.

[7] The statement that faith creates God may be misconstrued. What I mean is that faith discovers God and simultaneously God discovers the man. The discovery is mutual and takes place concomitantly. To use Buddhist terms, when Amida is enlightened all beings are enlightened, and when we are enlightened we realise that Amida attained his enlightenment whereby our rebirth into the Pure Land is assured. The objective interpretation betrays that the critic has not deeply delved into the matter.

the psychology of religion as well as those of psychology in general. I have touched on the subject in my books, but there are still many points I wish to clarify. The study naturally requires the cooperation of specialists not only of the West but of the East. This has so far never been attempted by anybody anywhere in the methodical way. Here is a field of religious study of the greatest import. I am not speaking just from the point of view of scientific interest, but mainly from the point of view of a world culture which is taking shape more or less tangibly in spite of the fact that we are at present facing a great confusion of thought political and otherwise. The world is becoming one as it should and the distinction of East and West is disappearing though slowly. Prejudices of all sorts are to give way to an age of illumination.

佛與先儒
三聖一醸
醸者春也
言曰如春

道人画

SENGAI

VI

UNIVERSAL
ZEN

The Three Sages, Buddha, Confucius, and Lao-tzu tasting peach wine. The wine has a different taste for each of them, but it is one and the same wine—by which Sengai implies that the doctrines of Buddhism, Confucianism, and Taoism all come from the same source and reach for the same truth.

VI UNIVERSAL ZEN

Zen teaching represents a time-tested body of experience and practice specifically designed to bring about a state of enlightened consciousness. The average Westerner who sets out to attain spiritual awakening by way of *zazen* and *sanzen*, *jodo* and *kufu*, the *koan* and the *mondo*, will unquestionably undergo a considerable degree of psychological reorientation. This fact, however, does not imply that the special Zen "awareness" is confined to one geographic sector of Asia. In all world cultures, poets, mystics, artists, and philosophers have shared in those particular intimations about the nature of reality to which the word Zen—when used as an adjective—is applicable. One of the first to place emphasis on the essential universality of Zen perceptions was R. H. Blyth. Encouraged by his pioneer efforts, I have undertaken to select, from both Western and Eastern writings, examples of Zen-like ways of looking, seeing, and feeling. Well aware of the possible dangers of lifting lines out of their context, I have tried in borrowing any part to take no undue liberties with the intention of the whole. The six categories in which these illustrations are grouped—*Who Am I?*, *Non-Attachment*, "*Is-ness*," "*Now-ness*," "*One-ness*," and *The Zen Eye*—are of my own choosing. As there is a definite plan to the order of appearance of the individual selections, it is hoped they will be read in sequence.   [N. W. R.]

> These are the thoughts of all men in all ages
> and lands, they are not original with me,
>   If they are not yours as much as mine they are
> nothing or next to nothing.
>   If they do not enclose everything they are next
> to nothing.
>   If they are not the riddle and the untying of the
> riddle they are nothing.
>   If they are not just as close as they are distant
> they are nothing.
>
>   —WALT WHITMAN,
>   *Leaves of Grass*

CHAPTER 1

Who Am I?

"I'm sure I'm not Ada, for her hair goes in such long ringlets, and mine doesn't go in ringlets at all; and I'm sure I can't be Mabel, for I know all sorts of things, and she, oh!, she knows such a very little! Besides, *she's she* and *I'm* I and—oh dear, how puzzling it all is! . . . ."

—LEWIS CARROLL,
Alice in Wonderland

A man has many skins in himself, covering the depths of his heart. Man knows so many things; he does not know himself. Why, thirty or forty skins or hides, just like an ox's or a bear's, so thick and hard, cover the soul. Go into your own ground and learn to know yourself there.

—MEISTER ECKHART

As I was going up the stair
I met a man who wasn't there,
He wasn't there again today.
I wish to God he'd go away.

—HUGHES MEARNS,
"Antigonish"

At the sound of the bell in the silent night, I wake from my dream in this dream-world of ours. Gazing at the reflection of the moon in a clear pool, I see, beyond my form, my real form.

—KOJISEI
(translated by R. H. Blyth)

. . . psychological, creative revolution in which the "me" is not, comes only when the thinker and the thought are one, when there is no duality such as the thinker controlling thought; and I suggest it is this experience alone that releases the creative energy which in turn brings about a fundamental revolution, the breaking up of the psychological "me."

—KRISHNAMURTI,
The First and Last Freedom

Zuigan called out to himself every day: "Master."
Then he answered himself: "Yes, sir."
And after that he added: "Become sober."
Again he answered: "Yes, sir."
"And after that," he continued,"do not be deceived by others."
"Yes, sir; yes, sir," he answered.

Mumon's comment: Old Zuigan sells out and buys himself. He is opening a puppet show. He uses one mask to call "Master" and another that answers the master. Another mask says, "Sober up" and another, "Do not be cheated by others." If anyone clings to any of his masks, he is mistaken, yet if he imitates Zuigan, he will make himself fox-like.

Some Zen students do not realize the true man in a mask.
Because they recognize ego-soul.
Ego-soul is the seed of birth and death,
And foolish people call it the true man.

—*The Gateless Gate*
(translated by Nyogen Senzaki and Paul Reps)

Between the idea
And the reality
Between the motion
And the act
Falls the Shadow.

. . . .

Between the conception
And the creation
Between the emotion
And the response
Falls the Shadow.

. . . .

Between the desire
And the spasm
Between the potency
And the existence

239

Between the essence
And the descent
Falls the Shadow.

. . . .

—T. S. ELIOT,
"The Hollow Men"

. . . For the alchemist it was clear that the "centre," or what we would call the self, does not lie in the ego but is outside it, "in us" yet not "in our mind," being located rather in that which we unconsciously are, the "quid" which we still have to recognize. Today we would call it the unconscious and we distinguish between a personal unconscious which enables us to recognize the shadow and an impersonal unconscious which enables us to recognize the archetypal symbol of the self.

—C. G. JUNG,
Aion

Every man is born as many men and dies as a single one.

—MARTIN HEIDEGGER

Alone I can never be.
Many before me going
And away from me flowing,
Were weaving,
Weaving
At the I that is me.

—RAINER MARIA RILKE
Gesammelte Werke
(translated by E. G. Butler)

I silently laugh at my own cenotaph,
And out of the caverns of rain,
Like a child from the womb, like a ghost from the tomb,
I arise and unbuild it again.

—SHELLEY,
"The Cloud"

A traveler—
Let my name be thus known—
This autumnal shower.

—BASHO

240

A star looks down at me
And says: "Here I and you
Stand, each in our degree:
What do you mean to do—
Mean to do?"

I say: "For all I know,
Wait, and let Time go by
Till my change come."—"Just so,"
The star says: "So mean I—
So mean I."

> —THOMAS HARDY,
> "Waiting Both"

Once, when our Master had just dismissed the first of the daily assemblies at K'ai Yuan Monastery near Hung Chou, I (P'ei Hsiu) happened to enter its precincts. Presently I noticed a wall-painting and, by questioning the monk in charge of the monastery's administration, learnt that it portrayed a certain famous monk.

"Indeed?" I said. "Yes, I can see his likeness before me, but where is the man himself?" My question was received in silence.

So I remarked: "But surely there ARE Zen monks here in this temple, aren't there?"

"Yes," replied the monastery administrator, "THERE IS ONE."

After that, I requested an audience with the Master and repeated to him my recent conversation.

"P'ei Hsiu!" cried the Master.

"Sir!" I answered respectfully.

"Where are YOU?"

Realizing that no reply was possible to such a question, I hastened to ask our Master to re-enter the hall and continue his sermon.

> —*The Zen Teaching of Huang Po on the
> Transmission of Mind.*
> (translated by John Blofeld)

Who need be afraid of the merge?

> —WALT WHITMAN,
> *Leaves of Grass*

Any man's death diminishes me, because I am involved in mankind;
And therefore never send to know for whom the bell tolls; It tolls for thee.

> —JOHN DONNE
> *Devotions. XVII*

241

God expects but one thing of you, and that is that you should come out of yourself in so far as you are a created being, and let God be God in you.

—MEISTER ECKHART

All meditation is based in the conviction that we have only to acknowledge and
assent to the Reality from which we have never in essence been separated to awake
from the long illusion of the ego. In doing so we shall cease to think about Truth
and realize Truth Itself. The transition from thinking to knowing, the fulfillment of
Mindfulness in "No-Mind" will have been effected.

—HUGH L'ANSON FAUSSET,
The Flame and the Light

As the Godhead is nameless, and all naming is alien to Him, so also the soul is
nameless; for it is here the same as God.

—MEISTER ECKHART

The poetical nature has no self—it is everything and nothing; it has no character.
. . . A poet has no identity—he is continually . . . filling some other body.

—JOHN KEATS
(from a letter)

I celebrate myself
And what I assume you shall assume,
For every atom belonging to me as good belongs to you.

—WALT WHITMAN,
Leaves of Grass

All reality is an activity which I share without being able to appropriate for myself. Where there is no sharing there is no reality.

—MARTIN BUBER

Dare we open our doors to the sources of our being? What are flesh and bones for?

—PAUL REPS,
Introduction to *Zen Flesh, Zen Bones*

If you work on your mind with your mind
How can you avoid an immense confusion?

—SENG-TS'AN

If a man wishes to be sure of the road he treads on, he must close his eyes and walk in the dark.

—ST. JOHN OF THE CROSS,
The Dark Night of the Soul

Birth is not one act; it is a process. The aim of life is to be fully born, though its tragedy is that most of us die before we are thus born. To live is to be born every minute. Death occurs when birth stops. Physiologically our cellular system is in a process of continual birth; psychologically, however, most of us cease to be born at a certain point.

—ERICH FROMM,
Zen Buddhism and Psychoanalysis

As many of the sacred books of the East emphasize, for sentient beings a human birth is difficult to win: as the Tibetan Teachers declare, "None but the foolish fritter away the mighty opportunity offered by having attained human birth."

—W. Y. EVANS-WENTZ,
Foreword to *The Diamond Sutra*
(translated by A. F. Price)

He [Heidegger] begins his lectures to students at Freiburg by referring to the university situation and the problems of contemporary life. Philosophy itself, he says, begins with the process by which we work out of ourselves into the immediate environment. *Was ist Philosophie? Philosophie ist philosophieren. Und was ist philosophieren? Philosophieren ist transcendieren.* And what is it to transcend? To transcend is to realize one's nature as a man in its bound-togetherness with circumstance yet its independence. It is to go directly to the object in the flash of awareness which Plato described by the metaphor of the kindling of a spark. It is to find the meaning of being by catching sight of being in yourself, as you face your work, your obligations, your social relationships, your common daily life. . . .

When we become aware not of the goodness or badness of a single act, nor of conscience as a prudential force keeping us out of trouble, but of the seriousness of life as a whole, in its aspect as the container of possibilities which must be realized in time and before death, we achieve *Existenz.* Only the self which exists in time and binds past and future together in the unity of present possibility can do this.

—JULIUS SEELYE BIXLER,
"The Contribution of Existenz Philosophie,"
Harvard Theological Review

243

"All that we are is the result of what we have thought: it is founded on our thoughts, it is made up of our thoughts. If a man speaks or acts with an evil thought, pain follows him, as the wheel follows the foot of the ox that draws the carriage.

"All that we are is the result of what we have thought; it is founded on our thoughts, it is made up of our thoughts. If a man speaks or acts with a pure thought, happiness follows him, like a shadow that never leaves him."

—The *Dhammapada* (words of the Buddha)

The Buddha said: "You should ponder on the fact that, though each of the four elements of which the body is made up has a name, they none of them (constitute any part of) the real self. In fact, the self is non-existent, like a mirage."

—*The Sutra of Forty-Two Sections*

. . . you should study the life processes of the salamander. It seems there is quite a simple and unaffected action of the whole organism with these little creatures, but then parts of them—a fore-limb, let us say—take on at times a quite independent, reflex action. These localized and independent departures in function assume betimes, I am told, a quite hoity-toity air. They even assume quite an "antagonistic" manner of behaviour toward the primary total action of the organism. I believe though that, in the salamander and kindred forms of life, these arbitrary and partial activities remain quite "discrete" as the biologists say. They do not assume any total or integrated or centred principle of individuality intact, as I understand it. There are these little side currents—these little eddyings of activity here and there— but "Who cares?" says salamander. As long as they do not get organized, do not form a union, as it were, they cannot really threaten the vested capital, so to speak, of the central salamander principality.

Man, too, began using these little physiological asides, these partial reactions, these reactions which are unintegrated with the "total action-pattern." That was long, long ago though, so long ago that you and I do not remember any more. But as I figure it out, these, at first, quite incidental and insignificant rebel activities began more and more to systematize themselves, to organize, to form trade unions, so to speak. They became specially strongly organized in the region of the cerebrum, and through it these "partitive" stimuli and responses found a ready inter-connection or inter-change socially. Then gradually the centre of gravity was shifted, or rather the organism began to act *as though* the centre of gravity were shifted. The principle of identity or of individuality was artificially displaced into this localized, cerebral zone of inter-change among us. These partial activities systematized themselves into something called "I," and this "I" constituted the identity that replaced the identity of the organism as a whole. This truancy, this misappropriation of feeling, this displacement of the centre of gravity, or of personality, so to speak, has registered itself in the tissues of the human organism. It is faintly, very delicately perceptible now of course after all these—heaven knows how many—hundreds of thousands of years of our inadvertent self-ostracism, but it is perceptible. This

who
is

partial, this cerebral innovation, this systematization of discrete functions is perceptible as being separate or discrete from the main trunk of man's feeling-life. It is probably some organic protest within the species against this arrogant shift of man's physiological centre of personality or authority that is the true account of the superficial symptoms we see today in man's social unrest, depression and outer disintegration generally.

> *—A Search for Man's Sanity:*
> *Selected Letters of Trigant Burrows*

Modern man, as a certain Dutch philosopher pointed out, is only a refined barbarian. By "barbarian" we mean all men in whom the avidities of the "I-process," and the violence arising from them, are in the fullness of their expression. . . . All our social, religious and moral structures are based on the reality of the "I-process" whose expression in all domains they encourage. Such is the fundamental drama of so-called "Christian" civilization. Were the absolute reality of the "I-process" to be assumed as the point of departure it is inevitable that it affirm itself with the violence and cruelty of which we are suffering the consequences in the tragic events of the present time. In radical opposition to the above, the basic idea of Buddhism is the impermanence of the "I-process" and of all things.

> —ROBERT LINSSEN,
> *Living Zen*

Bassui wrote the following letter to one of his disciples who was about to die:
"The essence of your mind is not born, so it will never die. It is not an existence, which is perishable. It is not an emptiness, which is a mere void. It has neither color nor form. It enjoys no pleasures and suffers no pains.

"I know you are very ill. Like a good Zen student, you are facing that sickness squarely. You may not know exactly who is suffering, but question yourself: What is the essence of this mind? Think only of this. You will need no more. Covet nothing. Your end which is endless is as a snowflake dissolving in the pure air."

> —PAUL REPS,
> *Zen Flesh, Zen Bones*

At the centre of myself, in this centre which is still unconscious today, resides the primordial man, united with the Principle of the Universe and through it with the whole of the Universe, totally sufficient unto himself, One from the beginning, neither alone or not-alone, neither affirmed nor denied, up-stream of all duality. It is the primordial Being, underlying all the egotistical "states" which cover it in my actual consciousness.

Because I am ignorant today concerning what are in reality my egotistical states these states constitute a sort of screen which separates me from my centre, from my

246

Real Self. I am unconscious of my essential identity with the All and I only consider myself as distinct from the rest of the Universe. . . . The Ego is illusory, since I am not in reality distinct; and all the egotistical states are equally illusory.

> —HUBERT BENOIT,
> *The Supreme Doctrine*

I have said that man is asked a question by the very fact of his existence, and that this is a question raised by the contradiction within himself—that of being in nature and at the same time of transcending nature by the fact that he is life aware of itself. Any man who listens to this question posed to him, and who makes it a matter of "ultimate concern" to answer this question, and to answer it as a whole man and not only by thoughts, is a "religious" man; and all systems that try to give, teach and transmit such answers are "religions." On the other hand any man— and any culture—that tries to be deaf to the existential question is irreligious. . . . No matter how often he *thinks* of God, or goes to church, or how much he believes in religious ideas, if he, the whole man, is deaf to the question of existence, if he does not have an answer to it, he is marking time, and he lives and dies like one of the million things he produces. He *thinks* of God, instead of experiencing *being* God.

> —ERICH FROMM,
> *Zen Buddhism and Psychoanalysis*

> He whose conquest nobody can conquer again,
> Into whose conquest nobody in this world can enter—
> By what track can you trace him,
> The awakened, of infinite range, the trackless?
> —The *Dhammapada* (words of the Buddha)

What is the price of Experience? Do men buy it for a song? Or wisdom for a dance in the Street? No, it is bought with the price of all that a man hath. . . .

> —WILLIAM BLAKE
> quoted by Mark Schorer in
> *William Blake, the Politics of Vision*

> Study what thou art
> Whereof thou art a part,
> What thou knowest of this art,
> This is really what thou art.
> All that is without thee
> Also is within,
> Thus wrote Trimosin.

> —SOLOMON TRIMOSIN (1598),
> quoted by C. G. Jung in *Psychology and Religion:*
> *East and West*

247

Look within, thou art the Buddha.
—Words of the Buddha

The Kingdom of Heaven is within you.
—Words of Jesus Christ

CHAPTER 2

Non-Attachment

Zen like a distant star which is seen most clearly (if at all) when we do not look straight at it, is best glimpsed when we are talking and thinking about something else—and are moving right along.

—HAROLD E. MCCARTHY,
"Poetry, Metaphysics and Zen,"
Philosophy East and West

Sitting quietly, doing nothing,
Spring comes, and the grass grows by itself.

—*Zenrin Kushu*

It may seem both strange and unreasonable that strong and intelligent men should simply sit still for hours on end. The Western mentality feels that such things are not only unnatural but a great waste of valuable time, however useful as a discipline for inculcating patience and fortitude. Although the West has its own contemplative tradition in the Catholic Church, the life of "sitting and looking" has lost its appeal, for no religion is valued which does not "improve the world. . . ." Yet it should be obvious that action without wisdom, without clear awareness of the world as it really is, can never improve anything. Furthermore, as muddy water is best cleared by leaving it alone, it could be argued that those who sit quietly and do nothing are making one of the best contributions to a world in turmoil. . . . One does not know the world simply in thinking about it and doing about it. One must first experience it more directly, and prolong the experience without jumping to conclusions.

—ALAN WATTS,
The Way of Zen

The wild geese fly back to country
After country without a calendar.

—SHUMPA
(translated by Miyamori)

The extinction of desire (Buddhism)—or detachment—or *amor fati*—or desire for the absolute good—these all amount to the same: to empty desire ... of all content, to desire in the void, to desire without any wishes.

To detach our desire from all good things and to wait. Experience proves that this waiting is satisfied. It is then we touch the absolute good.

—SIMONE WEIL,
Gravity and Grace

A man must become truly poor and as free from his own creaturely will as he was when he was born. And I tell you, by the eternal truth, that so long as you *desire* to fulfill the will of God and have any hankering after eternity and God, for just so long you are not truly poor. He alone has true spiritual poverty who wills nothing, knows nothing, desires nothing.

—MEISTER ECKHART

Blessed are the poor in spirit: for theirs is the kingdom of Heaven.
Blessed are the meek: for they shall inherit the earth.

—Matthew V:3, 5

My storehouse having been burnt down,
Nothing obstructs the view of the bright moon.

—MASAHIDE
(translated by Miyamori)

The thief
Left it behind—
The moon at the window.

—RYOKAN
(translated by R. H. Blyth)

Not even a hat—
and cold rain falling on me?
Tut-tut! think of that!

—BASHO
(translated by Harold Henderson)

In the selection of the following examples of Japanese and Chinese art, it has been the author's wish to illustrate certain choices of subject matter and manners of presentation which seem suggestive of Zen as we understand it today. In a few instances the artist is not a noted Zennist as such, nor is the painting itself "pure Zen" in treatment or technique. Each selection does, however, exemplify some particular grace or sensibility of the Eastern eye and brush, or it carries some hint of those subtle and ancient ways of thought which led Eastern painters to record, not alone the images of the passing world, but also their sense of that invisible "presence" which eternally and everywhere shows itself through the changing forms of nature.

Solitary Angler, attributed to Ma Yuan (Bayen), of the late twelfth century, a famous *sumiye* painting of "meaningful solitude," in which empty space is presented as a reality quite as significant as the man and the boat—"the permanence of space and the transience of substance."

Two sections of a painted scroll hitherto unreproduced, attributed to the twelfth-century Chinese Zen monk Fan-lung, that favorite Far Eastern theme of meditating figures in a landscape with waterfalls, rocks, trees. *Freer Gallery of Art, Washington, D.C.*

Two landscape paintings formerly attributed to the Chinese Sung emperor, Hui-tsung; one at the left a fine example of the "one corner style" showing a meditating figure gazing into space; at the right, a man sharing a storm as a part of nature itself.

Two landscapes by Sesshu, the great fifteenth-century Japanese master of wash drawing and an eminent Zen monk who traveled to China to study art but returned home to develop his own highly personal skills with line and his own rugged yet delicate style.

One of the greatest of Zen art treasures and n "Important Cultural Property" of Japan, his painting of *H'ui K'o (Eka) Offering His evered Arm to Bodhidharma as a Pledge* s a masterpiece by the noted artist Sesshu 420–1506). Painted with *sumi* ink on paper, depicts an episode famed in Zen legend: he moment when a fervent disciple, anxious o prove his ardor to the wall-gazing Master, evered his left arm with his own sword as roof of his sincerity.

The Second Patriarch in a Composed State of Mind and *Patriarch Meditating with a Tiger*, Shih K'o (Sekkaku), tenth century. Both pictures are considered masterpieces of brushwork in the highly controlled, seemingly casual Zen style.

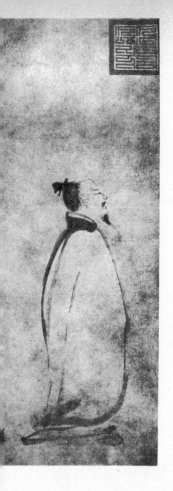

Right: *The Poet Li Po on a Stroll*, by Liang K'ai. Here a brilliant painter's "thrifty brush" manages to convey in a few strokes not only a sense of ineffable repose but also a total concentration of physical and mental forces. Early thirteenth century.

Left: *Hotei and Two Fighting Cocks*, painted by Miyamoto Musashi (Niten), a great swordsman and *sumiye* painter of feudal Japan. Here the popular "god of good fortune" (a personification of the inexhaustible resources of Nature), amusedly studies the birds' methods of attack while pondering—so it has been suggested—the Zen teaching that there is "no killing, no killer, no killed."

Tiger and *Shrike on a Bare Pine Bough*, both by Mu Ch'i (Mokkei). These thirteenth-century paintings are striking examples of the Eastern artist's ability to "harness his life for a moment to an object," in a sense to become his subject matter. "All things emerge from an abyss of mystery, and through every one of them we can have a peep into that abyss."

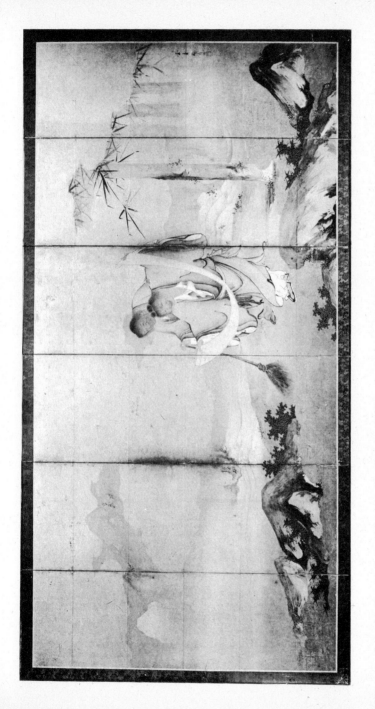

Kanzan and Jittoku, the two happy, irrepressible lunatics of Zen legend, in a famous painting by Kaihoku Yusho, another swords-man-artist of the sixteenth century. Of these two Zen lunatics Kanzan was a poet-recluse, Jittoku an orphan of unknown family. Their freedom from possessions and attachments, their carefree iconoclastic behavior have made them favorite subjects for the Zen brush.

Left: *Man Contemplating a Waterfall*, by Morikage (*circa* 1700), a familiar and favorite theme of Eastern art, expressing "not escape from life but rather an escape to life."

Right: *Landscape*, by Soami (1450–1530), a painter who loved to depict the elusive charms of rain and mist. Here the only hints of man's intrusion on nature are a house roof, a distant temple spire, and a small boat near shore.

Left: *Jittoku Laughing at the Moon* (artist unknown), one of the carefree "idiots" of Zen lore who find complete happiness in such simple pleasures as sweeping a garden path or viewing a moonrise. *Boston Museum of Fine Arts, Boston, Massachusetts*

An Early Zen Patriarch Tearing up a Scroll of Scriptures, by Liang K'ai. A great painter's treatment of an episode which serves to remind us of Zen's pragmatic attitude: direct experience and not canonical dogma is the way to self-realization.

Two Zen masters, portraits from the so-called Daruma Triptych painted by Soga Jasoku in the fifteenth century. The Master Rinzai has plainly just cried "Kwatz!" that exclamation of scorn which lets the aspirant monk before him know that he is still far from his goal. The Master Tokusan sits with the stick which he, as a master, uses when needed during training periods. Of this latter portrait the noted French art critic de Grousset has said, "One of the profoundest portraits of a thinker produced by the art of all time, and worthy of the Descartes by Franz Hals."

Man Crossing a Bridge While a Storm Threatens. With a great economy of brush stroke, Kano Tanyu (1602–1674) shows a little man stepping briskly forth across a roaring torrent, shielded only by a paper umbrella from the "Dragon" overhead. There is no fear, no hesitation, for "Is not all one with the Buddha Mind?" *Author's Collection*

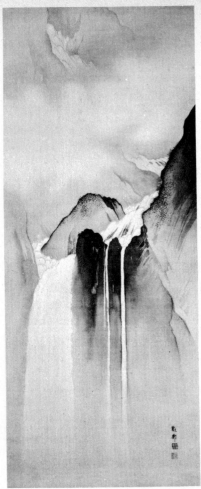

Left: *Bamboo* has always been a favorite subject with Eastern artists. The style of this particular eighteenth-century painting by Goshun is rather unconventional. Showing only a section of stem, a vigorous sprout, and a dwarf plant, the composition has been attributed to Goshun's taste for the stripped notations of *haiku* poetry.

Right: *Waterfall*, by Hashimoto Gaho. Although not strictly "Zen" in style or manner, it is a good nineteenth-century example of an enduring theme of Eastern art: flowing water expressing that which is "ever changing yet ever remaining."

Top: *Plants in Snow* (artist unknown). Nature is never "inanimate" to the Eastern painter. Useful lessons in nonresistance may be learned from observing how plants first yield to, and then gently slip off, their heavy burdens.

Bottom: *Deer Scroll*, by Nonomura Sotatsu (d. 1643). A section of a celebrated painting which well illustrates the rhythmic power of the brush in the hands of a master. *Seattle Art Museum, Seattle, Washington*

A Cow Herd, by Mori Sosen (1747–1821). This relatively modern painting is strongly reminiscent of the so-called Ox Herding Pictures, a series of episodes painted in many styles by Zen artists of the past. The Ox Herding Pictures depict the adventures of a boy, or a man, who is trying to find a lost animal (his lost "self"), and having found it, to bring it under control and return home peacefully riding it.

Some children were playing beside a river. They made castles of sand, and each child defended his castle and said, "This one is mine." They kept their castles separate and would not allow any mistakes about which was whose. When the castles were all finished, one child kicked over someone else's castle and completely destroyed it. The owner of the castle flew into a rage, pulled the other child's hair, struck him with his fist and bawled out, "He has spoilt my castle! Come along all of you and help me to punish him as he deserves." The others all came to his help. They beat the child with a stick and then stamped on him as he lay on the ground. . . . Then they went on playing in their sand-castles, each saying, "This is mine; no one else may have it. Keep away! Don't touch my castle!" But evening came; it was getting dark and they all thought they ought to be going home. No one now cared what became of his castle. One child stamped on his, another pushed his over with both his hands. Then they turned away and went back, each to his home.

> —*Yogacara Bhumi Sutra*,
> in *Buddhist Texts Through the Ages*

> Things are in the saddle,
> And ride mankind.

> —EMERSON
> "Ode"

> The Perfect Way is only difficult for those who pick and choose;
> Do not like, do not dislike; all will then be clear.
> Make a hairsbreadth difference, and Heaven and Earth are set
> apart;
> If you want the truth to stand clear before you, never be for
> or against.
> The struggle between "for" and "against" is the mind's worst
> disease.

> —Attributed to Seng-ts'an, Arthur Waley translation in
> *Buddhist Texts Through the Ages*

What is common to Jewish-Christian and Zen Buddhist thinking is the awareness that I must give up my "will" (in the sense of my desire to force, direct, strangle the world outside of me and within me) in order to be completely open, responsive, awake, alive. In Zen terminology this is often called "to make oneself empty"— which does not mean something negative, but means the openness to receive. In Christian terminology this is often called "to slay oneself and to accept the will of God." There seems to be little difference between the Christian experience and the Buddhist experience which lies behind the two different formulations. However, as far as the popular interpretation and experience is concerned, this formulation means that instead of making decisions himself, man leaves the decisions to an omniscient, omnipotent father, who watches over him and knows what is good for him. It is clear that in this experience man does not become open and responsive, but obedient and submissive. To follow God's will in the sense of true surrender of egoism is best done if there is no concept of God. Paradoxically, I truly follow God's will if I forget about God. Zen's concept of emptiness implies the true meaning of giving up one's will, yet without the danger of regressing to the idolatrous concept of a helping father.

—ERICH FROMM,
Zen Buddhism and Psychoanalysis

He that findeth his life shall lose it, and he that loseth his life for my sake shall find it.

—Matthew X:39

Once upon a time there was a man standing on a high hill. Three travellers, passing in the distance, noticed him and began to argue about him. One said: "He has probably lost his favourite animal." Another said: "No, he is probably looking for his friend." The third said: "He is up there only in order to enjoy the fresh air." The three travellers could not agree and continued to argue right up to the moment when they arrived at the top of the hill. One of them asked: "O friend, standing on this hill, have you not lost your favourite animal?" "No, Sir, I have not lost him." The other asked: "Have you not lost your friend?" "No, Sir, I have not lost my friend either." The third traveller asked: "Are you not here in order to enjoy the fresh air?" "No, Sir." "What then are you doing here, since you answer 'No' to all our questions?" The man on the hill replied: "I am just standing."

Reading this, the natural man will think in general that "to be just standing" has no meaning. "This man on the hill is an idiot," he will say to himself, "since he is *doing* nothing" (that is to say, since he is not seeking there any egotistical affirmation. One remembers the ironical phrase of Rimbaud: "*L'action, ce cher point du monde!*")

—Zen parable, quoted by Hubert Benoit in
The Supreme Doctrine

Do not permit the events of your daily lives to bind you, but never withdraw yourselves from them. Only by acting thus can you earn the title of "A Liberated One."

—*Wan Ling Record of the Zen Master Huang Po*
(translated by John Blofeld)

Suppose a boat is crossing a river and another boat, an empty one, is about to collide with it. Even an irritable man would not lose his temper. But suppose there was someone in the second boat. Then the occupant of the first would shout to him to keep clear. And if he did not hear the first time, nor even when called to three

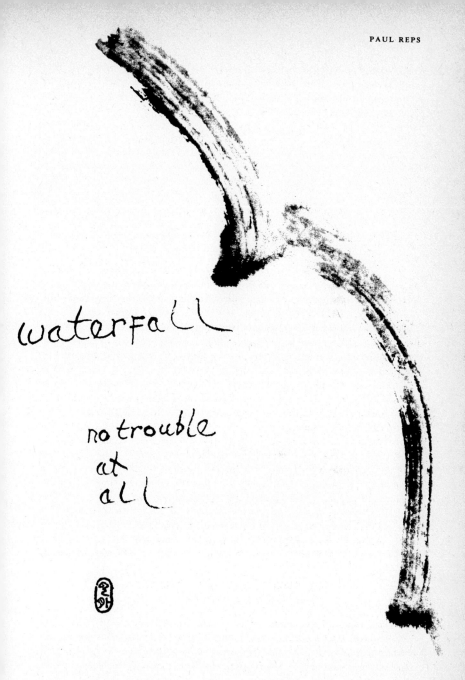

waterfall

no trouble
at
all

times, bad language would inevitably follow. In the first case there was no anger, in the second there was—because in the first case the boat was empty, in the second it was occupied. And so it is with man. If he could only pass empty through life, who would be able to injure him?

—CHUANG TZU

As long as I am this or that, or have this or that, I am not all things and I have not all things. Become pure till you neither are nor have either this or that; then you are omnipresent and, being neither this nor that, are all things.

—MEISTER ECKHART

Dispassion is called the Way. It is said "Through dispassion is one freed."
—*Visuddhimagga*, quoted in *Buddhist Texts*
Through the Ages

Sometimes contemplatives think that the whole end and essence of their life is to be found in recollection and interior peace and the sense of the presence of God. They become attached to these things. But recollection is just as much a creature as an automobile. The sense of interior peace is no less created than a bottle of wine. The experimental "awareness" of the presence of God is just as truly a created thing as a glass of beer. The only difference is that recollection and interior peace and the sense of the presence of God are spiritual pleasures and the others are material. Attachment to spiritual things is therefore just as much an attachment as inordinate love of anything else. The imperfection may be more hidden and more subtle: but from a certain point of view that only makes it all the more harmful because it is not so easy to recognize.

—THOMAS MERTON,
Seeds of Contemplation

Perfect detachment is without regard, without either lowliness or loftiness to creatures; it has no mind to be below nor yet to be above; it is minded to be master of itself, loving none and hating none, having neither likeness nor unlikeness, neither this nor that, to any creature; the only thing it desires to be is to be one and the same. For to be either this or that is to want something. He who is this or that is somebody; but detachment wants altogether nothing. It leaves all things unmolested.

—MEISTER ECKHART,
About Disinterest

Immersed in ignorance and obscured by delusion, the Knower (Mind) was afeared and confused. Then came the idea "I" and "Other" and hatred. As these gained force a continuous chain of Action (Karma) was produced. The Root Ignorance is the abysmal ground of the knower's unconscious Ignorance. The other Ignorance is that which regards self and others to be different and separate. The thought which regards beings as "two" begets a hesitating doubting state. A subtle feeling of Attachment arises, which if allowed to gain force, gradually resolves itself into strong attachment and a craving for food, clothing, dwellings, wealth and friends. . . . There is no end to the Action flowing from ideas of dualism.

—From a Tibetan Scripture
(translated by Marco Pallis)

DR. SUZUKI:

. . . What distinguishes Zen from all the rest of religious teaching, or from the rest of Buddhist teachings, perhaps, is this, psychologically speaking, *to become conscious of the unconscious. More, to be attached and not attached. Attachment, yet no attachment.*[1] Metaphysically speaking, perhaps, finite is infinite, infinite is finite. When you understand this then Zen is understood.

MR. SMITH:

Doctor Suzuki, you say that morally Zen is characterized by an attachment and detachment. What does this mean?

DR. SUZUKI:

Well, that's a very important part of Zen. In practical life as long as we live in a reality world we get attached to something good or something bad, something beautiful or something not so very beautiful. But in the Bible we read—it was perhaps one of Paul's letters—we live in the world as not being in the world. That expresses the idea of attachment, and yet not being attached.

So as long as we are relative, in a relative world, we get attached to the dualistic view of reality. But underneath, or in, or with, a relative world, we have another world which is not relative, which transcends it, but at the same time is in it, that is, *with* the relative world, and that world I may call a transcendental realm. In that world there is no attachment; there is no good, no evil, no guilt, or no ugliness.

The lotus flower grows out of dirty water but when it comes out of water how beautiful the flower is.

—From a transcript of an interview between Dr. Suzuki and Professor Huston Smith on the N.B.C. Wisdom Series, April 19, 1959.

Hast thou named all the birds without a gun?
Loved the wood-rose, and left it on its stalk?

—EMERSON,
"Forebearance"

---

[1] Italics mine. [N.W.R.]

Thinking about sense-objects
Will attach you to sense-objects;
Grow attached, and you become addicted;
Thwart your addiction, it turns to anger;
Be angry, and you confuse your mind;
Confuse your mind, you forget the lesson of experience;
Forget experience, you lose discrimination;
Lose discrimination, and you miss life's only purpose.

> —*Bhagavad-Gita*
> (translated by Swami Prabhavananda and
>   Christopher Isherwood)

Our claim to own our bodies and our world
Is our catastrophe. . . .

> —W. H. AUDEN,
> "Canzone"

CHAPTER 3

"Is-ness"

Like the empty sky it has no boundaries,
Yet it is right in this place, ever profound and clear.
When you seek to know it, you cannot see it.
You cannot take hold of it,
But you cannot lose it.
In not being able to get it, you get it.
When you are silent, it speaks;
When you speak, it is silent.
The great gate is wide open to bestow alms,
And no crowd is blocking the way.

> —"Cheng-tao Ke"
> (translated by Alan Watts in
> *The Way of Zen*)

It is too clear and so it is hard to see.
A dunce once searched for a fire with a lighted lantern.
Had he known what fire was,
He could have cooked his rice much sooner.

> —*The Gateless Gate*
> (translated by Nyogen Senzaki and Paul Reps)

For by thine eyes thou mayest not conceive of anything, unless it be by the length and the breadth, the smallness and the greatness, the roundness and the squareness, the farness and the nearness, and the color of it. And by thine ears, nought but noise or some manner of sound. By thine nose, nought but either stench or savour. And by thy taste, nought but either sour or sweet, salt or fresh, bitter or

257

pleasant. And by thy feeling, nought but either hot or cold, hard or tender, soft or sharp. And truly neither hath God nor ghostly things none of these qualities nor quantities. And therefore, leave thine outward wits, and work not with them, neither within nor without.

—*The Cloud of Unknowing*

Before a man studies Zen, to him mountains are mountains and waters are waters; after he gets an insight into the truth of Zen through the instruction of a good master, mountains to him are not mountains and waters are not waters; but after this when he really attains to the abode of rest, mountains are once more mountains and waters are waters.

—Old Zen Saying (first expressed by Ch'ing Yuan)

Do not, I beg of you, look for anything behind phenomena. They are themselves their own lesson.

—GOETHE

An assertion is Zen only when it is itself an act and does not refer to anything that is asserted in it.

—D. T. SUZUKI

The wild geese do not intend to cast their reflection
The water has no mind to receive their image.

—*Zenrin Kushu*

The poppy flowers;
How calmly
They fall.

—ETSUJIN
(translated by R. H. Blyth)

Let us open our leaves like a flower, and be passive and receptive.

—JOHN KEATS,
(from a letter)

Monk: "All these mountains and rivers and the great earth—where do they come from?"
Master: "Where does this question of yours come from?"

258

The woods decay, the woods decay and
    fall,
The vapours weep their burthen to the
    ground,
Man comes and tills the field and lies
    beneath
And after many a summer dies the swan.
        —TENNYSON,
        "Tithonus"

The falling leaves
fall and pile up; the rain
beats on the rain.
        —GYODAI
        (translated by Harold Henderson)

On how to sing
the frog school and the skylark school
are arguing.
        —SHIKI
        (translated by Harold Henderson)

The winds that blow—
ask them, which leaf of the tree
will be next to go!
        —SOSEKI
        (translated by Harold Henderson)

No sky at all;
no earth at all—and still
the snowflakes fall. . . .
        —HASHIN
        (translated by Harold Henderson)

A monk asked Fuketsu, "Speaking and silence belong to the absolute and the relative worlds; how can we escape both these errors?" Fuketsu said,
    "I always think of Konan in March;
    Partridges chirp among the scented blossoms."

When Joshu (Chao-chou) was asked what was the Tao (or the truth of Zen) he answered, "Your everyday life, that is the Tao."

    A monk asks, "What is the Buddha?"
    Tosu (the master) answers, "The Buddha."

259

Monk: "What is the Tao?"
Tosu: "The Tao."
Monk: "What is Zen?"
Tosu: "Zen."

The Master answers like a parrot, he is echo itself. In fact there is no other way of illuminating the monk's mind than affirming that what is is—which is the final fact of experience.

—D. T. SUZUKI,
Zen and Japanese Culture

When it is autumn do we get spring weather,
Or gather may of harsh northwindish time?

—EZRA POUND,
"Silet"

By a house collapsed
A pear tree is blooming;
Here a battle was fought.

—SHIKI
(translated by R. H. Blyth)

Aristotle says Characters are either Good or Bad; Now Goodness or Badness has nothing to do with Character; an Apple tree, a Pear tree, a Horse, a Lion are Characters but a Good Apple tree or a Bad is an Apple tree still; a Horse is not more a Lion for being a Bad Horse; that is its character: its Goodness or Badness is another consideration.

—WILLIAM BLAKE,
quoted in *Fearful Symmetry*, a *Study of William Blake*,
by Northrop Frye

Science no more than art—less than art, I imagine—attains "the thing in itself." It establishes the relations between "things." . . . Science, like art, is only a system of self deception, that is to say, of conquest.

—ELIE FAURE,
The Spirit of the Forms

Men know how to read printed books; they do not know how to read the unprinted ones. They can play on a stringed harp, but not on a stringless one. Applying themselves to the superficial instead of the profound, how should they understand music or poetry?

—KOJISEI
(translated by R. H. Blyth)

cucumber
unaccountably
cucumbering

Existenz is, in fact, as much like poetry as it is like phisosophy and a large part of its flavor is lost when it is translated into plodding prose. It makes less, that is to say, of the appeal to objective, verifiable truth than of subjective experience in its individual aspect. So far as it makes use of universal, communicable forms these are aesthetic rather than intellectual, and resemble more nearly the imaginative projections of a Schopenhauer or a Nietzsche than the logical essences of, say, a Plato. This appears to be true even in Heidegger's case, in spite of the fact that he inherited from his master, Husserl, an interest in the bracketed "reduced" logical essence which is reminiscent of the Platonic form. In Heidegger's hands *Phöno-menologie* by becoming *Existenz* has turned from the logical to the more imaginative and emotional side of experience. *Existenz* is thus a poetic and philosophical attempt to describe the subjective experiences of religion, and as such it depends for much of its appeal on its own medium of expression. In the urgency of his sense of the Absolute and for its inescapable influence on human life Kierkegaard makes us think of Francis Thompson. Jaspers is like Browning in his originality, his profoundly moving quality, and it must be added, in his objectivity. On the basis of the arbitrary waywardness of his style Heidegger can only be compared to Gertrude Stein. Like her he uses strange words in an ordinary setting or ordinary words in strange settings to jolt us out of our complacently accepted categories.

> —JULIUS SEELYE BIXLER,
> "The Contribution of Existenz Philosophie,"
> *Harvard Theological Review*

A rose is a rose is a rose.

> —GERTRUDE STEIN

Matter is less material and the mind less spiritual than is generally supposed. The habitual separation of physics and psychology, mind and matter is metaphysically indefensible.

—BERTRAND RUSSELL

CHAPTER 4

"Now-ness"

The philosophy of intuition takes time at its full value. It permits no ossification, as it were, of each moment. It takes hold of each moment as it is born from Sunyata [the Void]. Momentariness is therefore characteristic of this philosophy. Each moment is absolute, alive, and significant. The frog leaps, the cricket sings, a dewdrop glitters on the lotus leaf, a breeze passes through the pine branches, and the moonlight falls on the murmuring mountain stream.

—D. T. SUZUKI

To see a World in a grain of sand
And a Heaven in a wild flower,
Hold Infinity in the Palm of your hand
And Eternity in an hour.

—WILLIAM BLAKE,
"Auguries of Innocence"

The morning glory blooms but an hour
And yet it differs not at heart
From the giant pine that lives for a
    thousand years.

—MATSUNAGA TEITIKU

Truly, I say to you, whosoever does not receive the Kingdom of God like a child shall not enter it.

—Luke XVIII:17

> Look, children,
> Hail-stones!
> Let's rush out!
>
> —BASHO
> (translated by R. H. Blyth)

Man is a thinking reed but his great works are done when he is not calculating and thinking. "Childlikeness" has to be restored with long years of training in the art of self-forgetfulness. When this is attained, man thinks yet he does not think. He thinks like the showers coming down from the sky; he thinks like the waves rolling on the ocean; he thinks like the stars illuminating the nightly heavens; he thinks like the green foliage shooting forth in the relaxing spring breeze. Indeed, he is the showers, the ocean, the stars, the foliage.

> —D. T. SUZUKI,
> Introduction to *Zen in the Art of Archery*,
> by Eugen Herrigel

> The Cock is crowing,
> The stream is flowing,
> The small birds twitter,
> The lake doth glitter,
> The green fields sleep in the sun.
>
> —WORDSWORTH,
> "Written in March"

> O chestnut tree, great-rooted blossomer,
> Are you the leaf, the blossom or the bole?
> O body swayed to music, O brightening glance,
> How can we know the dancer from the dance?
>
> —W. B. YEATS,
> "Among School Children"

> What! Was it the moon
> That cried?
> A cuckoo!
>
> —BAISHITSU

The unique character of each moment of the present, its creative upsurge and its novelty continually escape us.

There is a key of fundamental importance which allows us to open the inner door which gives access to the plenitude of the Present, the heavy door which we have ourselves constructed. We can even say that it is ourselves. Its existence is due to our habitual inattention, to our constant negligence. . . .

The most fundamental distractions are not without; they are within us; they result from the potent magic of words and symbols inseparably connected with all our thoughts.

—ROBERT LINSSEN,
Living Zen

Zen's discipline is largely self-discipline. It is a constant self-recollectedness, a constant awareness, a state of being at all times "mindful and self-possessed." Asked how he exercised himself, a Master replied, "when I am hungry, I eat; when tired, I sleep." The reply was sharp. "That is what everybody does!" "When they eat," said the Master, "they eat, but are thinking of other things, thereby allowing themselves to be disturbed; when they sleep, they do not sleep, but dream of a thousand things." One thing at a time, in full concentration, is the mental discipline.

—CHRISTMAS HUMPHREYS,
Zen Buddhism

Without looking forward to tomorrow every moment, you must think only of this day and this hour. Because tomorrow is difficult and unfixed and difficult to know, you must think of following the Buddhist way while you live today. . . . You must concentrate on Zen practice without wasting time, thinking that there is only this day and this hour. After that it becomes truly easy. You must forget about the good and bad of your nature, the strength or weakness of your power.

—DOGEN,
Shobogenzo
(translated by Reiho Masunaga in *The Way of Zen*,
by Alan Watts)

When walking just walk,
When sitting, just sit,
Above all, don't wobble.
—YUN-MEN

. . . nirvana may well be waiting for us simply to give up and find it right here:—
You light the fire;
I'll show you something nice,—
A great ball of snow.

—JOSEPH CAMPBELL,
quoting a *haiku* by Basho

265

grain of
sand.
spins
round

child
too

Like late milkweed that blooms beside the lonely
And sunlit stone, peace bloomed all afternoon.

> —ROBERT PENN WARREN,
> "The Owl"

I raise my hand; I take a book from the other side of this desk; I hear the boys playing ball outside my window; I see the clouds blown away beyond the neighboring woods:—in all these I am practicing Zen, I am living Zen. No wordy discussion is necessary, nor any explanation.

> —D. T. SUZUKI

Nothing exists; all things are becoming.

> —REIHO MASUNAGA,
> *The Soto Approach to Zen*

Eternity is an infinite extent of time, in which every event is future at one time, present at another, past at another.

> —*Dictionary of Philosophy*,
> edited by Dagobert D. Runes

Today also,
Today also, a kite
Caught on the enoki-tree.

> —ISSA
> (translated by R. H. Blyth)

"One thing I remember
Spring came on forever,
Spring came on forever,"
Said the Chinese nightingale.

> —VACHEL LINDSAY,
> "The Chinese Nightingale"

Seeing myself well lost once more, I sighed,
"Where, where in heaven am I? But don't tell me,"
I warned the clouds, "by opening me wide!
Let's let my heavenly lostness overwhelm me."

> —ROBERT FROST,
> "Lost in Heaven"

267

Four-souled like the wind am I,
Voyaging an endless sky,
Undergoing destiny.

—AMY LOWELL,
"Shooting the Sun"

CHAPTER 5

"One-ness"

The object of Zenism is to make us intuitively sure that we have discovered in the depths of our soul the entity which goes beyond and takes the place of all individual differences and temporary changes. This entity is known as spirit, or soul, or as the fundamental nature of the universe and the spirit. It implies the supreme unity of existence, a latent unity which permeates individual beings and their changing forms, a unity which should not be sought in the outer world, but can be found directly within ourselves. So soon as the discipline of Zen has endowed one with the consciousness of this fundamental nature or primordial quality of the self and of the universe alike, one has absorbed the universe into oneself which amounts to saying that one has identified oneself with the cosmos.

> —M. ANESAKI,
> *Buddhist Art in Its Relation to Buddhist Ideals*

Even when Zen indulges in intellection, it never subscribes to a pantheistic interpretation of the world. For one thing, there is no One in Zen. If Zen ever speaks of the One as if it recognized it, this is a kind of condescension to common parlance. To Zen students, the One is the All and the All is the One; and yet the One remains the One and the All the All. "Not two!" may lead the logician to think, "It is One." But the master would go on saying, "Not One either." "What then?" we may ask. We here face a blind alley, as far as verbalism is concerned. Therefore, it is said that "If you wish to be in direct communion (with Reality) I tell you, "Not two!"

> —D. T. SUZUKI,
> *Zen and Japanese Culture*

For double the vision my Eyes do see,
And a double vision is always with me.

With my inward Eye 'tis an old Man grey:
With my outward, a Thistle across my way.

—WILLIAM BLAKE

To wear out one's intellect in an obstinate adherence to the individuality of things, not recognizing the fact that all things are ONE—this is called *Three in the Morning.*

Chuang Tzu, the Chinese sage who made this comment, explained his meaning of the expression "three in the morning" by the following story:

A keeper of monkeys said with regard to their ration of chestnuts that each monkey was to have three in the morning and four at night. But at this the monkeys were very angry, so the keeper said they might have four in the morning and three at night, with which arrangement they were all well pleased. The actual number of chestnuts remained the same, but there was an adaptation to the likes and dislikes of those concerned. Such is the principle of putting oneself into subjective relation with externals.

—CHUANG TZU

God is so omnipresent . . . that God is an angel in an angel, and a stone in a stone, and a straw in a straw.

—JOHN DONNE,
Sermon VII

This identity out of the One into the One and with the One is the source and fountainhead and breaking forth of glowing Love.

—MEISTER ECKHART

Who is God? I can think of no better answer than, He who is. Nothing is more appropriate to the eternity which God is. If you call God good, or great, or blessed, or wise, or anything else of this sort, it is included in these words, namely, He is.

—ST. BERNARD

Far or forgot to me is near;
Shadow and sunlight are the same;
The vanquished gods to me appear;
And one to me are shame and fame.

They reckon ill who leave me out;
When me they fly, I am the wings;
I am the doubter and the doubt,
And I the hymn the Brahmin sings.

—EMERSON,
"Brahma"

When the Ten Thousand things are viewed in their one-ness we return to the Origin and remain where we have always been.

> —SENG-TS'AN

O My God, how does it happen in this poor old world that Thou art so great and yet nobody finds Thee, Thou art so near and nobody feels Thee, that Thou give Thyself to everybody and nobody knows Thy name? Men flee from Thee and say they cannot find Thee; they turn their backs and say they cannot see Thee; they stop their ears and say they cannot hear Thee.

> —HANS DENK,
> quoted by Aldous Huxley in *The Perennial Philosophy*

I met a seer.
He held in his hands
The book of wisdom.
"Sir," I addressed him,
"Let me read."
"Child—" he began.
"Sir," I said,
"Think not that I am a child,
For already I know much
Of that which you hold;
Aye, much."

He smiled.
Then he opened the book
And held it before me.
Strange that I should have grown
So suddenly blind.

> —STEPHEN CRANE,
> "The Book of Wisdom"

Only a narrow wall stands 'tween us both
Through no design; for it might be
A call from Thee or even me would make
It soon give way
Without alarm or noise.
Out of Thy Symbols is the wall built up.

> —RAINER MARIA RILKE,
> *Das Stunden Buch*
> quoted by Frederic Spiegelberg in *The Religion of No Religion*

The central theme of the Upanishads is to seek unity in the midst of diversity. "What is it that, by knowing which, everything in the universe is known?" The answer is to be found in the conception of God, or Brahman, as the Ultimate Cause of the universe: Since the effect is not different from the cause, it is possible to know the universe by knowing Brahman, "as by knowing one lump of clay, all that is made of clay is also known; for the modification is but an effort of speech, a name, and the only reality is the clay."

—SWAMI MADHAVANANDA,
The Cultural Heritage of India

To the question "Where does the soul go when the body dies?" Jacob Boehme answered: "There is no necessity for it to go anywhere."

The One remains, the many change and pass;
Heaven's light forever shines, earth's shadows fly;
Life, like a dome of many-colored glass,
Stains the white radiance of Eternity.

—SHELLEY,
"Adonais"

And we, spectators always, everywhere,
looking at, never out of, everything!
It fills us. We arrange it. It decays.
We re-arrange it, and decay ourselves.

Who's turned us round like this, so that we always,
do what we may, retain the attitude
of someone who's departing? Just as he,
on the last hill, that shows him all his valley
for the last time, will turn and stop and linger,
we live our lives, for ever taking leave.

—RAINER MARIA RILKE,
Duino Elegies

The wheel goes back and I shall live again,
But the wave turns, my birth arrives and spills
Over my breast the world bearing my grave.

—MURIEL RUKEYSER,
"Ajanta"

. . . death and life are not serious alternatives.

—ROBINSON JEFFERS,
"May-June, 1940"

when god lets my body be

From each brave eye shall sprout a tree
fruit that dangles therefrom

the purpled world will dance upon
Between my lips which did sing

a rose shall beget the spring
that maidens whom passion wastes

will lay between their little breasts
My strong fingers beneath the snow

Into strenuous birds shall go
my love walking in the grass

their wings will touch with her face
and all the while shall my heart be

With the bulge and nuzzle of the sea

—E. E. CUMMINGS,
"When God Lets My Body Be"

A university student while visiting Gasan asked him: "Have you ever read the Christian Bible?"

"No, read it to me," said Gasan.

The student opened the Bible and read from St. Matthew: "And why take ye thought for raiment? Consider the lilies of the field, how they grow. They toil not, neither do they spin, and yet I say unto you that even Solomon in all his glory was not arrayed like one of these. . . . Take therefore no thought for the morrow, for the morrow shall take thought for the things of itself."

Gasan said: "Whoever uttered those words I consider an enlightened man."

The student continued reading: "Ask and it shall be given you, seek and ye shall find, knock and it shall be opened unto you. For everyone that asketh receiveth, and he that seeketh findeth, and to him that knocketh, it shall be opened."

Gasan remarked: "That is excellent. Whoever said that is not far from Buddhahood."

—PAUL REPS,
Zen Flesh, Zen Bones

"Now there are diversities of gifts but the same Spirit. And there are differences of administrations but the same Lord. And there are diversities of operations, but it is the same God which worketh all in all. *For as the body is one, and hath many members, and all the members of that one body, being many, are one body:* so also is Christ. Now ye are the body of Christ, and members in particular."

(I Corinthians, chap. XII, vv. 4–6, 12, 27)

During the Last Supper, Jesus took some bread, broke it, and gave it to his disciples saying, "Take, eat, *this is my body*," and then He passed round the cup saying "Drink ye all of it for this is my blood." The Zen masters interpret these words in a manner different from that of the Christians: to the former *everything is the "Body of Buddha"* so if Jesus said "the bread is my body" it was because *all things without distinction* are the "real Body," that of the Totality-that-is-One of the Universe; not a single grain of dust lies outside this Reality.

—ROBERT LINSSEN,
Living Zen

The *Chandogya Upanishad* tells a story about Svetaketu, a young man of ancient India who, on returning to his home after twelve years of studying the Vedas, appeared to his father to be somewhat set up about his vast learning. The father therefore set out to teach him some homely but profound wisdom not necessarily gleaned from books.   [N. W. R.]

"Bring me," he said to his son, "a fruit from a banyan tree."
"Here is one, sir."
"Break it."
"It is broken, sir."
"What do you see there?"
"Some seeds, sir, exceedingly small."
"Break one of these."
"It is broken, sir."
"What do you see there?"
"Nothing at all."
The father said, "My son, that subtle essence which you do not perceive there—in that very essence stands the being of the great banyan tree. In that which is the subtle essence all that exists has its self. That is the True, that is the Self, and thou, Svetaketu, art That."
"Pray, sir," said the son, "tell me more."
For the second lesson the father gave his son a bag of salt, saying, "Place this salt in a vessel of water and come to me tomorrow morning with the vessel."
When the son appeared the next day the father commanded, "Bring me the salt which you put in the water."

consciousness
deLighting
as crane

But the salt of course had disappeared.
"Taste the water from the surface of the vessel and tell me how it is."
"Salty," said the son.
"And from the middle?"
"Salty."
"And from the bottom?"
"Salty also."
Then the father said, "Here likewise in this body of yours, my son, you do not perceive the True; but there in fact it is. In that which is the subtle essence, all that exists has its self. That is the True, that is the Self, and thou, Svetaketu, art That."

Chandogya Upanishad

... thou canst not stir a flower
Without troubling of a star.

—FRANCIS THOMPSON,
"The Mistress of Vision"

And I have felt ... a sense sublime
Of something far more deeply interfused,
Whose dwelling is the light of setting suns,
And the round ocean and the living air,
And the blue sky, and in the mind of man;
A motion and a spirit, that impels
All thinking things, all objects of all
     thought,
And rolls through all things.

—WORDSWORTH,
"Tintern Abbey"

CHAPTER 6

The Zen Eye

Similarities between *haiku* and certain poems of the late Wallace Stevens, in particular a series called "Thirteen Ways of Looking at a Blackbird" have been pointed out by Earl Miner in his book, *The Japanese Tradition in British and American Literature*[1]:   [N. W. R.]

[Stevens'] most impressionistic and most nearly Japanese poems are those which give a series of several quasi-Impressionistic pictures, apprehensions, or impressions of one subject. The most important of these for our purposes are "Six Significant Landscapes" and "Thirteen Ways of Looking at a Blackbird" from *Harmonium* and "Study of Two Pears" and "Variations on a Summer Day" from *Parts of a World* (1942). The titles of these poems recall such series of Japanese prints as Hiroshige's "Eight Views of Ōmi," Hokusai's "Thirty-Six Views of Fuji," or Utamaro's "Seasons." These poems are also closest to the Imagist method and haiku technique, and are especially reminiscent of Amy Lowell's "Twenty-Four Hokku on a Modern Theme." The best example from among these poems of the highly pictorial method merged with haiku-like technique is "Thirteen Ways of Looking at a Blackbird." The blackbird is the constant, objective reality which means different things according to the mood and impression of the observer. Several of the sections of the poem are most extraordinarily like the Japanese in their method and in their use of natural imagery.

I

Among twenty snowy mountains
The only moving thing
Was the eye of the blackbird.

---

[1] Princeton University Press, Princeton, 1958.

277

III

The blackbird whirled in the autumn winds.
It was a small part of the pantomime.

IX

When the blackbird flew out of sight,
It marked the edge
Of one of many circles.

XII

The river is moving.
The blackbird must be flying.

XIII

It was snowing all afternoon.
It was snowing
And it was going to snow.
The blackbird sat
In the cedar-limbs.

The third and twelfth sections are haiku-like in spirit, because they assume the interrelatedness of all nature. The river, for example, is a Taoist symbol for motion; it moves, and the blackbird may therefore also be expected to be in flight. Only one of the thirteen sections—but also perhaps the basic image of the poem as a whole, the blackbird in autumn—seems to echo a specific haiku, and this the thirteenth with its darkening scene and the dark bird sitting in the tree. This poem recalls one of the best-known haiku, Basho's "On a Withered Bough."

On a withered bough
A crow has stopped to perch,
And autumn darkens.

The haiku-like elements in these stanzas are, then, their short, condensed quality, the poetic weight placed upon a few natural images, and the interrelatedness of the elements in a natural scene.

Many Zennists feel an affinity for the life and work of Thoreau. From the writings of the sage of Walden Pond, Blyth has made a number of selections which he compares to a Japanese literary form known as *haibun:* [N. W. R.]

We see men haying far in the meadow, their heads waving like the grass they cut. In the distance, the wind seemed to bend all alike.

All day fireflies husbanded their light under the grass and leaves against the night.

The barking of the house-dogs, from the loudest and hoarsest bark, to the faintest serial palpitation under the eaves of heaven.

Our thoughts too begin to rustle.

> —THOREAU,
> *A Week on the Concord and Merrimack Rivers*

Out across the wave
All is bare.
Not a scarlet leaf
Not a flower there!
Only over thatched huts falling brief
Twilight, and the lonely autumn air.

> —SADA-IHE,
> quoted by Okakura in *The Book of Tea*

A poem should be equal to:
Not true

For all the history of grief
An empty doorway and a maple leaf

For love
The leaning grasses and two lights
above the sea—

A poem should not mean
But be.

> —ARCHIBALD MACLEISH,
> "Ars Poetica"

The desolation of winter;
Passing through a small hamlet,
A dog barks.

> —SHIKI
> (translated by R. H. Blyth)

... In the dusk when, like an eyelid's soundless blink
The dewfall-hawk comes crossing the shades to alight
Upon the wind-warped upland thorn. ...

> —THOMAS HARDY,
> "Afterwards"

279

Wind on the lagoon, the south wind breaking roses.

—EZRA POUND,
"Canto XXVI"

We gaze
Even at horses
This morn of snow.

—BASHO
(translated by R. H. Blyth)

The tall rock
The mountain, and the deep and gloomy wood,
Their colours and their forms, were then to me
An appetite, a feeling and a love,
That had no need of a remoter charm,
By thought supplied, nor any interest
Unborrowed from the eye.

—WORDSWORTH,
"Tintern Abbey"

. . . the poet is he who never ceases to have confidence precisely because he does not attach himself to any port, does not fasten himself by any anchor, but pursues this one form that flies through the storm and is lost unceasingly in the eternal becoming.

—ELIE FAURE,
The Spirit of the Forms

Nothing is so beautiful as spring—
When weeds, in wheels, shoot long and lovely and lush
Thrush's eggs look like little low heavens, and thrush
Through the echoing timber does so rinse and wring
The ear, it strikes like lightning to hear him sing;
The glassy peartree leaves and blooms, they brush
The descending blue; that blue is all in a rush
With richness; the racing lambs too have fair their fling.

What is all this juice and all this joy?
A strain of the earth's sweet being in the beginning. . . .

—GERARD MANLEY HOPKINS,
"Spring"

SPECIAL ORDER

YOUR PH. NO. (206) 866 23 5N0.3

NO. COPIES 1   DATE 10-14-86

AUTHOR Robert Linssen

TITLE "Judo and Psycho—
Physical Unity," in Living
Zen

PUBL. G. Allen & Unwin London 1954

PAPER BACK ☒ HARD BACK ☐   DEPOSIT
PAID $ 2.00
ISBN   + tax

3.95

Mike Bricks
NAME

3138 Overhulse Rd NW # 82
ADDRESS

Olympia WA 98502
CITY   STATE   ZIP

866 2353

SAN 102-52d7
PH. 206-866-6000 EXT. 6216
THE EVERGREEN STATE COLLEGE
BOOKSTORE
OLYMPIA   WA 98505

My religion consists of a humble admiration of the illimitable superior spirit who reveals himself in the slight details we are able to perceive with our frail and feeble mind.

—ALBERT EINSTEIN

If "compression is the first grace of style,"
you have it. Contractility is a virtue
as modesty is a virtue.
It is not the acquisition of any one thing
that is able to adorn,
or the incidental quality that occurs
as a concomitant of something well said,
that we value in style,
but the principle that is hid:
in the absence of feet, "a method of conclusions";
"a knowledge of principles,"
in the curious phenomenon of your occipital horn.

—MARIANNE MOORE,
"To a snail"
Selected Poems

Head or tail,
which is which, one can't be sure—
sea snail!

—KYORAI
(translated by Harold Henderson)

The dragonfly:
his face is very nearly
only eye.

—CHISOKU
(translated by Harold Henderson)

A thrush is tapping a stone
With a snail-shell in its beak;
A small bird hangs from a cherry
Until the stem shall break.
No waking song has begun,
And yet birds chatter and hurry
And throng in the elm's gloom
Because an owl goes home.

—GORDON BOTTOMLEY,
"Dawn"

The song of birds, the voices of insects, are all means of conveying truth to the mind; in flowers and grasses we see messages of the Way. The scholar pure and clear of mind, serene and open of heart, should find in everything what nourishes him.

—KOJISEI
(translated by R. H. Blyth)

The wood-pecker looks for dead trees,
Among the cherry-trees in bloom.

—JOSO
(translated by Miyamori)

Thou shalt be in league with the stones of the field, and the beasts of the field shall be at peace with thee.

—*Book of Job*

With love exceeding a simple love of the things
That glide in grasses and rubble of woody wreck;
Or change their perch on a beat of quivering wings
From branch to branch, only restful to pipe and peck;
Or, bristled, curl at a touch their snouts in a ball;
Or cast their web between bramble and thorny hook;
The good physician Melampus, loving them all,
Among them walked, as a scholar who reads a book.
For him the woods were a home and gave him the key
Of knowledge, thirst for their treasures in herbs and
    flowers.
The secrets held by the creatures nearer than we
To earth he sought, and the link of their life with ours:
And where alike we are, unlike where, and the vein'd
Division, vein'd parallel, of a blood that flows
In them, in us, from the source of man unattain'd
Save marks he well what the mystical woods disclose . . .

—GEORGE MEREDITH,
"Melampus"

And do not change. Do not divert your love from visible things. But go on loving what is good, simple and ordinary; animals and things and flowers, and keep the balance true.

—RAINER MARIA RILKE,
(from a letter)

Each clustered bouquet of the snows is
Like stephanotis and white roses.

> —EDITH SITWELL,
> "Winter"

Now of my threescore years and ten,
Twenty will not come again,
And take from seventy springs a score,
It only leaves me fifty more.

And since to look at things in bloom
Fifty springs are little room,
About the woodlands I will go
To see the cherry hung with snow.

> —A. E. HOUSMAN,
> *A Shropshire Lad*

Of their worship of the blossoming cherry which bears only a small bitter fruit, the Japanese say that it teaches "the subtle use of the useless."

> [N. W. R.]

The willow paints the wind
Without using a brush.

> SARYU,
> (translated by Miyamori)

When all aloud the wind doth blow,
And coughing drowns the parson's saw,
And birds sit brooding in the snow,
And Marian's nose looks red and raw;
When roasted crabs hiss in the bowl—
Then nightly sings the staring owl
"To-whit! To-whoo!" A merry note,
While greasy Joan doth keel the pot.

> —SHAKESPEARE,
> Song from *Love's Labour's Lost*

Ever fresh the broad creation
A divine improvisation. . . .

> —EMERSON,
> *Woodnotes*

... think not it is with God as with a human carpenter, who works or works not as he chooses, who can do or leave undone at his good pleasure. It is not thus with God; but finding thee ready, he is obliged to act, to overflow into thee; just as the sun must needs burst forth when the air is bright, and is unable to contain itself. . . . If the painter had to plan out every brush mark before he made his first he would not paint at all.

> —MEISTER ECKHART,
> quoted by Ananda K. Coomaraswamy in
> *Transformation of Nature in Art*

The artist must atune himself to that which wants to reveal itself and permit the process to happen through him.

> —MARTIN HEIDEGGER

In reality, the individual never creates anything; if man creates it is as universal man, anonymous, and as manifestations of the Principle. In ages of truer wisdom artists, scholars and thinkers did not dream of attaching their names to the works which took form through them.

> —HUBERT BENOIT,
> *The Supreme Wisdom*

Analytical intellect is chiefly concerned with breaking down complex phenomena into ever smaller components in order to observe and classify them, and give them practical application, while intuition, wittingly or unwittingly, sees the *oneness* of purpose and meaning behind the multitude of phenomena. But this is not all, for intuition, being akin to the creative spirit itself, is man's instrument for creativeness as well as comprehension.

> —FRANZ E. WINKLER,
> *Man the Bridge Between Two Worlds*

I paint to rest from the phenomena of the external world—to pronounce it—and to make notations of its essence with which to verify the inner eye.

> —MORRIS GRAVES

> so much depends
> upon
>
> a red wheel
> barrow
>
> glazed with rain
> water

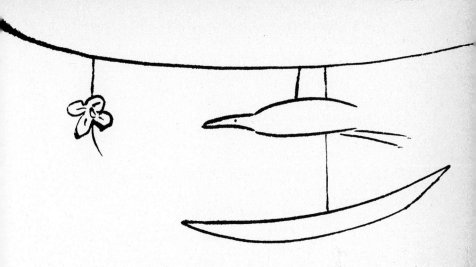

paper flower
paper bird
paper moon

who walks
the wild earth
any more?

beside the white
chickens.

—WILLIAM CARLOS WILLIAMS,
"The Red Wheelbarrow"

The mountain ant
Stands out clear
On the white peony.

—BUSON
(translated by R. H. Blyth)

The legs of the crane
Have become short
In the summer rains.

—BASHO
(translated by R. H. Blyth)

Now I hung the moon
On the pine
Now took it off again.

—HOKUSHI
(translated by Miyamori)

Up the barley rows,
stitching, stitching them together,
a butterfly goes.

—SORA
(translated by Harold Henderson)

. . . cautious,
I offered him a crumb,
And he unrolled his feathers
And rowed him softer home

Than oars divide the ocean,
Too silver for a seam,
Or butterflies, off banks at noon,
Leap, plashless, as they swim.

—EMILY DICKINSON,
"A Bird Came Down the Walk"

As for the outside world, the artist is confronted by what he sees; but what he sees is primarily what he looks at.

—ANDRE MALRAUX,
The Creative Act

Meanwhile the intense color and nobility of sunrise,
Rose and gold and amber, flowed up the sky. Wet rocks were
    shining, a little wind
Stirred the leaves of the forest and the marsh flag-flowers;
    the soft valley between the low hills
Became as beautiful as the sky;

—ROBINSON JEFFERS,
"Original Sin"

. . . In [Japanese] flower arrangement the unfilled empty spaces are to be regarded as belonging to the total picture. . . . They too manifest the inexpressible, irrepresentable, wordless silence. Rhythmically included in the unsymmetrical harmony, these empty spaces can be given particularly eloquent and clear expression.

—GUSTIE L. HERRIGEL,
Zen in the Art of Flower Arrangement

When I resided at the Zen monastery I was given a sumi-ink painting of a large free brush circle to meditate upon. What was it? Day after day I would look at it. Was it selflessness? Was it the Universe—where I could lose my identity? Perhaps I didn't see its aesthetic and missed the fine points of the brush which to a trained Oriental eye would reveal much about the character of the man who painted it. But after my visit I found I had new eyes. . . . When I saw a great dragon painted in free brush style on a ceiling in a temple in Kyoto I thought of the same rhythmical power of Michelangelo—the rendering of the form was different—the swirling clouds accompanying his majestic flight in the heavenly sphere were different—but the same power of the spirit pervaded both.

—MARK TOBEY
(from a paper read at a UNESCO Conference held in San Francisco in 1957)

Always beyond the particular object whatever it may be, we have to fix our will on the void, to will the void. For the good which we can neither picture nor define is a void for us. But this void is fuller than all fullnesses.

If we get as far as this we shall come through all right, for God fills the void. It has nothing to do with an intellectual process in the present-day sense. The intelligence has nothing to discover, it has only to clear the ground. It is only good for servile tasks. . . . This nothingness is not unreal. Compared with it everything in existence is unreal.

—SIMONE WEIL,
Gravity and Grace

In the Noh plays and the old legends performed in the Kabuki theatre, the most striking and most significant passages are those where nothing is spoken at all, and the actor has to express everything wordlessly from within, by the most economical and yet concentrated mime and gestures.

—GUSTIE L. HERRIGEL,
Zen in the Art of Flower Arrangement

Among the great things which are to be found among us, the Being of Nothingness is the greatest.

—LEONARDO DA VINCI,
Diaries and Notes

CHAPTER 7

The Archer, The Judoka, Puppets, Swords, and a Tame Bear

The following excerpts bear an interesting relationship not only to each other but to an early nineteenth-century German classic, *The Marionette Theatre*, by Heinrich von Kleist, which is the fourth of five examples I have arbitrarily placed together to illustrate such Zen attributes as "constant awareness" and "obedience to the nature of things."

The first excerpt, from Eugen Herrigel's now famous little book, *Zen in the Art of Archery*, tells how a European finally learned, under the wise guidance of a Japanese master, how *not* to shoot the arrow but to let "It" shoot for him. The essay following, from Robert Linssen's *Living Zen*, speaks of Judo's use of the "instinctive wisdom of the body." The third contribution, by one of Japan's most noted swordsmen, Takano Shigeyoshi, suggests a connection between the art of swordsmanship and the notable Japanese theatrical art of the puppeteer. In von Kleist's story we move from the marionette theatre of nineteenth-century Germany to a fencing scene with a tame bear.

If connections between Herrigel's bow and arrow, Linssen's judo, Shige-yoshi's sword and puppets, and von Kleist's tame bear and marionettes can be perceived, it should be easy enough for the reader to move on to the fictional tale of an imaginary Chinese archery expert named Chi Ch'ang, of whom it could finally be written, "So attuned had he become to the underlying laws of the universe, so far removed from the insecurities and contradictions of things apparent, that in the evening of his life he no longer knew

289

the difference between 'I' and 'he,' between 'this' and 'that.' The kaleidoscope of sensory impressions no longer concerned him; for all he cared, his eye might have been an ear, his ear a nose, his nose a mouth." [N. W. R.]

THE ART OF ARCHERY[1]

By EUGEN HERRIGEL

One day I asked the Master: "How can the shot be loosed if 'I' do not do it?"

" 'It' shoots," he replied.

"I have heard you say that several times before, so let me put it another way: How can I wait self-obliviously for the shot if 'I' am no longer there?"

" 'It' waits at the highest tension."

"And who or what is this 'It'?"

"Once you have understood that, you will have no further need of me. And if I tried to give you a clue at the cost of your own experience, I would be the worst of teachers and would deserve to be sacked! So let's stop talking about it and go on practicing."

. . . .

Then, one day, after a shot, the Master made a deep bow and broke off the lesson. "Just then 'It' shot!" he cried, as I stared at him bewildered. And when I at last understood what he meant I couldn't suppress a sudden whoop of delight.

"What I have said," the Master told me severely, "was not praise, only a statement that ought not to touch you. Nor was my bow meant for you, for you are entirely innocent of this shot. You remained this time absolutely self-oblivious and without purpose in the highest tension, so that the shot fell from you like a ripe fruit. Now go on practicing as if nothing had happened.'

. . . .

"I'm afraid I don't understand anything more at all," I answered, "even the simplest things have got in a muddle. Is it 'I' who draw the bow, or is it the bow that draws me into the state of highest tension? Do 'I' hit the goal, or does the goal hit me? Is 'It' spiritual when seen by the eyes of the body, and corporeal when seen by the eyes of the spirit—or both or neither? Bow, arrow, goal and ego, all melt into one another, so that I can no longer separate them. And even the need to separate has gone. For as soon as I take the

---

[1] From *Zen in the Art of Archery*, by Eugen Herrigel. Pantheon Books, New York, 1953.

bow and shoot, everything becomes so clear and straightforward and so ridiculously simple. . . ."

"Now at last," the Master broke in, "the bow-string has cut right through you."

. . . .

JUDO AND PSYCHO-PHYSICAL UNITY[1]

By ROBERT LINSSEN

The Zen masters, Hatha Yoga, and Judo teach us that the human races of today have lost all trace of an instinctive wisdom of the body. The physical body which is disdained by many Occidental mystics, spiritually minded persons and intellectuals, *is Cosmic Mind* in the same way as are the highest mental attainments.

We can still rediscover an instinctive wisdom of the body drawing its essence from obscure biological memories going back to the beginnings of the world. The possibilities of physical life from this angle are immense.

That is the reason which leads many Zen sympathizers to practise Judo. We will not assume the responsibility here of asserting that the practise of Judo leads to the experience of Satori. Nevertheless it gives a certain suppleness to the physical body, a flexibility, a muscular and nervous relaxation which can be of great use. Judo also brings about a pacification and non-violence of thought. We know, indeed, that this pacification and non-violence apply to the peripheral, the most "physical" layers of the mind, and do not affect the "I-process" in its ultimate refuge. Nevertheless the results obtained can be of considerable help.

Chinese tradition gives us some interesting details concerning the origin of Judo long before the form given it by the Master Kano in the last century.

Its principles of non-resistance and non-violence were born one day in the mind of an observer who noticed that the branches of a fir-tree snapped under the weight of the snow, whilst the simple reeds, weaker but more supple, emerged victorious from the trial. This suppleness and this non-resistance figure among the bases of Judo.

We are often broken by circumstances, for we resist the law of Life.

We are no longer adequate. We no longer have the relaxation, neither the physical suppleness nor the mental agility with which to reply adequately to

---

[1] From "Judo and Psycho-Physical Unity," in *Living Zen*, by Robert Linssen. George Allen and Unwin, Ltd., London, 1954.

circumstances. Our disordered mental activity and too fertile imagination cut us off from the outside world.

The practise of Judo forces us to an attention which is completely physical and non-mental. In Judo, he who thinks is immediately thrown. Victory is assured to the combatant who is both physically and mentally non-resistant. We suppose wrongly that only thought-out and calculated moves are sound.

The practise of Judo helps us to revalue the vegetative life which our hyper-intellectualized generations too often despise. We should rid ourselves of our excessive intellectuality.

As we have seen above, mental activity conceals a fundamental character of violence whose importance escapes us. Violence and fear are the distinctive signs of thought in its deepest levels. We are often unaware of this. In the first period of training the attentive judoka can surprise in himself signs of this mental violence and fear. He will notice that they are radically opposed to the reflexes arising from the instinctive wisdom of the body. The gestures suggested by violence and fear express tense, agitated and often aggressive attitudes. The great art of Judo consists precisely in using to the maximum the force of the adversary against himself. If we try to resist him we are immediately thrown off balance, and our fall is inevitable. If we free ourselves from all mental suggestions of resistance and, on the contrary, adopt an extremely supple attitude, the defeat of our adversary is certain.

The practise of Judo is of great benefit to the impenitent "hypercerebral." The intensity of the exercise, and the completely physical attention required, bring a happy compensation. Equilibrium is assured because the judoka is *obliged* to exercise a vigilant and non-mental observation. He is *obliged* to rediscover the dormant corporeal reflexes of an instinctive wisdom which is directly linked with the profound nature of all things and his own being.

THE PSYCHOLOGY OF SWORDPLAY[1]

By TAKANO SHIGEYOSHI

When I have a bamboo sword most suited to my personal taste in respect of weight, formation, tone, etc., I can enter more readily into a state of identity where my body and the sword I hold become one. It goes without saying that as soon as one cherishes the thought of winning the contest or dis-

---

[1] From an essay quoted in *Zen and Japanese Culture*, by D. T. Suzuki. Bollingen Series LXIV. Pantheon Books, New York, 1959.

playing one's skill in technique, swordsmanship is doomed. When all these thoughts are done away with, including also the idea of the body, one can realize the state of oneness in which you are the sword and the sword is you—for there is no more distinction between the two. This is what is known as the psychology of *muga* ("no-ego" or "no-mind"). This perhaps corresponds to what Buddhism calls a state of emptiness. It is then that all thoughts and feelings, which are likely to hinder the freest operation of whatever technique one has mastered, are thoroughly purged, and one returns to one's "original mind" divested of its bodily encumbrances.

I sometimes feel that when the marionette master puts his mind wholly into the play his state of mind attains something of the swordsman's. He is then not conscious of the distinction between himself and the doll he manipulates. The play becomes really an art when the master enters into a state of emptiness. Some may feel like seeing a difference between the marionette master and the swordsman, because of the latter's confronting a living personality who is aiming every moment at striking you down. But my way of thinking is different, inasmuch as both have realized the state of identity it must operate alike regardless of its objectives.

When the identity is realized, I as swordsman see no opponent confronting me and threatening to strike me. I seem to transform myself into the opponent, and every movement he makes as well as every thought he conceives are felt as if they were all my own and I intuitively, or rather unconsciously, know when and how to strike him. All seems to be so natural.

THE MARIONETTE THEATRE[1]

By HEINRICH VON KLEIST

One evening in the winter of 1801 as I walked in the park, I happened to meet Mr. C. . . . who was engaged as first dancer in the opera, a man very popular with the public. I told him, in passing, that I had seen him several times at an outdoor marionette theatre that had been set up in the market square to entertain the common-folk with songs and dances and short dramatic burlesques.

---

[1] "The Marionette Theatre," by Heinrich von Kleist, from *Five Essays on Paul Klee*, designed and edited by Merle Armitage. Duell, Sloan and Pearce, distributors, New York, 1940. Written at the turn of the nineteenth century for the *Berliner Abendblatter*, this essay became and still is one of the literary treasures of the German-speaking peoples of Europe.

He assured me that I need not be surprised at his delight in the pantomime of these puppets; and he hinted that the puppets could be very effective teachers of the dance. Since he did not seem to be indulging a mere whim about these marionettes, I sat down with him to discuss this strange theory in which puppets seemed to become teachers.

He asked me if I had not been impressed by the elegance and gracefulness of the movement of these puppets, particularly of the smaller ones.

I could not deny that I had been impressed. A group of four peasants dancing a fast Rondo could not have been portrayed with more beauty and charm by the most famous Flemish painters of village scenes.

I inquired about the mechanical control of these figures. How was it possible to direct the small limbs in the intricate rhythms of the dance? How did the puppeteer manage without having his hands tied in a confusion of strings?

He replied that I should not be deceived into thinking that each limb was separately controlled in all the phases of the dance. "Each puppet," he said, "has a focal point in movement, a center of gravity, and when this center is moved, the limbs follow without any additional handling. After all, the limbs are pendula, echoing automatically the movement of the center.

"These movements of the center are very simple. Every time the center of gravity is guided in a straight line, the limbs describe curves that complement and extend the basically simple movement. Many times when the puppets are merely shaken arbitrarily, they are transformed into a kind of rhythmic movement that in itself is very similar to the dance."

These remarks seemed at first to throw light on his enjoyment of the marionette theatre, but I did not as yet have any concept of the consequences of his ideas.

I asked him whether he thought that the puppeteer himself should be a dancer, or whether at least the puppeteer should have some sense of the beauty in dance.

He replied: "Even if the manipulation is easy, it is not necessarily performed without feeling. The line which the center of gravity has to describe is, at any rate, very simple and in most cases straight. In cases where the line is curved, the curve remains simple, at the most complicated, elliptic; and the ellipse (because of the joints) seems to be the natural curve for movement of the human body. The drawing of an ellipse does not demand any great artistry on the part of the puppeteer. On the other hand there is something very enigmatic about an ellipse. It is actually the course that the soul of the dancer takes when the dancer moves, and I doubt whether this course can be traced if the puppeteer does not enter the center of gravity of his puppet; in other words, the puppeteer himself must dance."

I replied that I had regarded the handling of puppets as something rather spiritless, approximate to the turning of the crank that plays a hand organ.

"Not in the least," he said, "the action of the puppeteer's fingers is directly related to the movements of his puppet, just as numbers relate to their logarithms; but then it may be true that this last vestige of human spirit can be eliminated from the marionettes; and then their dance would be completely mechanized, performed with a crank as you have suggested."

I was surprised that he favored this minor variation of a great art form, surprised not only that he thought it capable of development but also that he seemed to concern himself with its development.

He smiled and said: "I will even dare to maintain that if an artisan would follow the directions that I want to give and build a marionette for me, I could have that marionette perform a dance which neither I nor any other capable dancer of this era could duplicate."

I stared at the pavement between my feet. "Have you," he asked, "seen the artificial legs that British artisans are manufacturing for amputees?"

I said no; I had never seen anything of the sort.

"I am sorry," he answered, "because if I tell you that amputees dance with these legs, I rather fear you will not believe me."

"What," I said, "dance?"

"Yes, their sphere of movement is limited, but the movements that they command they perform with a poise, ease and gracefulness that would astound you."

I said jokingly that he had found his man. The artisan who was able to build such a remarkable leg should, doubtless, be able to build a marionette to his specifications.

It was his turn to stare silently at the pavement. "What," I asked, "are the specific demands you want to make for your marionette?"

"Nothing," he said, "nothing that is unusual; simple harmonious proportion, mobility, ease of manipulation; but each of these qualities must be developed to a higher degree; and most particularly the placement of the center of gravity must be more true to nature than in the common marionette."

"And what advantage would these puppets of yours have over the human dancer?"

"Advantage? . . . at first only a negative one. The puppet would never slip into affectation (if we think of affectation as appearing when the center of intention of a movement is separated from the center of gravity of the movement). Since the puppeteer has no control over any point other than the center of gravity, and since this center is his only means of starting an intended movement, all the limbs follow the law of gravity and are what they ought to be: dead, mere pendula. We look in vain for this quality in the majority of our dancers.

"Look at Miss P. . . ." he continued, "when she plays Daphne, persecuted by Apollo, she looks back at him; the soul, the center of intention, is located in the lumbar vertebra; she bends down as if she would break; and young F. . . . when, as Paris, he stands among the goddesses and presents the apple to Venus, his soul is (oh painful to behold) in his elbow.

"Great blunders," he added, "are inevitable. We have eaten from the tree of knowledge; the paradise of Eden is locked up; and the Cherubim is behind us. We must wander about the world and see if, perhaps, we can find an unguarded back door."

I laughed. Certainly, I thought, the spirit cannot err when it is nonexistent. But I saw that he had more on his mind and I asked him to continue.

"These puppets," he said, "have another advantage. They haven't discovered the law of gravity. They know nothing about the inertia of matter. In other words they know nothing of those qualities most opposed to the dance. The force that pulls them into the air is more powerful than that which shackles them to the earth. What would not our dear G. . . . give to be sixty pounds lighter or to have a force that would lift her for her entrechats and pirouettes. These marionettes, like fairies, use the earth only as a point of departure; they return to it only to renew the flight of the limbs with a momentary pause. We, on the other hand, need the earth: for rest, for repose from the effort of the dance; but this rest of ours is, in itself, obviously not dance; and we can do no better than disguise our moments of rest as much as possible."

I said that however cleverly he managed his paradoxes he would never make me believe that there was more grace in a jointed mechanical doll than there is in the structure of the human body.

He replied: "It is simply impossible for a human being to reach the grace of the jointed doll. Only a god can duel with matter on this level, and it is at this point that the two ends of the ring-formed world grasp each other."

I was more surprised than before, and I did not know how to reply to these strange statements.

"It would seem," he said, "that you have not read the third chapter of Genesis with sufficient attention; and if one does not understand the first period of human culture, it is difficult enough to talk about the periods that follow but almost impossible to discuss the very last period."

I said: "I know all too well the disorder that self-consciousness imposes on the natural grace of the human being. Before my very eyes, a young acquaintance of mine 'lost his innocence,' and he has never recovered his lost paradise despite his efforts. But what consequences can you draw from that?"

He asked me what had happened.

"About three years ago," I said, "I was bathing with a young man who at that time had a wonderful quality of physical grace. He was about sixteen years old; and since he had only very vaguely attracted the attention of women, the first traces of vanity were barely discernible. It happened that we had both just seen the statue of the youth removing a splinter from his foot; (the cast of this sculpture is included in most German collections). As my young friend was drying himself, he put his foot on a stool; a glance at his reflection in a large mirror reminded him of the statue. He smiled and told me his discovery. In fact I had made the same discovery at that very moment, but to counter his vanity I laughed and replied that he was seeing ghosts. He blushed and lifted his foot a second time to show me. Of course, the experiment failed. Confused, he lifted his foot a third and fourth time; he lifted it possibly ten times in all and in vain. He was incapable of reproducing the gesture; in fact, the movement that he made had such an element of oddity that it was hard for me to repress my laughter.

"From that day on, practically from that very moment, the young man was changed. Day after day he stood before a mirror, and one by one his charms fell away from him. An invisible and inconceivable pressure (like an iron net) seemed to confine the free flow of his gestures, and after a year had passed there remained not a trace of that loveliness that had so delighted everyone."

Mr. C. . . . began very gently: "On this occasion I must tell you yet another story. You will understand easily how it relates.

"On my journey to Russia I stayed at the estate of Herr von G. . . . , a Lithuanian nobleman, whose sons were at that time intense in their practice of fencing. The older one, just back from the university, styled himself a virtuoso and one morning offered me a rapier. We fenced, and it happened that I was victorious. His passion had added to his confusion; and almost every thrust that I made was a hit until finally his rapier was knocked from his hand.

"As he picked it up, half in joke, half in irritation, he said that he had found his master, indeed that everyone in the world eventually found his master and that he would show me mine. The brother laughed heartily and shouted: 'Let's go to the woodshed.' And with that they took me by the arm and led me to a bear which their father had had raised in the yard.

"As I approached, the bear stood erect with his back against the pole to which he was chained. He looked me in the eye, his right paw raised; he was in fencing position. For a moment, confronted by this strange rival, I thought I was dreaming. 'Foil, foil,' said Herr von G. . . . 'see if you can strike him.' When I had recovered from my astonishment, I thrust at him with the rapier; the bear flipped his paw; the thrust was parried. I tried to seduce him with a feint; the bear did not budge. With a sudden lunge I thrust again; I would absolutely have hit a human opponent; the bear flipped his paw, parried the thrust. I was in the same spot that young Herr von G. . . . had been. The bear's concentration added to my loss of composure. I alternated thrusts and feints; I sweated, in vain! Like the finest fencer in the world, the bear met and parried each thrust, but he did not respond to feints; (no fencer in the world could have matched him in that). Eye to eye, as if he read my soul, he stood with his paw lifted, ready to fight; and if I did not intend my thrust, he remained immobile.

"Do you believe this story?"

"Absolutely!" I exclaimed, applauding him. "I would believe it of anyone and how much more of you."

"Now then," said Mr. C. . . . "you have in your possession every means to understanding me. We see that in the natural world, as the power of reflection darkens and weakens, grace comes forward, more radiant, more dominating. . . . But that is not all; two lines intersect, separate and pass through infinity and beyond, only to suddenly reappear at the same point of intersection. As we look in a concave mirror, the image vanishes into infinity and appears again close before us. Just in this way, after self-consciousness has, so to speak, passed through infinity, the quality of grace will reappear; and this reborn quality will appear in the greatest purity, a purity that has either no consciousness or consciousness without limit; either the jointed doll or the god."

"Therefore," I said, a little distracted, "we must eat from the tree of knowledge again and fall back into a state of innocence."

"By all means," he replied, "that is the last chapter in the history of the world."

THE EXPERT[1]

By NAKASHIMA TON

It is the philosophy of Taoism that underlies the determined efforts of the hero of *The Expert*, the story which follows. The close relationship between Zen and this ancient Chinese teaching, referred to earlier, is further clarified by Arthur Waley's illuminating comments cited in the following introductory note by Ivan Morris, the story's translator.   [N. W. R.]

Art, indeed, all types of skill play an important part in Taoism. As Dr. Waley points out (*The Way and Its Power*, p. 58), "The Taoists saw in many arts and crafts the utilisation of a power akin to if not identical with that of Tao. The wheel-wright, the carpenter, the butcher, the bowman, the swimmer, achieve their skill not by accumulating facts concerning their art, nor by the energetic use either of muscles or outward senses; but through utilising the fundamental kinship which, underneath apparent distinctions and diversities, unites their own Primal Stuff to the Primal Stuff of the medium in which they work."

Chi Ch'ang's dictum that "the ultimate state of activity is inactivity" echoes the opening lines of Chapter 38 of the *Tao Te Ching* (Waley, op. cit., p. 189):

> "The man of highest 'power' does not reveal
>   himself as a possessor of 'power';
> Therefore he keeps his 'power.'
> The man of inferior 'power' cannot rid it of
>   the appearance of 'power';
> Therefore he is in truth without 'power.'
> The man of highest 'power' (does not)
>   act . . .
> The man of inferior 'power' acts . . . "

There lived in the city of Hantan, the capital of the ancient Chinese state of Chao, a man called Chi Ch'ang who aspired to be the greatest archer in the

---

[1] "The Expert," by Nakashima Ton, translated by Ivan Morris. *Encounter*, May, 1958.

world. After many enquiries, he ascertained that the best teacher in the country was one Wei Fei. So great was this Master's skill in archery that he was able, by repute, to shoot a quiverful of arrows into a single willow-leaf at the distance of a hundred paces. Chi Ch'ang journeyed to the far-away province where Wei Fei lived and became his pupil.

First Wei Fei ordered him to learn not to blink. Chi Ch'ang returned home and as soon as he entered his house, crept under his wife's loom and lay there on his back. It was his plan to stare without blinking at the treadle as it rushed up and down directly before his eyes. His wife was amazed to see him in this posture and said that she could not weave with a man, albeit her husband, watching from this strange angle. She was, however, constrained to work the treadle despite her embarrassment.

Day after day Chi Ch'ang took up his peculiar station under the loom and practised staring. After two years he had reached the point of not blinking even if one of his eye-lashes was caught in the treadle. When Chi Ch'ang finally crawled out for the last time from under the machine, he realised that his lengthy discipline had been effective. Nothing now could make him blink— not a blow on the eyelid, nor a spark from the fire, nor a cloud of dust raised suddenly before his eyes. So thoroughly had he trained his eye-muscles to inactivity that even when he slept his eyes remained wide open. One day as he sat staring ahead of him, a small spider wove its web between his eye-lashes. Now at last he felt sufficiently confident to report to his teacher.

"To know how not to blink is only the first step," said Wei Fei when Chi Ch'ang had eagerly recounted the story of his progress. "Next you must learn to look. Practise looking at things, and if the time comes when what is minute seems conspicuous, and what is small seems huge, visit me once more."

Again Chi Ch'ang returned home. This time he went to the garden and searched for a tiny insect. When he had found one barely visible to the naked eye, he placed it on a blade of grass and hung this by the window of his study. Now he took up his post at the end of the room and sat there day after day staring at the insect. At first he could barely see it, but after ten days, he began to fancy that it was slightly bigger. At the end of the third month it seemed to have grown to the size of a silk-worm and he could now clearly make out the details of its body.

As Chi Ch'ang sat staring at the insect, he scarcely noticed the changing of the seasons—how the glittering spring sun changed to the fierce glare of summer; how before long the geese were flying through a limpid autumn sky;

and how autumn in turn gave way to the sleety grey winter. Nothing seemed to exist now but the little animal on the blade of grass. As each insect died or disappeared, he had his servant replace it by another one equally minute. But in his eyes they were constantly becoming larger.

For three years he hardly left his study. Then one day he perceived that the insect by the window was as big as a horse. "I've done it!" he exclaimed, striking his knee, and so saying he hurried out of the house. He could scarcely believe his eyes. Horses seemed as big as mountains; pigs looked like great hills, and chickens like castle-towers. Bounding with joy, he ran back to his house and immediately notched a slender Shuo P'êng arrow on a Swallow bow. He took aim and shot the insect straight through the heart without so much as touching the blade of grass on which it rested.

He lost no time in reporting to Wei Fei. This time his teacher was sufficiently impressed to say, "Well done!"

It was five years since Chi Ch'ang had embarked on the mysteries of archery and he felt that his rigorous training had indeed borne fruit. No feat of bowmanship now seemed beyond his powers. To confirm this, he set himself a series of exacting tests before returning home.

First he decided to emulate Wei Fei's own accomplishment, and at the distance of a hundred yards he succeeded in shooting every arrow through a willow-leaf. A few days later he undertook the same task, using his heaviest bow and balancing on his right elbow a cup filled to the brim with water; not a drop was spilt and again every arrow found its mark.

The following week he took a hundred light arrows and shot them in rapid succession at a distant target. The first one hit the bull's-eye; the second one pierced the first arrow straight in the notch; the third arrow lodged itself in the notch of the second; and so it continued until in a twinkling all hundred arrows were joined in a single straight line extending from the target to the bow itself. So true had he aimed that even after he had finished, the long line of arrows did not fall to the ground but remained quivering in mid-air. At this, even the Master Wei Fei, who had watched from the side, could not help clapping and shouting, "Bravo!"

When after two months Chi Ch'ang finally returned home, his wife, chafing at his long neglect, started to rail at him. Thinking to correct her shrewishness, Chi Ch'ang quickly notched a Ch'i Wei arrow on a Raven bow, drew the string to its fullest extension and fired just above her eye. The arrow removed three of her lashes, but so great was its speed and so sure the aim that she was not even aware that anything had happened, and without so much as blinking, continued to nag at her husband.

There was nothing more for Chi Ch'ang to learn from his teacher Wei Fei. He seemed close to the achievement of his ambition. Yet one obstacle remained, he realised with an unpleasant jolt: that obstacle was Wei Fei himself. So long as the Master lived, Chi Ch'ang could never call himself the greatest archer in the world. Though he now equalled Wei Fei in bowmanship, he felt sure that he could never excel him. The man's life was a constant denial of his own great purpose.

Walking through the fields one day, Chi Ch'ang caught sight of Wei Fei far in the distance. Without a moment's hesitation, he raised his bow, fixed an arrow and took aim. His old master, however, had sensed what was happening and in a flash had also notched an arrow on his bow. Both men fired at the same moment. Their arrows collided half way and fell together to the ground. Chi Ch'ang immediately shot another arrow, but this was stopped in mid-air by a second unerring arrow from Wei Fei's bow. So the strange duel continued until the Master's quiver was empty but one arrow still remained to the pupil. "Now's my chance!" muttered Chi Ch'ang and at once aimed the final arrow. Seeing this, Wei Fei broke off a twig from the thorn-bush beside him. As the arrow whistled towards his heart, he flicked the point sharply with the tip of one of the thorns and brought it to the ground at his feet.

Realising that his evil design had been thwarted, Chi Ch'ang was filled with a fine sense of remorse, which, to be sure, he would have been far from feeling had any of his arrows lodged where he intended. Wei Fei, on his side, was so relieved at his escape and so satisfied with this latest example of his own virtuosity that he could feel no anger for his would-be assassin. The two men ran up to each other and embraced with tears of devotion. (Strange indeed were the ways of ancient times! Would not such conduct be unthinkable to-day? The hearts of the men of old must have differed utterly from our own. How else explain that when the Duke Huan one evening demanded a new delicacy, the Director of the Imperial Kitchen, by name I Ya, baked his own son and begged the Duke to sample it; or that the fifteen-year-old youth, who was to be the first Emperor of the Shin Dynasty, did not scruple on the very night his father died to make love three times to the old man's favourite concubine?)

Even as he embraced his head-strong pupil in forgiveness, Wei Fei was aware that his life might any day be threatened again. The only way to rid himself of this constant menace was to divert Chi Ch'ang's mind to some new goal.

"My friend," he said, standing aside, "I have now, as you realise, transmitted to you all the knowledge of archery that I possess. If you wish to delve further into these mysteries, cross the lofty Ta Hsing Pass in the western country and climb to the summit of Mount Ho. There you may find the aged Master Kan Ying, who in the art of archery knows no equal in this or any age. Compared to his skill, our bowmanship is as the puny fumbling of children. There is no man in the world but the Master Kan Ying to whom you can now look for instruction. Seek him out, if indeed he be still alive, and become his pupil."

Chi Ch'ang immediately set out for the West. To hear his achievements described as child's play had pricked his pride and made him fear that he might still be far from realising his great ambition. He must lose no time in climbing Mount Ho and matching his own achievements against those of this old Master.

He crossed the Ta Hsing Pass and made his way up the rugged mountain. His shoes were soon worn out and his feet and legs were cut and bleeding. Quite undaunted, he clambered up perilous precipices and traversed narrow planks set over huge chasms. After a month he reached the summit of Mount Ho and burst impetuously into the cave where dwelt Kan Ying. He proved to be an aged man with eyes as gentle as a sheep's. He was, indeed, quite frighteningly old—far older than anyone Chi Ch'ang had ever seen. His back was bent, and as he walked his white hair trailed along the ground.

Thinking that anyone of such an age must needs be deaf, Chi Ch'ang announced in a loud voice, "I have come to find out if I am indeed as great an archer as I believe." Without waiting for Kan Ying's reply, he took the great poplar bow, which he was carrying on his back, notched a Tsu Chieh arrow and aimed at a flock of migrating birds which were passing by high overhead. Instantly five birds came hurtling down through the clear blue sky.

The old man smiled tolerantly and said, "But my dear Sir, this is mere shooting with bow and arrow. Have you not yet learned to shoot without shooting? Come with me."

Ruffled by his failure to impress the old hermit, Chi Ch'ang followed him in silence to the edge of a great precipice some two hundred paces from the cave. When he glanced down, he thought that he must indeed have come into the presence of "the great screen three thousand cubits high" described of old by

Chang Tsai. Far below he saw a mountain-stream winding its way like a shining thread over the rocks. His eyes became blurred and his head began to spin. Meanwhile the Master Kan Ying ran lightly on to a narrow ledge which jutted straight out over the precipice and, turning round, said, "Now show me your real skill. Come where I am standing and let me see your bowmanship."

Chi Ch'ang was too proud to decline the challenge, and without hesitation changed places with the old man. No sooner had he stepped on to the ledge, however, than it began to sway slightly to and fro. Assuming a boldness that he was far from feeling, Chi Ch'ang took his bow and with trembling fingers tried to notch an arrow. Just then a pebble rolled off the ledge and began to fall thousands of feet through space. Following it with his eye, Chi Ch'ang felt that he was going to lose his balance. He lay down on the ledge, clutching its edges firmly with his fingers. His legs shook and the perspiration flowed from his whole body.

The old man laughed, reached out his hand and helped Chi Ch'ang down off the ledge. Jumping on to it himself, he said, "Allow me, Sir, to show you what archery really is."

Though Chi Ch'ang's heart was pounding and his face was deadly white, he still had sufficient presence of mind to notice that the Master was empty-handed.

"What about your bow?" he asked in a sepulchral voice.

"My bow?" said the old man. "My bow?" he repeated laughing. "So long as one requires bow and arrow, one is still at the periphery of the art. Real archery dispenses with both bow and arrow!"

Directly above their heads a single kite was wheeling in the sky. The hermit looked up at it and Chi Ch'ang followed his gaze. So high was the bird that even to his sharp eyes it looked like a tiny sesame seed. Kan Ying notched an invisible arrow on an incorporeal bow, drew the string to its full extension and released it. Chi Ch'ang seemed to hear a swishing sound; the next moment the kite stopped flapping its wings and fell like a stone to the ground.

Chi Ch'ang was aghast. He felt that now for the first time he had glimpsed the limit of the art which he had so glibly undertaken to master.

For nine years he stayed in the mountains with the old hermit. What disciplines he underwent during this time, none ever knew. When in the tenth year he descended from the mountains and returned home, all were amazed at the change in him. His former resolute and arrogant countenance had disappeared; in its place had come the expressionless, wooden look of a simpleton. His old teacher, Wei Fei, come to visit him, said after a single glance, "Now I can see that you have indeed become an expert! Such as I are no longer worthy ever to touch your feet."

The inhabitants of Hantan hailed Chi Ch'ang as the greatest archer in the land and impatiently awaited the wonderful feats which he no doubt would soon display. But Chi Ch'ang did nothing to satisfy their expectations. Not once did he put his hands to a bow or arrow. The great poplar bow which he had taken with him on his journey he evidently had left behind. When someone asked him to explain, he answered in a languid tone, "The ultimate stage of activity is inactivity; the ultimate stage of speaking is to refrain from speech; the ultimate in shooting is not to shoot."

The more perceptive citizens of Hantan at once understood his meaning and stood in awe before this great expert archer who declined to touch a bow. It was his very refusal to shoot that now caused his reputation to grow.

All sorts of rumours and tales were bruited abroad about Chi Ch'ang. It was reported that always after midnight one could hear the sound of someone pulling an invisible bow-string on the roof of his house. Some said that this was the god of archery, who dwelt each day within the Master's soul and at night escaped to protect him from all evil spirits. A merchant who lived nearby circulated a rumour that one night he had clearly seen Chi Ch'ang riding on a cloud directly above his own house; for once he was carrying his bow, and he was matching his accomplishments against those of Hou I and Yang Yu-chi, the famous archers of legendary times. According to the merchant's story, the arrows fired by the three Masters disappeared in the distance between Orion and Sirius, trailing bright blue lights in the black sky.

There was also a thief who confessed that, as he had been about to climb into Chi Ch'ang's house, a sudden blast of air had rushed through the window and struck him so forcefully on the forehead that he had been knocked off the wall. Thenceforth all those who harboured evil designs avoided the precincts of Chi Ch'ang's house, and it was said that even flocks of migrating birds kept clear of the air above his roof.

As his renown spread through the land, reaching to the very clouds, Chi Ch'ang grew old. More and more he seemed to have entered the state in which both mind and body look no longer to things outside but exist by themselves in restful and elegant simplicity. His stolid face divested itself of every vestige of expression; no outside force could disturb his complete impassiveness.

一箭一箭
遮穀中中
吾不白射
籤人以弓

SENGAI

This drawing shows the famous master Sek-kyo preaching by means of a bow, a type of train-ing that he learned from the great master Baso, thus adding to his initial skill as a hunter (which Sekkyo at one time was) an understanding of the deeper significance of the archer, the bow, and the target.

The verse reads:

"One arrow to one target
The distance being right, a hit.
I do not shoot the bow;
You are tested by it."

It was rare now for him to speak, and presently one could no longer tell whether or not he still breathed. Often his limbs seemed stark and lifeless as a withered tree. So attuned had he become to the underlying laws of the universe, so far removed from the insecurities and contradictions of things apparent, that in the evening of his life he no longer knew the difference between "I" and "he," between "this" and "that." The kaleidoscope of sensory impressions no longer concerned him; for all he cared, his eye might have been an ear, his ear a nose, his nose a mouth.

Forty years after he had come down from the mountains, Chi Ch'ang peacefully left the world, like smoke disappearing in the sky. During these forty years he had never once mentioned the subject of archery, let alone taken up a bow and arrow.

Of his last year, the story is told that one day he visited a friend's house and saw lying on a table a vaguely familiar utensil whose name and use he could, however, not recall. After vainly searching his memory, he turned to his friend and said, "Pray tell me: that object on your table—what is it called and for what is it used?" His host laughed as if Chi Ch'ang was joking. The old man pressed his question but his friend laughed again, though this time somewhat uncertainly. When he was questioned seriously for a third time, a look of consternation appeared on the friend's face. He gazed intently at Chi Ch'ang and, having made sure that he had heard correctly and also that the old man was neither mad nor speaking in jest, he stammered out in an awe-struck tone, "Oh, Master. You must indeed be the greatest Master of all times. Only so can you have forgotten the bow—both its name and its use!"

It was said that for some time after this in the city of Hantan painters threw away their brushes, musicians broke the strings of their instruments, and carpenters were ashamed to be seen with their rules.

Zen and Science — "No-Knowledge"

By R. G. H. SIU

In their efforts to pass beyond the intellect, the Zen Buddhists have emphasized the experience of the moment. Deliberation should not be permitted to interfere with the immediacy of the response. Just as the sound does not wait to issue forth when the bell is struck, man should develop that consciousness of mind that focuses infinite experience into instant intuition. The spontaneity of reaction is stressed continuously by the Zen Master to his disciples. In the art of fencing the counter movements must be made without slow logic or hesitant reasoning. The intuition springs forth as a wordless and thoughtless message translated into integrated and immediate action. . . .

We may observe an inkling of a similar rapidity of response among our kith and kin of the animal world. The frog's tonguing a bee does not wait for the syllogisms. The spider spins a workable web the first time it tries. The weaver birds plait artistic nests even when kept for generations away from nesting material. These illustrations are not presented to press a Bergsonian similarity of human intuition to animal instinct. They are merely listed as further weights to the thesis that rational knowledge is not the only generative force behind reasonable actions.

Rational knowledge is rational only because it is obtainable through reason. The others obtainable through means other than reason are not irrational; they are extrarational. The gift of the gods is to recognize which is which—

---

1 From "No-Knowledge," in *The Tao of Science*, by R. G. H. Siu. Published jointly by The Technology Press, Massachusetts Institute of Technology, and John Wiley and Sons, New York, 1957.

ideas that are susceptible to rational analysis and ideas that are not. For the executive, sensing the propriety of a particular intuitional judgment is as important as recognizing the soundness of a particular scientific proof.

Broadly speaking, intellectual progress is an advancement in concepts which man has formulated and handed down. But let us dissect the statement further. We should contrast rational knowledge and intuitive knowledge. The role of discovery is quite different in these two forms. In rational knowledge it plays a prominent part; this is where science has contributed greatly. In intuitive knowledge, discovery, of the patent office variety, plays a minor role. Science has not accelerated human development in this area. If anything, she may have dulled man's sensibilities to intuitive riches by her passive and in some instances antagonistic attitudes. All that is intuitively known has been recognized by persons living before, in other settings perhaps, but practiced to equal perfection. Political decisions in international statesmanship, maneuvers and countermaneuvers in military campaigns, estimates of the surges of people in elections, inspiration of poets, painters, and sculptors, conscience of holy men—all have been repetitiously exhibited through the ages. The great works of art of antiquity have never been surpassed or antiquated. The Ecclesiastes and Horace give as much enjoyment to us today as they did to the Hebrews and the Romans before Christ. The silent and formless depth of life had passed many times before the mind of man in its full sweep. This type of knowledge is not enkindled by mathematical formulae and scientific treatises. To pursue this latter means of communication is to remain in the realm of the rational. The inspiration can be shared only by those willing to accept the extrarational sources of enlightenment and keep the flow free from the dam of rational analysis.

Although much advance has been made in the analysis of rational knowledge, intuitive knowledge has not gained the same clarity of assertion and definition. While logic is susceptible to patterned discourse, intuition cannot be systematized in a comparable fashion. This realization tempted many people to regard rational knowledge and intuitive knowledge as opposing schools competing for disciples. Logicians deprecate the fuzziness of intuition; the intuitionists decry the strictures of logic. Actually, there is no exclusiveness of one over the other. Discursive reasoning is not possible without intuition. Consider Langer's example of the syllogism. To her syllogisms are merely devices to lead a person from one intuition to the next. The ability to react with intuitive understanding at each step is a prerequisite to rational analysis.

The emergence of meaning is considered always a matter of logical intuition or insight. In real life this intuitive understanding is not built up step-by-step, as is the case with logical discourse. Instead it is grasped as an immediate total apprehension.

Yet even intuitive knowledge itself is not the ultimate stretch. Sooner or later we hesitate at the limits of rational and intuitive knowledge. Our faltering mind must then seek repose and cure in what it cannot know. At this point the concept of sage-knowledge or no-knowledge is introduced by the Taoists. This is really not knowledge in the ordinary sense. Knowledge, as we understand it in the West, involves the selection of a certain event or quality as the object of knowledge. Sage-knowledge does not do so. It concerns an understanding of what the East calls *Wu* or nonbeing. The *Wu* transcends events and qualities; it has no shape, no time. As a result it cannot be the object of ordinary knowledge. At the higher level of cognizance, the sage forgets distinctions between things. He lives in the silence of what remains in the undifferentiable whole.

An important difference exists between "having-no" knowledge and having "no-knowledge." The former is merely a state of ignorance; the latter is one of ultimate enlightenment and universal sensibilities. To the confirmed rationalist, no-knowledge may appear to be the huggermuggery of the mystagogue. Nevertheless, it is precisely its ineffability that lends force to its reality. The mysteries of nature appear to be mysteries only to those who refuse to participate in them.

It is in this area of no-knowledge that all nature shares a kindred voice. Its utterance is not restricted to the rationality of one species nor to the grammar of one language. It is the reservoir of the evolutionary vestiges shared by all, as they differentiated into their respective genera and forms. There is something of primordial man in the fish; there is something of primordial fish in the man.

Man does not gain simplicity by leading the life of unlettered shepherds or by relinquishing his command of rational knowledge. He gains humility by widening his awareness of the vastness of nature through ungrudging communion with her. Man need not creep on all fours to share the naturalness of the animals, as rabid followers of Rousseau may suggest; he need only converse in the common domain of no-knowledge. It is the art of participation in these pastures that infuses the true zoologist with the deep feeling for the sentiments of animals, so that the observed creatures themselves speak through his data. It is no-knowledge that enables the true botanist to transfuse his own understanding empathetically into the plant kingdom, so that his works breathe through its stomata. . . . It is no-knowledge that stimulates the Taoist artist to paint a forest "as it would appear to the trees themselves" and capture the "tigerishness of the tiger," thereby imparting a feeling of nature that is rarely equaled in Occidental paintings with their anthropocentric overcast.

With rational knowledge, the scientist is a spectator of nature. With no-knowledge, he becomes a participant in nature. There is a communion of understandings. He no longer shares that tragic suffering of many individuals, who [have a] "fear of finding oneself alone," as André Gide describes it, "and so they don't find themselves at all."

To quote the Zen Buddhists:

> An old pine tree preaches wisdom,
> And a wild bird is crying out truth.

. . . Integrity and humility pervade the realm of no-knowledge. There is no question of fame, by-lines, awards, titles, honors. There is only participation. Man does not know selflessness until he has shared no-knowledge with nature.

Creation in research is the fluorescence of no-knowledge. It is the reaching into this area of ineffability and pulling out its rational synonym in a form expressible in our human language. Transformation of one rational cog into another, adaptation of a theory to new systems, conversion of a hypothesis into practical hardware are not creative research. These are merely varieties of tautological research. Such accomplishments, we must hasten to add, are worthy pursuits. They forge the link between theory and utility, between laboratory dreams and human welfare. But they are not creative.

The average scientist regards creativity as an extension of rationality. Prevailing ideas of thermodynamics, quantum mechanics, enzyme-substrate complexes, and so on, are to be thrown like baited hooks into the ocean of knowledge. If this is repeated with sufficient persistence, some hitherto unknown may be hauled in by the lucky fisherman. But such is not the way of creativity. Rational hooks do not sink in the waters of no-knowledge. To plumb the depths of no-knowledge, one must rely on his own ineffable awareness of the ineffable. During this stage rational and factual knowledge is a hindrance and the investigator should keep his mind clear of it. He should try for the complete fusion of his own no-knowledge with the no-knowledge of the comprehended. Only after that ineffable union is affected is an attempt made to transfigure it into a conscious and rational analogue. Current rational knowledge is then tested for adaptability; new, conscious forms of expressions are developed; or the indescribable is left unmentioned. The capacity to realize these difficult syntheses is a rare endowment, and this is why creative genius comes seldom.

There has also been much groping in the West for this concept of no-knowledge. It is unfortunate, however, that considerable effort has been wasted in rationalizing no-knowledge or opposing it competitively with rational knowledge. This belief in the mutual exclusiveness of rational knowledge and no-knowledge traps us into thinking that the absence of one generates the presence of the other. This is not so. . . . If we deal in such "truths of the common sense," we would lose all touch with "truths in the higher sense."

Surrealism as an art form has sought a new knowledge from the subconscious and irrational. Dreams with their mixed reality become a guidepost. In the paintings of Salvador Dali, we see peculiar mixtures of photographically accurate details and incongruous juxtapositions of corpses on the piano, sea shells as eyes, and sewing machines on dissecting tables. These paradoxes were meant to suggest a "second reality" and an inclusion of everything within the whole. The kinship between the subconscious of the surrealist and that of no-knowledge, however, is remote. The dogmatic, aggressive pursuit of the irrational in the former case stands in sharp contrast to the serene reflective passivity in the latter.

Sorokin's analysis of cognition may be taken as an introduction to the Taoist concept of no-knowledge. He recognizes three systems of truth. The first group of propositions deals with sensory aspects of the world. These are confined to the responses of sense organs and are known as Sensate Truth. The second group, or Rational Truth, is obtained through logic, reason, and the scientific method. The third group, or Ideational Truth, is superrational and supersensory. In this last group we may include the direct intuition, revelations, and sudden enlightenment of the Buddhists.

There is only a small departure from Sorokin's triad to the rational, intuitive, and no-knowledge triad presented in this chapter. The Sensate Truth of Sorokin is combined with his Rational Truth in our rational knowledge. Our Intuitive knowledge and no-knowledge are possibly both implied by Sorokin in his Ideational Truth but are separated in our own treatment. In the present discourse intuitive knowledge is considered to be knowledge from a superrational source but generally limited to the human mind. It is an instantaneous integration of unexpressed human thought. No-knowledge is also superrational in origin but is not restricted to the human mind in conception. It is indigenous to all nature. Hence, no-knowledge is not a projection of one's ego into nature; it is nature's ego shared by all. It alone makes man actively intimate with nature. With rational knowledge, one is in tune with the scientific man; with intuitive knowledge added, one is in tune with the total man; with no-knowledge added, one is in tune with nature.

One of the best Taoist poems inspired by no-knowledge is that by Tao Ch'ien of the fourth century. To borrow from Arthur Waley's translation:

> I built my hut in a zone of human habitation,
> Yet near me there sounds no noise of horse or coach,
> > Would you know how that is possible?
> A heart that is distant creates a wilderness around it.
> I pluck chrysanthemums under the eastern hedge,
> Then gaze long at the distant summer hills.
> The mountain air is fresh at the dusk of day;
> The flying birds two by two return.
> In these things there lies a deep meaning;
> Yet when we would express it, words suddenly fail us.

Despite the cool reception by positivists and scientists, the aesthetic sensibilities of the East are not strangers to the West. Shelley's dwelling on the elusiveness of objects and Wordsworth's passion in nature have expressed the feeling of ineffability with intimacy. So have St. Augustine, Nicolas of Cusa, and other Western mystics. What can be more Taoist than Wordsworth's lines:

> To every natural form, rock, fruits or flower
> Even the loose stones that cover the highway,
> I gage a moral life: I saw them feel,
> Or linked them to some feeling: The great mass
> Lay imbedded in a quickening soul, and all
> That I beheld respired with inward meaning.

One of the most sensitive and recent expressions of no-knowledge in the Occidental literature is given by Eugene O'Neill. In the words of the youngest son, Edmund Tyrone, in *Long Day's Journey into Night*, the reminiscence flows on:

When I was on the Squarehead square rigger bound for Buenos Aires. Full moon in the Trades. The old hooker driving 14 knots. I lay on the bowsprit, facing astern, with the water foaming into spume under me. I became drunk with the beauty and singing rhythm of it and for a moment I lost myself—actually lost my life. I dissolved in the sea, became white sails and flying spray, became beauty and rhythm, became moonlight and the ship and the high dim-starred sky. I belonged, without past or future, within peace and unity and a wild joy, within something greater than my own life, or the life of Man, to Life itself! To God, if you want to put it that way.

But how can no-knowledge, which is indescribable and born of silence, be elicited from ourselves? In this respect we should gain some insight into the methodology of learning and inspiration from the East. As Northrop has so well elaborated, there are three conceptual types in the Eastern way of thought. First, there is the concept of the "Differentiated Aesthetic Continuum." This is the initial all-embracing, immediately apprehended totality. The "continuum" emphasizes the all-embracing characteristic; the "differentiated" means that some parts within the continuum are different from others; the "aesthetic" means that there are certain features in the continuum which are qualitatively ineffable. Second, there is the notion of the "Undifferentiated Aesthetic Continuum." This is the continuum component of the parent "Differentiated Aesthetic Continuum" apart from the differentiations. Third, there is the idea of "Differentiations," which are the concrete properties apart from the continuum.

The difference in viewpoint between the East and the West is particularly emphasized in consideration of the concept of the "Undifferentiated Aesthetic Continuum." The idea probably appears untenable to the empirical mind, to which the continuum can but be the total aggregate of the many qualities. The positivism of the West therefore differs from that of the East. The former maintains that the three versions of the East are reducible to the single thought of "Differentiations." The complete meaning is obtained by immediate observations upon atomic objects and properties. It is clear, therefore, that the scientific Westerner would approach a situation by direct and positive assertions and postulations. Things can be theorized about or examined. Nothing need be left undescribed or unsaid.

To the Taoist, there are many observations and sentiments of ineffability. Even in the immediately apprehended, there is the important "Undifferentiated Aesthetic Continuum." It is inconceivable that postulations and positive statements provide us with any contact with such wordless regions of apprehension. As a result of these differences in orientation, the respective methodologies of acquiring knowledge differ significantly between the East and the West. Each has developed techniques especially suitable for the primary interests of its own precincts. The scientific West adopts the positive method and the Taoist East the negative. In the positive method the item under question is intentionally pointed out and described. In the negative method, it is specifically not discussed. By not dissecting the ineffable x in question but merely restricting discourse to objects that it is not, the features of the x are revealed in our dim consciousness.

Many of the parables in the Bible are versions of the negative approach. Even in fields of activity not necessarily close to the church and the book, there is keen appreciation of the indescribability of essences. . . .

One may contrast the negative approach in resistance to evil in Christ's "Turn the other cheek" with the positive approach of the older Hebraic "An eye for an eye." We recall the negative challenge that Garibaldi voiced to his men when the defense of Rome appeared hopeless, "Let them who dare to keep fighting the stranger follow me. I give neither pay nor sustenance. I offer only hunger, forced marches, battle and death." We may also compare the positive approach to attaining independence by Washington's fighting army with the negative approach of Gandhi's passive resistance.

Even among executives we notice not infrequent exploitation of negative methods in imparting the art of leadership. Many of the most effective leaders do not use positive tactics in describing the ways of men and the means of their control and direction. Instead, they merely state to their subordinates what is to be done and criticize inept implementing actions. They do not offer apparently or obviously helpful guidance and advice—a practice contrary to all the good books of management. Sooner or later, if the followers are susceptible to inspirations from the province of no-knowledge, they would gain sudden enlightenment on the ineffable principles of human behavior.

Closely tied to this outlook on the development of executives is the selection of the raw material with which to begin. The advice of Confucius along this line goes something like this:

Refusal to instruct one who is capable of learning entails the waste of a man; instruction of one who is incapable of learning entails the waste of words.

In a similar vein, Chuang-tze tells the story of the Spirit of the Ocean speaking to the Spirit of the River:

You cannot speak of ocean to a well-frog—the creature of a narrower sphere. You cannot speak of ice to a summer insect—the creature of a season. You cannot speak of Tao to a pedagogue; his scope is too limited. But now that you have emerged from your narrow sphere and have seen the great ocean, you know your own insignificance and I can speak to you of great principles.

A subtle use of the negative technique in teaching is also illustrated in the Ch'an story: It seems that a certain teacher stuck out his thumb and remained silent whenever he was asked to explain the Tao. His boy attendant would imitate him. One day when this mimicry occurred, the teacher suddenly chopped off the boy's thumb. Whereupon the boy ran away crying. The teacher called out to him. Just as the boy turned, the teacher again stuck out his thumb. Then and there the boy gained sudden enlightenment.

The positive and the negative strategies are not contradictory nor even distinctly separable. They are complementary facets of the one access to total knowledge. As long as we restrict ourselves to the positive, we merely touch the obvious. To tap the secret springs of deep awareness, we must expand into the negative. Because of emphasis on the latter, however, the Orient has never fully developed the positive skills. For this reason the Orient lacked the clear, logical, and methodical empiricism so necessary for material and industrial progress. In its place it has refined the inscrutable smile of the negative.

For ease of presentation the previous pages discussed separately rational knowledge, intuitive knowledge, and no-knowledge. The classification is more didactic than real. Actually they compose an inseparable unity. They may be looked upon as reflections from different angles of the basic quality that makes man man. As in the case of an athlete, one may develop the agility at running, at shooting a sphere through a hoop, at hooking a disc over ice, at parrying a thrust in mid-air. The respective skills are just various forms of expression of the same native "athletic talent." One does not seek different ghosts within the athlete, which are to be allocated to the respective sports. A special training must be selected, however, to sharpen the proficiency in a given direction. The analogy can be extended to rational knowledge, intuitive knowledge, and no-knowledge and the applicable techniques of the positive and the negative. Each of the forms of knowledge is especially effective for certain games in life. Since we are called upon to play the entire series, unlike the athlete who can select only one sport, we should be equipped with the complete spectrum of understanding.

. . . The chief value of science lies in the introduction of a new way of thought. The method relies on postulation, based on rational knowledge. During the past three hundred years this technique has opened up expansive and heretofore inaccessible vistas. But the acquisition of new jewels does not exhaust the treasure troves of old. The wisdom of the sages, amalgamating the elements of intuitive and no-knowledge, remains untarnished. It is still the basic guidance behind the important decisions affecting man as man. Wisdom is the artful way in which rational knowledge, intuitive knowledge, and no-knowledge are mastered, handled, integrated, and applied. Segmented knowledge, as science is wont to offer through its emphasis on rationality, is hardly wisdom. As Cassirer clearly recognized, the "crisis in man's knowledge of himself" today is the fact that "a central power capable of directing all individual efforts ceased to exist." Unfortunately, Cassirer and others have sought this centralizing power within the exclusive nature of man. . . . In order to penetrate the nature of man, a language beyond the confines of man must be employed. Man cannot know himself through his own knowledge. He must resort to the language of universal scope, that of no-knowledge. This is an important chord for the research executive to remember who is seeking harmony between science and nature.

Lao-tzu: Poems[1]

Existence is beyond the power of words
To define:
Terms may be used
But are none of them absolute.
In the beginning of heaven and earth there
   were no words,
Words came out of the womb of matter;
And whether a man dispassionately
Sees to the core of life
Or passionately
Sees the surface,
The core and the surface
Are essentially the same,
Words making them seem different
Only to express appearance.
If name be needed, wonder names them both:
From wonder into wonder
Existence opens.

    This is the first poem in *The Way of Life*, Witter Bynner's poetic version of Lao-tzu's *Tao Te Ching*. In this Chinese classic, written over two thousand years ago, there is much of the Zen viewpoint. The philosopher Lao-tzu, a contemporary of Confucius was a rare combination of pragmatist and mystic. He maintained that through specific meditative disciplines it was possible—

[1] *The Way of Life, according to Laotzu*, An American Version by Witter Bynner. John Day Company, New York, 1944.

as the Buddha had also affirmed—for any man to make connection with the Absolute. "The way to do is to be," said Lao-tzu. [N. W. R.]

· · · · · · · · ·

> The universe is deathless,
> Is deathless because, having no finite self,
> It stays infinite.
> A sound man by not advancing himself
> Stays the further ahead of himself,
> By not confining himself to himself
> Sustains himself outside himself:
> By never being an end in himself
> He endlessly becomes himself.

· · · · · · · · ·

> Keep stretching a bow
> You repent of the pull,
> A whetted saw
> Goes thin and dull,
> Surrounded with treasure
> You lie ill at ease,
> Proud beyond measure
> You come to your knees:
> Do enough, without vieing,
> Be living, not dying.

· · · · · · · · ·

> Nature does not have to insist,
> Can blow for only half a morning,
> Rain for only half a day,
> And what are these winds and these rains but
>   natural?
> If nature does not have to insist,
> Why should man?
> It is natural too
> That whoever follows the way of life feels alive,
> That whoever uses it properly feels well used,
> Whereas he who loses the way of life feels lost,
> That whoever keeps to the way of life
> Feels at home,
> Whoever uses it properly
> Feels welcome,
> Whereas he who uses it improperly

Feels improperly used:
"Fail to honor people,
They fail to honor you."

. . . .

Everyone says that my way of life is the way
    of a simpleton.
Being largely the way of a simpleton is what
    makes it worth while.
If it were not the way of a simpleton
It would long ago have been worthless,
These possessions of a simpleton being the
    three I choose
And cherish:
To care,
To be fair,
To be humble.
When a man cares he is unafraid,
When he is fair he leaves enough for others,
When he is humble he can grow;
Whereas if, like men of today, he be bold
    without caring,
Self-indulgent without sharing,
Self-important without shame,
He is dead.
The invincible shield
Of caring
Is a weapon from the sky
Against being dead.

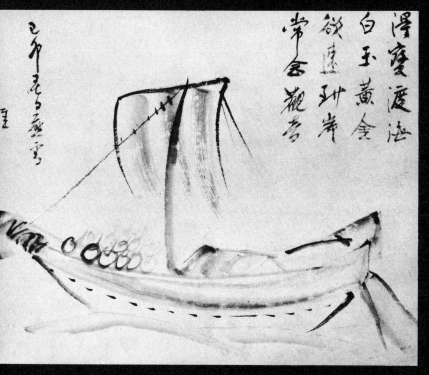

SENGAI

"They are crossing the oceans
Hunting for the treasure
Of white jade and yellow gold
If they wish soon to reach "the other shore"
Let them always be mindful of Kwannon."

(Kwannon is the Goddess of Mercy in the Buddhist pantheon; her great desire is the salvation of all human beings.)

VII ZEN AND THE WEST

1. Spring Sesshin at Shokoku-ji
   Gary Snyder

2. Beat Zen, Square Zen and Zen
   Alan Watts

3. Zen for the West
   William Barrett

CHAPTER 1

Spring Sesshin at Shokoku-ji[1]

By GARY SNYDER

Shokoku Temple is in northern Kyoto, on level ground, with a Christian college just south of it and many blocks of crowded little houses and stone-edged dirt roads north. It is the mother-temple of many branch temples scattered throughout Japan, and one of the several great temple-systems of the Rinzai Sect of Zen. Shokoku-ji is actually a compound: behind the big wood gate and tile-topped crumbling old mud walls are a number of temples each with its own gate and walls, gardens, and acres of wild bamboo grove. In the center of the compound is the soaring double-gabled Lecture Hall, silent and airy, an enormous dragon painted on the high ceiling, his eye burning down on the very center of the cut-slate floor. Except at infrequent rituals the hall is unused, and the gold-gilt Buddha sits on its high platform at the rear untroubled by drums and chanting. In front of the Lecture Hall is a long grove of fine young pines and a large square lotus-pond. To the east is a wooden bell-tower and the unpretentious gate of the *Sodo*, the training school for Zen monks, or Unsui.[2] They will become priests of Shokoku-ji temples. A few,

---

1 "Spring Sesshin at Shokoku-ji," by Gary Snyder. *Chicago Review* Volume 12, Number 2, Summer 1958.

2 *Unsui.* The term is literally "cloud, water"—taken from a line of an old Chinese poem, "To drift like clouds and flow like water." It is strictly a Zen term. The Japanese word for Buddhist monks and priests of all sects is *bozu* (bonze). One takes no formal vows upon becoming an Unsui, although the head is shaved and a long Chinese-style robe called *koromo* is worn within Sodo walls. Unsui are free to quit the Zen community at any time. During the six months of the year in which the Sodo is in session (spring and fall) they eat no meat, but during the summer and winter off-periods they eat, drink, and wear what they will. After becoming temple priests (*Osho*, Chinese *Ho-shang*) the great majority of Zen monks marry and raise families. The present generation of young Unsui is largely from temple families.

after years of *za-zen* (meditation), *koan* study, and final mastery of the *Avatamsaka* (*Kegon*) philosophy, become *Roshi* (Zen Masters), qualified to head Sodos, teach lay groups, or do what they will. Laymen are also permitted to join the Unsui in evening *Zendo* (meditation hall) sessions, and some, like the Unsui, are given a *koan* by the Roshi and receive regular *sanzen*—the fierce face-to-face moment where you spit forth truth or perish—from him. Thus being driven, through time and much *za-zen*, to the very end of the problem.

In the routine of Sodo life, there are special weeks during the year in which gardening, carpentry, reading, and such, are suspended, and the time given over almost entirely to *za-zen*. During these weeks—called *sesshin*, "concentrating the mind"—*sanzen* is received two to four times a day and hours of *za-zen* in the Zendo are much extended. Laymen who will observe the customs of Sodo life and are able to sit still are allowed to join in the *sesshin*. At Shokoku-ji, the spring *sesshin* is held the first week of May.

The *sesshin* starts in the evening. The participants single-file circle into the mat-floored Central Hall of the Sodo and sit in a double row in dim light. The Roshi silently enters, sits at the head, and everyone drinks tea, each fishing his own teacup out of the deep-sleeved black robe. Then the *Jikijitsu*—head Unsui of the Zendo (a position which revolves among the older men, changing every six months)—reads in formal voice the rules of Zendo and *sesshin*, written in medieval Japanese. The Roshi says you all must work very hard; all bow and go out, returning to the Zendo for short meditation and early sleep.

At three A.M. the *Fusu* (another older Zenbo who is in charge of food, finances and meeting people) appears in the Zendo ringing a hand-bell. Lights go on—ten-watt things tacked under the beams of a building lit for centuries by oil lamps—and everyone wordlessly and swiftly rolls up his single quilt and stuffs it in a small cupboard at the rear of his mat, leaps off the raised platform that rings the hall, to the stone floor, and scuffs out in straw sandals to dash icy water on the face from a stone bowl. They come back quickly and sit crosslegged on their *za-zen* cushions, on the same mat used for sleeping. The Jikijitsu stalks in and sits at his place, lighting a stick of incense and beginning the day with the rifleshot crack of a pair of hardwood blocks whacked together and a ding on a small bronze bell. Several minutes of silence, and another whack is heard from the Central Hall. Standing up and slipping on the sandals, the group files out of the Zendo trailing the Jikijitsu—

who hits his bell as he walks—and goes down the roofed stone path, fifty yards long, that joins the Zendo and the Central Hall. Forming two lines and sitting on the mats, they begin to chant *sutras*. The choppy Sino-Japanese words follow the rhythm of a fish-shaped wooden drum and a deep-throated bell. They roar loud and chant fast. The Roshi enters and between the two lines makes deep bows to the Buddha-image before him, lights incense, and retires. The hard-thumping drum and *sutra*-songs last an hour, then suddenly stop and all return to the Zendo. Each man standing before his place, they chant the *Prajna-paramita-hridaya Sutra*, the Jikijitsu going so fast now no one can follow him. Then hoisting themselves onto the mats they meditate. After half an hour a harsh bell-clang is heard from the Roshi's quarters. The Jikijitsu bellows "Getout!" and the Zenbos dash out racing, feet slapping the cold stones and robes flying, to kneel in line whatever order they make it before the *sanzen* room. A ring of the bell marks each new entrance before the Roshi. All one hears from outside is an occasional growl and sometimes the whack of a stick. The men return singly and subdued from *sanzen* to their places.

Not all return. Some go to the kitchen, to light brushwood fires in the brick stoves and cook rice in giant black pots. When they are ready they signal with a clack of wood blocks, and those in the Zendo answer by a ring on the bell. Carrying little nested sets of bowls and extra-large chopsticks, they come down the covered walk. It is getting light, and at this time of year the camellias are blooming. The moss-floored garden on both sides of the walk is thick with them, banks under pine and maple, white flowers glowing through mist. Even the meal, nothing but salty radish pickles and thin rice gruel, is begun and ended by whacks of wood and chanting of short verses. After breakfast the Zenbos scatter: some to wash pots, others to mop the long wood verandas of the central hall and sweep and mop the Roshi's rooms or rake leaves and paths in the garden. The younger Unsui and the outsiders dust, sweep, and mop the Zendo.

The Shokoku-ji Zendo is one of the largest and finest in Japan. It is on a raised terrace of stone and encircled by a stone walk. Outside a long overhang roof and dark unpainted wood—inside round log posts set on granite footings—it is always cool and dark and very still. The floor is square slate laid diagonal. The raised wood platform that runs around the edge has mats for forty men. Sitting in a three-walled box that hangs from the center of the ceiling, like an overhead crane operator, is a life-size wood statue of the

Buddha's disciple Kasyapa, his eyes real and piercing anyone who enters the main door. In an attached room to the rear of the Zendo is a shrine to the founder of Shokoku-ji, his statue in wood, eyes peering out of a dark alcove.

By seven A.M. the routine chores are done and the Jikijitsu invites those cleaning up the Zendo into his room for tea. The Jikijitsu and the Fusu both have private quarters, the Fusu lodging in the Central Hall and the Jikijitsu in a small building adjoining the Zendo. The chill is leaving the air, and he slides open the paper screens, opening a wall of his room to the outside. Sitting on mats and drinking tea they relax and smoke and quietly kid a little, and the Jikijitsu—a tigerish terror during the *za-zen* sessions—is very gentle. "You'll be a Roshi one of these days," a medical student staying the week said to him. "Not me, I can't grasp *koans*," he laughs, rubbing his shaved head where the Roshi has knocked him recently. Then they talk of work to be done around the Sodo. During *sesshin* periods work is kept to a minimum, but some must be done. Taking off robes and putting on ragged old dungarees everyone spreads out, some to the endless task of weeding grass from the moss garden, others to the vegetable plots. The Jikijitsu takes a big mattock and heads for the bamboo-grove to chop out a few bamboo shoots for the kitchen. Nobody works very hard, and several times during the morning they find a warm place in the sun and smoke.

At ten-thirty they quit work and straggle to the kitchen for lunch, the main meal. *Miso*-soup full of vegetables, plenty of rice, and several sorts of pickles. The crunch of bicycles and shouts of children playing around the bell-tower can be heard just beyond the wall. After lunch the laymen and younger Unsui return to the Zendo. More experienced men have the greater responsibilities of running the Sodo, and they keep busy at accounts, shopping, and looking after the needs of the Roshi. Afternoon sitting in the Zendo is informal—newcomers take plenty of time getting comfortable, and occasionally go out to walk and smoke a bit. Conversation is not actually forbidden, but no one wants to talk.

Shortly before three, things tighten up and the Jikijitsu comes in. When everyone is gathered, and a bell heard from the Central Hall, they march out for afternoon *sutra*-chanting. The *sutras* recited vary from day to day, and as the leader announces new titles some men produce books from their sleeves to read by, for not all have yet memorized them completely. Returning to the Zendo, they again recite the *Prajna-paramita-hridaya Sutra*, and the Jikijitsu chants a piece alone, his voice filling the hall, head tilted up to the statue of Kasyapa, hand cupped to his mouth as though calling across miles.

After sitting a few minutes the signal is heard for evening meal, and all file into the kitchen, stand, chant, sit, and lay out their bowls. No one speaks. Food is served with a gesture of "giving" and one stops the server with a gesture of "enough." At the end of the meal—rice and pickles—a pot of hot water is passed and each man pours some into his bowls, swashes it around and drinks it, wipes out his bowls with a little cloth. Then they are nested again, wrapped in their cover, and everyone stands and leaves.

It is dusk and the Zendo is getting dark inside. All the Zenbos begin to assemble now, some with their cushions tucked under arm, each bowing before Kasyapa as he enters. Each man, right hand held up before the chest flat like a knife and cutting the air, walks straight to his place, bows toward the center of the room, arranges the cushions, and assumes the crosslegged "half lotus" posture. Others arrive too—teachers, several college professors, and half a dozen university students wearing the black uniforms that serve for classrooms, bars, and temples equally well—being all they own. Some enter uncertainly and bow with hesitation, afraid of making mistakes, curious to try *za-zen* and overwhelmed by the historical weight of Zen, something very "Japanese" and very "high class." One student, most threadbare of all, had a head shaved like an Unsui and entered with knowledge and precision every night, sitting perfectly still on his cushions and acknowledging no one. By seven-thirty the hall is half-full—a sizeable number of people for present-day Zen sessions—and the great bell in the bell-tower booms. As it booms the man ringing it, swinging a long wood beam ram, sings out a *sutra* over the shops and homes of the neighborhood. When he has finished, the faint lights in the Zendo go on and evening *za-zen* has begun.

The Jikijitsu sits at the head of the hall, marking the half-hour periods with wood clackers and bell. He keeps a stick of incense burning beside him, atop a small wood box that says "not yet" on it in Chinese. At the end of the first half-hour he claps the blocks once and grunts"*kinhin*." This is "walking za-zen," and the group stands—the Unsui tying up sleeves and tucking up robes—and at another signal they start marching single file around the inside of the hall. They walk fast and unconsciously in step, the Jikijitsu leading with a long samurai stride. They circle and circle, through shadow and under the light, ducking below Kasyapa's roost, until suddenly the Jikijitsu claps his blocks and yells "Getout!"—the circle broken and everyone dashing for the door. Night *sanzen*. Through the next twenty minutes they return to resume meditation—not preparing an answer now, but considering the Roshi's response.

Za-zen is a very tight thing. The whole room feels it. The Jikijitsu gets up, grasps a long flat stick and begins to slowly prowl the hall, stick on shoulder, walking before the rows of sitting men, each motionless with eyes half-closed and looking straight ahead downward. An inexperienced man sitting out of balance will be lightly tapped and prodded into easier posture. An Unsui sitting poorly will be without warning roughly knocked off his cushions. He gets up and sits down again. Nothing is said. Anyone showing signs of drowsiness will feel a light tap of the stick on the shoulder. He and the Jikijitsu then bow to each other, and the man leans forward to receive four blows on each side of his back. These are not particularly painful—though the loud whack of them can be terrifying to a newcomer—and serve to wake one well. One's legs may hurt during long sitting, but there is no relief until the Jikijitsu rings his bell. The mind must simply be placed elsewhere. At the end of an hour the bell does ring and the second *kinhin* begins—a welcome twenty minutes of silent rhythmic walking. The walking ends abruptly and anyone not seated and settled when the Jikijitsu whips around the hall is knocked off his cushion. Zen aims at freedom but its practice is disciplined.

Several Unsui slip out during *kinhin*. At ten they return—they can be heard coming, running full speed down the walk. They enter carrying big trays of hot noodles, *udon*, in large lacquer bowls. They bow to the Jikijitsu and circle the room setting a bowl before each man; giving two or even three bowls to those who want them. Each man bows, takes up chopsticks, and eats the noodles as fast as he can. Zenbos are famous for fast noodle-eating and no one wants to be last done. As the empty bowls are set down they are gathered up and one server follows, wiping the beam that fronts the mats with a rag, at a run. At the door the servers stop and bow to the group. It bows in return. Then one server announces the person—usually a friend or patron of the Sodo—who footed the bill for the *sesshin* noodles last night. The group bows again. Meditation is resumed. At ten-thirty there is another rest period and men gather to smoke and chat a little in back. "Are there really some Americans interested in Zen?" they ask with astonishment—for their own countrymen pay them scant attention.

At eleven, bells ring and wood clacks, and final *sutras* are chanted. The hall is suddenly filled with huge voices. The evening visitors take their cushions and leave, each bowing to the Jikijitsu and Kasyapa as he goes. The others flip themselves into their sleeping quilts immediately and lie dead still. The Jikijitsu pads once around, says "Take counsel of your pillow," and walks out. The hall goes black. But this is not the end, for as soon as the lights go out, everyone gets up again and takes his sitting cushion, slips outside, and practices *za-zen* alone wherever he likes for another two hours. The next day begins at three A.M.

This is the daily schedule of the *sesshin*. On several mornings during the week, the Roshi gives a lecture (*teisho*) based on some anecdote in the Zen textbooks—usually from *Mumonkan* or *Hekiganroku*. As the group sits in the Central Hall awaiting his entrance, one Zenbo stands twirling a stick around the edge-tacks of a big drum, filling the air with a deep reverberation. The Roshi sits crosslegged on a very high chair, receives a cup of tea, and delivers lectures that might drive some mad—for he tells these poor souls beating their brains out night after night that "The Perfect Way is without difficulty" and he means it and they know he's right.

In the middle of the week everyone gets a bath and a new head-shave. There is a Zen saying that "while studying *koans* you should not relax even in the bath" but this one is never heeded. The bath-house contains two deep iron tubs, heated by brushwood fires stoked below from outside. The blue smoke and sweet smell of crackling *hinoki* and *sugi* twigs, stuffed in by a fire-tender, and the men taking a long time and getting really clean. Even in the bath-house you bow—to a small shrine high on the wall—both before and after bathing. The Jikijitsu whets up his razor and shaves heads, but shaves his own alone and without mirror. He never nicks himself any more.

On the day after bath they go begging (*takuhatsu*). It rained this day, but putting on oiled-paper slickers over their robes and wearing straw sandals they splashed out. The face of the begging Zenbo can scarcely be seen, for he wears a deep bowl-shaped woven straw hat. They walk slowly, paced far apart, making a weird wailing sound as they go, never stopping. Sometimes they walk for miles, crisscrossing the little lanes and streets of Kyoto. They came back soaked, chanting a *sutra* as they entered the Sodo gate, and added up a meagre take. The rain sluiced down all that afternoon, making a green twilight inside the Zendo and a rush of sound.

The next morning during tea with the Jikijitsu, a college professor who rents rooms in one of the Sodo buildings came in and talked of *koans*. "When you understand Zen, you know that the tree is really *there*."—The only time anyone said anything of Zen philosophy or experience the whole week. Zenbos never discuss *koans* or *sanzen* experience with each other.

The *sesshin* ends at dawn on the eighth day. All who have participated gather in the Jikijitsu's room and drink powdered green tea and eat cakes. They talk easily, it's over. The Jikijitsu, who has whacked or knocked them all during the week, is their great friend now—compassion takes many forms.

CHAPTER 2

Beat Zen, Square Zen, and Zen[1]

By ALAN WATTS

It is as difficult for Anglo-Saxons as for the Japanese to absorb anything quite so Chinese as Zen. For though the word "Zen" is Japanese and though Japan is now its home, Zen Buddhism is the creation of T'ang dynasty China. I do not say this as a prelude to harping upon the incommunicable subtleties of alien cultures. The point is simply that people who feel a profound need to justify themselves have difficulty in understanding the viewpoints of those who do not, and the Chinese who created Zen were the same kind of people as Lao-tzu, who, centuries before, had said, "Those who justify themselves do not convince." For the urge to make or prove oneself right has always jiggled the Chinese sense of the ludicrous, since as both Confucians and Taoists—however different these philosophies in other ways—they have invariably appreciated the man who can "come off it." To Confucius it seemed much better to be human-hearted than righteous, and to the great Taoists, Lao-tzu and Chuang-tzu, it was obvious that one could not be right without also being wrong, because the two were as inseparable as back and front. As Chuang-tzu said, "Those who would have good government without its correlative misrule, and right without its correlative wrong, do not understand the principles of the universe."

To Western ears such words may sound cynical, and the Confucian admiration of "reasonableness" and compromise may appear to be a weak-kneed lack of commitment to principle. Actually they reflect a marvelous under-

---

[1] *Beat Zen, Square Zen, and Zen*, by Alan Watts. City Lights Books, San Francisco, 1959.

standing and respect for what we call the balance of nature, human and otherwise—a universal vision of life as the Tao or way of nature in which the good
and the evil, the creative and the destructive, the wise and the foolish are the
inseparable polarities of existence. "Tao," said the *Chung-yung*, "is that from
which one cannot depart. That from which one can depart is not the Tao."
Therefore wisdom did not consist in trying to wrest the good from the evil
but in learning to "ride" them as a cork adapts itself to the crests and troughs
of the waves. At the roots of Chinese life there is a trust in the good-and-evil
of one's own nature which is peculiarly foreign to those brought up with the
chronic uneasy conscience of the Hebrew-Christian cultures. Yet it was always obvious to the Chinese that a man who mistrusts himself cannot even
trust his mistrust, and must therefore be hopelessly confused. . . .

. . . There is no single reason for the extraordinary growth of Western interest in Zen during the last twenty years. The appeal of Zen arts to the
"modern" spirit in the West, the work of Suzuki, the war with Japan, the
itchy fascination of "Zen-stories," and the attraction of a non-conceptual,
experiential philosophy in the climate of scientific relativism—all these are
involved. One might mention, too, the affinities between Zen and such purely
Western trends as the philosophy of Wittgenstein, Existentialism, General
Semantics, the metalinguistics of B. L. Whorf, and certain movements in the
philosophy of science and in psychotherapy. Always in the background there
is our vague disquiet with the artificiality or "anti-naturalness" of both
Christianity, with its politically ordered cosmology, and technology, with
its imperialistic mechanization of a natural world from which man himself
feels strangely alien. For both reflect a psychology in which man is identified
with a conscious intelligence and will standing apart from nature to control
it, like the architect-God in whose image this version of man is conceived.
The disquiet arises from the suspicion that our attempt to master the world
from outside is a vicious circle in which we shall be condemned to the per-
petual insomnia of controlling controls and supervising supervision *ad in-
finitum*.

To the Westerner in search of the reintegration of man and nature there
is an appeal far beyond the merely sentimental in the naturalism of Zen—
in the landscapes of Ma-yuan and Sesshu, in an art which is simultaneously
spiritual and secular, which conveys the mystical in terms of the natural,
and which, indeed, never even imagined a break between them. Here is a
view of the world imparting a profoundly refreshing sense of wholeness to a

culture in which the spiritual and the material, the conscious and the un-conscious, have been cataclysmically split. For this reason the Chinese humanism and naturalism of Zen intrigue us much more strongly than Indian Buddhism or Vedanta. These, too, have their students in the West, but their followers seem for the most part to be displaced Christians—people in search of a more plausible philosophy than Christian supernaturalism to carry on the essentially Christian search for the miraculous. The ideal man of Indian Buddhism is clearly a superman, a *yogi* with absolute mastery of his own nature, according perfectly with the science-fiction ideal of "men beyond mankind." But the Buddha or awakened man of Chinese Zen is "ordinary and nothing special"; he is humorously human like the Zen tramps portrayed by Mu-chi and Liang-k'ai. We like this because here, for the first time, is a conception of the holy man and sage who is not impossibly remote, not super-human but fully human, and, above all, not a solemn and sexless ascetic. Furthermore, in Zen the *satori* experience of awakening to our "original in-separability" with the universe seems, however elusive, always just around the corner. . . .

. . . Above all, I believe that Zen appeals to many in the post-Christian West because it does not preach, moralize and scold in the style of Hebrew-Christian prophetism. Buddhism does not deny that there is a relatively limited sphere in which human life may be improved by art and science, reason and good-will. However, it regards this sphere of activity as important but nonetheless subordinate to the comparatively limitless sphere in which things are as they are, always have been, and always will be—a sphere entirely beyond the categories of good and evil, success and failure, and individual health and sickness. . . .

. . . The Hebrew-Christian universe is one in which moral urgency, the anxiety to be right, embraces and penetrates everything. God, the Absolute itself, is good as against bad, and thus to be immoral or in the wrong is to feel oneself an outcast not merely from human society but also from existence itself, from the root and ground of life. To be in the wrong therefore arouses a metaphysical anxiety and sense of guilt—a state of eternal damnation—utterly disproportionate to the crime. This metaphysical guilt is so insupportable that it must eventually issue in the rejection of God and his laws—which is just what has happened in the whole movement of modern secularism, mate-rialism, and naturalism. Absolute morality is profoundly destructive of morality, for the sanctions which it invokes against evil are far, far too heavy.

One does not cure the headache by cutting off the head. The appeal of Zen, as of other forms of Eastern philosophy, is that it unveils behind the urgent realm of good and evil a vast region of oneself about which there need be no guilt or recrimination, where at last the self is indistinguishable from God.

But the Westerner who is attracted by Zen and who would understand it deeply must have one indispensable qualification: he must understand his own culture so thoroughly that he is no longer swayed by its premises unconsciously. He must really have come to terms with the Lord God Jehovah and with his Hebrew-Christian conscience so that he can take it or leave it without fear or rebellion. He must be free of the itch to justify himself. Lacking this, his Zen will be either "beat" or "square," either a revolt from the culture and social order or a new form of stuffiness and respectability. For Zen is above all the liberation of the mind from conventional thought, and this is something utterly different from rebellion against convention, on the one hand, or adapting foreign conventions, on the other.

Conventional thought is, in brief, the confusion of the concrete universe of nature with the conceptual things, events, and values of linguistic and cultural symbolism. For in Taoism and Zen the world is seen as an inseparably interrelated field or continuum, no part of which can actually be separated from the rest or valued above or below the rest. It was in this sense that Hui-neng, the Sixth Patriarch, meant that "fundamentally not one thing exists," for he realized that things are *terms*, not entities. They exist in the abstract world of thought, but not in the concrete world of nature. Thus one who actually perceives or feels this to be so no longer feels that he is an ego, except by definition. He sees that his ego is his *persona* or social role, a somewhat arbitrary selection of experiences with which he has been taught to identify himself. (Why, for example, do we say "I think" but not "I am beating my heart?") Having seen this, he continues to play his social role without being taken in by it. He does not precipitately adopt a new role or play the role of having no role at all. . . .

The "beat" mentality as I am thinking of it is something much more extensive and vague than the hipster life of New York and San Francisco. It is a younger generation's nonparticipation in "the American Way of Life," a revolt which does not seek to change the existing order but simply turns away from it to find the significance of life in subjective experience rather than objective achievement. It contrasts with the "square" and other-directed mentality of beguilement by social convention, unaware of the correlativity of right and wrong. . . .

Beat Zen is a complex phenomenon. It ranges from a use of Zen for justifying sheer caprice in art, literature, and life to a very forceful social criticism and "digging of the universe" such as one may find in the poetry of Ginsberg, Whalen and Snyder, and, rather unevenly, in Kerouac, who is always a shade too self-conscious, too subjective, and too strident to have the flavor of Zen.

. . . It is indeed the basic intuition of Zen that there is an ultimate standpoint from which "anything goes." In the celebrated words of the master Yun-men, "Every day is a good day." Or as is said in the *Hsin-hsin Ming:*

> If you want to get the plain truth,
> Be not concerned with right and wrong.
> The conflict between right and wrong
> Is the sickness of the mind.

But this standpoint does not exclude and is not hostile towards the distinction between right and wrong at other levels and in more limited frames of reference. The world is seen to be beyond right and wrong when it is not framed: that is to say, when we are not looking at a particular situation by itself—out of relation to the rest of the universe. Within this room there is a clear difference between up and down; out in interstellar space there is not. Within the conventional limits of a human community there are clear distinctions between good and evil. But these disappear when human affairs are seen as part and parcel of the whole realm of nature. Every framework sets up a restricted field of relationships, and restriction is law or rule.

Now a skilled photographer can point his camera at almost any scene or object and create a marvelous composition by the way in which he frames and lights it. An unskilled photographer attempting the same thing creates only messes, for he does not know how to place the frame, the border of the picture, where it will be in relation to the contents. How eloquently this demonstrates that as soon as we introduce a frame anything does *not* go. But every work of art involves a frame. A frame of some kind is precisely what distinguishes a painting, a poem, a musical composition, a play, a dance, or a piece of sculpture from the rest of the world. Some artists may argue that they do not want their works to be distinguishable from the total universe, but if this be so they should not frame them in galleries and concert halls. Above all they should not sign them nor sell them. This is as immoral as selling the moon or signing one's name to a mountain. . . .

Today there are Western artists avowedly using Zen to justify the indiscriminate framing of simply anything—blank canvases, totally silent music, torn up bits of paper dropped on a board and stuck where they fall, or dense masses of mangled wire. . . .

Just as the skilled photographer often amazes us with his lighting and framing of the most unlikely subjects, so there are painters and writers in the West, as well as in modern Japan, who have mastered the authentically Zen art of controlling accidents. Historically this first arose in the Far-East in the appreciation of the rough texture of brush-strokes in calligraphy and painting, and in the accidental running of the glaze on bowls made for the tea-ceremony. One of the classical instances of this kind of thing came about through the shattering of a fine ceramic tea-caddy, belonging to one of the old Japanese tea-masters. The fragments were cemented together with gold, and its owner was amazed at the way in which the random network of thin gold lines enhanced its beauty. It must be remembered, however, that this was an *objet trouvé*—an accidental effect selected by a man of exquisite taste, and treasured as one might treasure and exhibit a marvelous rock or a piece of driftwood. For in the Zen-inspired art of *bonseki* or rock-gardening, the stones are selected with infinite care, and though the hand of man may never have changed them it is far from true that any old stone will do. Furthermore, in calligraphy, painting, and ceramics, the accidental effects of running glaze or of flying hair-lines of the brush were only accepted and presented by the artist when he felt them to be fortuitous and unexpected marvels within the context of the work as a whole.

What governed his judgment? What gives *certain* accidental effects in painting the same beauty as the accidental outlines of clouds? According to Zen feeling there is no precise rule, no rule, that is to say, which can be formulated in words and taught systematically. On the other hand, there is in all these things a principle of order which in Chinese philosophy is termed *li*, and which Joseph Needham has translated "organic pattern." *Li* originally meant the markings in jade, the grain in wood, and the fiber in muscle. It designates a type of order which is too multi-dimensional, too subtly interrelated, and too squirmingly vital to be represented in words or mechanical images. The artist has to know it as he knows how to grow his hair. He can do it again and again, but can never explain how. In Taoist philosophy this power is called *te*, or "magical virtue." It is the element of the miraculous which we feel both at the stars in heaven and at our own ability to be conscious.

It is the possession of *te*, then, which makes all the difference between mere scrawls and the "white writing" of Mark Tobey which admittedly derived its inspiration from Chinese calligraphy. It was by no means a purely haphazard drooling of paint or uncontrolled wandering of the brush, for the character and taste of such an artist is visible in the grace (a possible equivalent of *te*) with which his strokes are formed even when he is not trying to represent anything except strokes. It is also what makes the difference between mere patches, smudges, and trails of black ink and the work of such Japanese moderns as Sabro Hasegawa and Onchi, which is after all in the *haboku* or "rough style" tradition of Sesshu. Anyone can write absolutely illegible Japanese, but who so enchantingly as Ryokwan? If it is true that "when the wrong man uses the right means, the right means work in the wrong way," it is often also true that when the right man uses the wrong means, the wrong means work in the right way.

The real genius of Chinese and Japanese Zen artists in their use of controlled accidents goes beyond the discovery of fortuitous beauty. It lies in being able to express, at the level of artistry, the realization of that ultimate standpoint from which "anything goes" and at which "all things are of one suchness." The mere selection of any random shape to stick in a frame simply confuses the metaphysical and the artistic domains; it does not express the one in terms of the other. Set in a frame, any old mess is at once cut off from the totality of its natural context, and for this very reason its manifestation of the Tao is concealed. The formless murmur of night noises in a great city has an enchantment which immediately disappears when formally presented as music in a concert hall. A frame outlines a universe, a microcosm, and if the contents of the frame are to rank as art they must have the same quality of relationship to the whole and to each other as events in the great universe, the macrocosm of nature. In nature the accidental is always recognized in relation to what is ordered and controlled. The dark *yin* is never without the bright *yang*. Thus the painting of Sesshu, the calligraphy of Ryokwan, and the ceramic bowls of the Hagi or Karatsu schools reveal the wonder of accidents in nature through accidents in a context of highly disciplined art.

The realization of the unswerving "rightness" of whatever happens is no more manifested by utter lawlessness in social conduct than by sheer caprice in art. As Zen has been used as a pretext for the latter in our times, its use as a pretext for the former is ancient history. Many a rogue has justified himself with the Buddhist formula, "Birth-and-death (*samsara*) is Nirvana; worldly

337

passions are Enlightenment." This danger is implicit in Zen because it is implicit in freedom. Power and freedom can never be safe. They are dangerous in the same way that fire and electricity are dangerous. But it is quite pitiful to see Zen used as a pretext for license when the Zen in question is no more than an idea in the head, a simple rationalization. To some extent "Zen" is so used in the underworld which often attaches itself to artistic and intellectual communities. After all, the Bohemian way of life is primarily the natural consequence of artists and writers being so absorbed in their work that they have no interest in keeping up with the Joneses. It is also a symptom of creative changes in manners and morals which at first seem as reprehensible to conservatives as new forms in art. But every such community attracts a number of weak imitators and hangers-on, especially in the great cities, and it is mostly in this class that one now finds the stereotype of the "beatnik" with his phony Zen. Yet if Zen were not the pretext for this shiftless existence, it would be something else. . . .

Now the underlying protestant lawlessness of beat Zen disturbs the square Zennists very seriously. For square Zen is the Zen of established tradition in Japan with its clearly defined hierarchy, its rigid discipline, and its specific tests of *satori*. More particularly, it is the kind of Zen adopted by Westerners studying in Japan, who will before long be bringing it back home. . . . It is . . . square because it is a quest for the *right* spiritual experience, for a *satori* which will receive the stamp (*inka*) of approval and established authority. There will even be certificates to hang on the wall.

If square Zen falls into any serious excess it is in the direction of spiritual snobbism and artistic preciousness, though I have never known an orthodox Zen teacher who could be accused of either. These gentlemen seem to take their exalted office rather lightly, respecting its dignity without standing on it. The faults of square Zen are the faults of any spiritual in-group with an esoteric discipline and degrees of initiation. . . .

The student of square Zen is also inclined at times to be niggling in his recognition of parallels to Zen in other spiritual traditions. Because the essentials of Zen can never be accurately and fully formulated, being an experience and not a set of ideas, it is always possible to be critical of anything anyone says about it, neither putting up nor shutting up. Any statement about Zen, or about spiritual experience of any kind, will always leave some aspect, some subtlety, unexpressed. No one's mouth is big enough to utter the whole thing. The Western follower of Zen should also resist the temptation to associate himself with an even worse form of snobbery, the intellectual snobbery so largely characteristic of Far-Eastern studies in American universities. In this particular field the fad for making humanistic studies "scientific" has gone to such wild extremes that even Suzuki is accused of being a "popularizer" instead of a serious scholar—presumably because he is a little unsystematic about footnotes and covers a vast area instead of confining himself with rigor to a single problem, e. g., "An Analysis of Some Illegible and Archaic Character-forms in the Tun-huang Manuscripts of the Sutra of the Sixth Patriarch." There is a proper and honorable place in scholarship for the meticulous drudge, but when he is on top instead of on tap his dangerous envy of real intelligence drives all creative scholars from the field.[2]

In its artistic expression square Zen is often rather tediously studied and precious, a fate which all too easily befalls a venerable aesthetic tradition when its techniques are so highly developed that it takes a lifetime to master any one of them. No one has then the time to go beyond the achievements of the old masters, so that new generations are condemned to endless repetition and imitation of their refinements. The student of *sumi*-painting, calligraphy, *haiku*-poetry, or tea-ceremony can therefore get trapped in a tiresomely repetitive affectation of styles, varied only with increasingly esoteric allusions to the work of the past. When this comes to the point of imitating the old masters' happy accidents in such a way that "primitive" and "rough" effects are produced by the utmost practice and deliberation, the whole thing becomes so painful that even the wildest excesses of beat Zen art look refreshing. Indeed, it is possible that beat Zen and square Zen will so complement and rub against one another that an amazingly pure and lively Zen will arise from the hassle.

For this reason I see no really serious quarrel with either extreme. There was never a spiritual movement without its excesses and distortions. The experience of awakening which truly constitutes Zen is too timeless and universal to be injured. The extremes of beat Zen need alarm no one, since, as Blake said, "the fool who persists in his folly will become wise." As for square Zen, "authoritative" spiritual experiences have always had a way of wearing

---

[2] Suzuki, incidentally, is a very rare bird among contemporary Asians—an original thinker. He is no mere mouthpiece for any fixed tradition, and has come forth with some ideas about comparative religion and the psychology of religion which are of enormous importance, quite aside from what he has done to translate and interpret the literature of Zen. But it is just for this reason that people in square Zen and academic sinology have their qualms about accepting him.

thin, and thus of generating the demand for something genuine and unique which needs no stamp.

... *Satori* can lie along both roads. It is the concomitant of a "non-grasping" attitude of the senses to experience, and grasping can be exhausted by the discipline of directing its utmost intensity to a single, ever-elusive objective. But what makes the way of effort and will-power suspect to many Westerners is not so much an inherent laziness as a thorough familiarity with the wisdom of our own culture. The square Western Zennists are often quite naïve when it comes to an understanding of Christian theology or of all that has been discovered in modern psychiatry, for both have long been concerned with the fallibility and unconscious ambivalence of the will. Both have posed problems as to the vicious circle of seeking self-surrender or of "free-associating on purpose" or of accepting one's conflicts to escape from them, and to anyone who knows anything about either Christianity or psychotherapy these are very real problems. The interest of Chinese Zen and of people like Bankei is that they deal with these problems in a most direct and stimulating way, and begin to suggest some answers. But when Herrigel's Japanese archery master was asked, "How can I give up purpose on purpose?" he replied that no one had ever asked him that before. He [Herrigel] had no answer except to go on trying blindly, for five years.

Foreign religions can be immensely attractive and highly overrated by those who know little of their own, and especially by those who have not worked through and grown out of their own. This is why the displaced or unconscious Christian can so easily use either beat or square Zen to justify himself. The one wants a philosophy to justify him in doing what he pleases. The other wants a more plausible authoritative salvation than the Church or the psychiatrists seem to be able to provide. . . .

The old Chinese Zen masters were steeped in Taoism. They saw nature in its total interrelatedness, and saw that every creature and every experience is in accord with the Tao of nature just as it is. This enabled them to accept themselves as they were, moment by moment, without the least need to justify anything . . .

> In the landscape of Spring there is neither better
>   nor worse;
> The flowering branches grow naturally, some long,
>   some short.

CHAPTER 3

Zen for the West[1]

By WILLIAM BARRETT

I

Zen Buddhism presents a surface so bizarre and irrational, yet so colorful and striking, that some Westerners who approach it for the first time fail to make sense of it, while others, attracted by this surface, take it up in a purely frivolous and superficial spirit. Either response would be unfortunate. The fact is that Zen, as Dr. Suzuki demonstrates, is an essential expression of Buddhism and Buddhism is one of the most tremendous spiritual achievements in human history—an achievement which we Westerners probably have not yet fully grasped. We have to remember how recent it is that we have sought out any knowledge of the East. Only a century separates us from Schopenhauer, the first Western philosopher who attempted a sympathetic interpretation of Buddhism, a brilliant and sensational misunderstanding on the basis of meagre translations. Since then great strides have been made in Oriental studies, but a curiously paradoxical provincialism still haunts the West: the civilization which has battered its way into every corner of the globe has been very tardy in examining its own prejudices by the wisdom of the non-Western peoples. Even today when the slogan "One World!" is an incessant theme of Sunday journalism and television, we tend to interpret it in a purely Western sense to mean merely that the whole planet is now bound together in the net of modern technology and communications. That the phrase may imply a necessity for coming to terms with our Eastern opposite

[1] "Zen for the West," by William Barrett. Introduction to *Zen Buddhism*, by D. T. Suzuki. Anchor Books, New York, 1956.

and brother, seems to pass publicly unnoticed. There are many signs, however, that this tide must turn.

I consider it a great stroke of personal good fortune to have stumbled (and quite by chance) upon the writings of D. T. Suzuki years ago. I emphasize the word "personal" here because I am not a professional Orientalist and my interest in Suzuki's writings has been what it is simply because these writings shed light upon problems in my own life—one proof that Zen does have a much needed message for Westerners. There are now a good many books available on Buddhism, but what makes Suzuki unique—and unique not only among writers on Buddhism but among contemporary religious writers generally—is that he starts from the assumption that Buddhism is a living thing that began some 2500 years ago with Gotama's experience of enlightenment, has been developing ever since, and is still alive and growing. Hence the extraordinary freshness and vitality of his writings, so that if you go on from them to other books on Buddhism you will find that these latter take on a life from him that they themselves would never have initially for the Westerner. Suzuki has steeped himself thoroughly in Chinese Buddhism, and the practical and concrete Chinese spirit probably provides an introduction to Buddhism more congenial to the Westerner than the soaring metaphysical imagination of the Indians. One picture is worth a thousand words, as the old Chinese saying has it, and this Chinese genius for the concrete may never have been better realized than in the anecdotes, paradoxes, poems of the Zen masters. Westerners usually think that the religious and philosophic thought of China is summed up in the two names of Lao-tsu and Confucius; Suzuki shows us that some of the great figures of Chinese Buddhism were at least the equal of these two. And if his writings did nothing else, they would still be important for giving us knowledge of this great chapter of Buddhist history that had been virtually unknown to us hitherto.

But do these ancient Oriental masters have anything to say to us who belong to the present-day West? Very much so, I think; and the reason is that we Westerners have only recently come to face certain realities of life with which the Oriental has been living for centuries. This is a large claim, and requires some itemized documentation.

What we call the Western tradition is formed by two major influences, Hebraic and Greek, and both these influences are profoundly dualistic in spirit. That is, they divide reality into two parts and set one part off against the other. The Hebrew makes his division on religious and moral grounds: God absolutely transcends the world, is absolutely separate from it; hence there follow the dualisms of God and creature, the Law and the erring members, spirit and flesh. The Greek, on the other hand, divides reality along intellectual lines. Plato, who virtually founded Western philosophy single-handed—Whitehead has remarked that 2500 years of Western philosophy is but a series of footnotes to Plato—absolutely cleaves reality into the world of the intellect and the world of the senses. The great achievement of the Greeks was to define the ideal of rationality for man; but in doing so, Plato and Aristotle not only made reason the highest and most valued function, they also went so far as to make it the very center of our personal identity. The Orientals never succumbed to this latter error; favoring intuition over reason, they grasped intuitively a center of the personality which held in unity the warring opposites of reason and unreason, intellect and senses, morality and nature. So far as we are Westerners, we inherit these dualisms, they are part of us: an irrationally nagging conscience from the Hebrews, an excessively dividing rational mind from the Greeks. Yet the experience of modern culture, in the most diverse fields, makes them less and less acceptable.

Medieval Christianity still lives in the rational world of the Greeks. The universe of St. Thomas Aquinas is the same bandbox universe of Aristotle, a tight tiny tidy rational whole, where all is in apple-pie order, and everything occupies its logical and meaningful place in the absolute hierarchy of Being. When we turn from such humanized universes to Indian thought, we are at first staggered by the vision of vast spaces, endless aeons of time, universe upon universe, against which man looks very small and meaningless; then we realize these are the spaces and times of modern astronomy, and the Indian idea is therefore closer to us. The distinguished Protestant theologian Paul Tillich has described the essential experience of modern man as an encounter with "meaninglessness": lost in the vastness of the universe, man begins to think that his own existence and that of the universe are "meaningless." The God of Theism, says Tillich echoing Nietzsche, is dead, and Western man must find a God beyond the God of Theism: the God offered us by rational theology is no longer acceptable. From the point of view of the medieval Catholic (and many still survive) the very premises of Buddhist thinking would look "meaningless"; they are also more difficult and grim, but they look much closer to what we moderns may have to swallow.

In science itself, modern developments have combined to make our inherited rationalism more shaky. Physics and mathematics, the two most advanced of Western sciences, have in our time become paradoxical: that is, arrived at the state where they breed paradoxes for reason itself. One hundred fifty years ago the philosopher Kant attempted to show that there were ineluctable limits to reason, but the Western mind, positivistic to the core, could be expected to take such a conclusion seriously only when it showed up in science itself. Well, science in this century has at last caught up with Kant: almost simultaneously Heisenberg in physics, and Godel in mathematics, have shown ineluctable limits to human reason. Heisenberg's Principle of Indeterminacy shows essential limits to our ability to know and predict physical states of affairs, and opens up to us the glimpse of a nature irrational and chaotic at bottom. Godel's results would seem to have even more far-reaching consequences when one reflects that in the Western tradition, from the Pythagoreans and Plato onward, mathematics has inspired the most absolute claims of rationalism. Now it turns out that even in his most precise science—in the province where his reason had seemed omnipotent—man cannot escape his essential finitude: every system of mathematics that he constructs is doomed to incompleteness. Mathematics is like a ship in mid-ocean that has sprung leaks (paradoxes) which have been temporarily plugged, but our reason can never guarantee that the ship will not spring other leaks. That this human insecurity should manifest itself in what had hitherto been the very citadel of reason, mathematics, marks a new turn in Western thinking. The next step would be to recognize the essentially paradoxical nature of reason itself.

This step has been taken by some modern philosophers. The most original and influential philosopher now alive on the European continent is the German Existentialist Martin Heidegger. A German friend of Heidegger told me that one day when he visited Heidegger he found him reading one of Suzuki's books; "If I understand this man correctly," Heidegger remarked, "this is what I have been trying to say in all my writings." This remark may be the slightly exaggerated enthusiasm of a man under the impact of a book in which he recognizes some of his own thoughts; certainly Heidegger's philosophy in its tone and temper and sources is Western to its core, and there is much in him that is not in Zen, but also very much more in Zen that is not in Heidegger; and yet the points of correspondence between the two, despite their disparate sources, are startling enough. For what, after all, is Heidegger's final message but that Western philosophy is a great error, the result of the dichotomizing intellect that has cut man off from unity with Being itself and from his own Being. This error begins (in Plato) with locating truth in the intellect; the world of nature thereby becomes a realm of objects set over against the mind, eventually objects to be manipulated by scientific and practical calculation. Twenty-five hundred years of Western metaphysics move from Plato's intellectualism to Nietzsche's Will to Power, and concurrently man does become in fact the technological master of the whole planet; but the conquest of nature merely estranges him from Being itself and from his own Being and delivers him over to an ever ascending, ever more frantic will to power. "Divide and conquer" might thus be said to be the motto which Western man has adopted toward Being itself; but this of course is the counsel of power not of wisdom. Heidegger repeatedly tells us that this tradition of the West has come to the end of its cycle; and as he says this, one can only gather that he himself has already stepped beyond that tradition. Into the tradition of the Orient? I should say at least that he has come pretty close to Zen.

If these happenings in science and philosophy indicate changed ways of thinking in the West, our modern art would seem to indicate very new ways of feeling. Whatever may be said on the thorny subject of modern art, the one fact that is clear is that to the artistic conservative it represents a scandal and a break with the tradition. Our modern art presents a surface so irrational, bizarre, and shocking that it must be considered a break with the older more rational canons of Western art. That Western painters and sculptors in this century have gone outside their tradition to nourish themselves with the art of the rest of the world—Oriental, African, Melanesian—signifies that what we knew as *the* tradition is no longer able to nourish its most creative members; its confining mould has broken, under pressures from within. Our painting has detached itself from three-dimensional space, the arena of Western man's power and mobility; detached itself from the object, the supreme fixation of Western man's extroversion; and it has become subjective, contrary to the whole tenor of our Western life. Is all this merely malaise and revolt, or prophecy of a different spirit to come? In the past, new styles in painting have often been thus prophetic. In the art of literature, of course, the writer can be vocal about the new and revolutionary thing, and we find a novelist like D. H. Lawrence preaching against the bloodless rationalism of his culture. Lawrence urged the necessity of something he called "mindlessness," of becoming "mindless," if the meddlesome and self-conscious intellect

345

were not in the end to cut off Western man irreparably from nature and even the possibility of real sexual union. Oddly enough, this "mindlessness" of Lawrence is a groping intuition after the doctrine of "no-mind" which Zen Buddhism had elaborated a thousand years before. . . . Unlike Lawrence, however, the Zen masters developed this doctrine without falling into primitivism and the worship of the blood. In Lawrence's behalf it must be remembered that his culture gave him no help at all on these matters, and he had to grope in the dark pretty much on his own. And to change to one final literary example that involves no preaching or thesis whatsoever: the most considerable work of prose in English in this century is probably James Joyce's *Ulysses*, and this is so profoundly Oriental a book that the psychologist C. G. Jung recommended it as a long-needed bible for the white-skinned peoples. Joyce shattered the aesthetic of the Georgians that would divide reality into a compartment of the Beautiful forever separate from the opposite compartments of the Ugly or Sordid. *Ulysses*, like the Oriental mind, succeeds in holding the opposites together: light and dark, beautiful and ugly, sublime and banal. The spiritual premise of this work is an acceptance of life that no dualism—whether puritanical or aesthetic—could ever possibly embrace.

Admittedly, all these happenings I have cited—from science, philosophy, art—make up a very selective list; this list could be expanded greatly; nevertheless even as it stands, these instances make up a body of "coincidence" so formidable that they must make us pause. When events run parallel this way, when they occur so densely together in time and in such diverse fields, they can no longer be considered as mere meaningless "coincidence" but as very meaningful symptoms; in this case symptoms that the West in its own depths begins to experience new things, begins in fact to experience its own opposite. In this new climate a concern with something like Zen Buddhism can no longer be taxed as idle exoticism, for it has to do with the practical daily bread of the spirit.

The really somber paradox about all these changes is that they have happened in the deep and high parts of our culture, while in the areas in between everything goes on as usual. Despite the discoveries of its artists, philosophers, theoretical scientists, the West, in its public and external life at any rate, is just as Western as ever, if not more so. Gadgets and traffic accumulate, the American way of life (or else the Russian) spreads all over the globe, the techniques for externalizing life become year by year more slick and clever.

All of which may only show what a creature of contradictions Western man has become. And now that at last his technology has put in his hands the hydrogen bomb, this fragmented creature has the power to blow himself and his planet to bits. Plain common sense would seem to advise that he turn to look inward a little.

II

None of the above considerations has to do with Zen itself. Or rather—to put it abruptly as Zen likes to do—Zen has nothing at all to do with them. They deal with the complicated abstractions of the intellect—philosophy, culture, science, and the rest—and what Zen seeks above all is the concrete and the simple that lie beyond the snarled tangles of intellectualization. Zen *is* the concrete itself. Zen eschews abstractions, or uses them only to get beyond them. Even when Zen declares against abstractions, it has to put the matter concretely: thus when the great Master Tokusan has his enlightenment, he does not merely say in pallid fashion that concepts are not enough; no, he burns all his philosophic texts, declaring, "All our understanding of the abstractions of philosophy is like a single hair in the vastness of space." Let the Western reader fasten upon this image and he will find it harder to miss the point. Or when another Master remarks on the difficulty of solving one of the Zen questions—which is equivalent to answering the riddle of existence itself—he does not merely say that it is difficult or so very very difficult that it is well-nigh impossible, but this: "It is like a mosquito trying to bite into an iron bull." The image lives because the image suggests the meaning beyond conceptualization.

Now it is just this concreteness of expression, this extraordinary profusion of images and examples, that can make Zen most helpful to the Westerner, who in fact derives from a more highly abstract culture. But it would be a mistake for the Western reader to imagine that these are merely so many literary devices or adornments adopted by the Zen masters. On the contrary, the language of Zen is of the essence, the manner of expression is one with the matter. Zen expresses itself concretely because Zen is above all interested in facts not theories, in realities and not those pallid counters for reality which we know as concepts. "Fact" may suggest to the Western mind something merely quantitative or statistical—therefore also a lifeless and abstract thing. Zen wants, rather, the facts as living and concrete. In this sense, Zen might be described as Radical Intuitionism—if the Westerner wishes a handle by which to lay hold of it. This does not mean that it is merely a philosophy of intuition like Bergson's, though it agrees with Bergson that the conceptualizing intellect does not reach reality; rather, it is radical intuition in the act itself. Radical Intuitionism means that Zen holds that thinking and sensing live, move, and have their being within the vital medium of intuition. We see with the two eyes only insofar as we are also seeing (though we may not know it) with the third eye—the eye of intuition. Hence, any sensory facts will do for Zen provided they serve to awaken the third eye, and we encounter in the Zen writings the most extraordinary incidents of illumination in connection with the most humble objects. In the end all language is pointing: we use language to point beyond language, beyond concepts to the concrete. The monk asks the Master, "How may I enter in the Way?", and the Master, pointing to the mountain spring, responds, "Do you hear the sound of that torrent? There you may enter." Another time Master and monk are walking upon the mountain, and the Master asks, "Do you smell the mountain laurel?" "Yes." "There, I have held nothing back from you."

In its emphasis upon the living fact over the mere idea, Zen is true to the essential teaching of Buddha. Buddha cared very little for the philosophers; there were said to be already some 63 schools in existence in his time, and he had occasion to observe from their wrangling how imprisoned in the labyrinths of the intellect the human spirit can become. Thus Zen itself is not a philosophy (the Western reader must be warned here), though there lie behind it some of the great philosophies of Mahayana Buddhism. Though Buddha began by opposing the philosophers, nevertheless in the course of its history Buddhism evolved one of the greatest and most profound philosophies ever created. Is this a contradiction of the original spirit of the founder? No; for Buddhist philosophy is activated by an altogether different purpose from that of Western philosophy: Buddhism takes up philosophy only as a device to save the philosopher from his conceptual prison; its philosophy is, as it were, a non-philosophy, a philosophy to undo philosophy. A comparison of the minds of Buddha and Plato—probably the greatest intellects of East and West—may make us understand how sharply East and West diverge on this crucial point. For Plato philosophy is a discipline that leads us from the lower to the higher world, from the world of the senses to the world of ideas, to leave us abiding in this latter world as much as is humanly possible; for the Buddhist, philosophy should lead us beyond the intellect back into the one real world that was always there in its undivided wholeness. Zen presupposes this view of philosophy, but goes beyond the mere restatement of it to make actual use of it in its practical and concrete Chinese fashion.

This passion for the living fact accounts for that quality in the Zen masters which must seem most amazing to the Westerner: their supreme matter-of-factness. "What is the Tao (the way, the truth)?" asks the disciple. "Your everyday mind," replies the Master; and he goes on to amplify: "When I am hungry, I eat; when tired, I sleep." The disciple is puzzled, and asks whether this is not what everybody else does too. No, the Master replies; most people are never wholly in what they are doing; when eating, they may be absent-mindedly preoccupied with a thousand different fantasies; when sleeping, they are not sleeping. The supreme mark of the thoroughly integrated man is to be without a divided mind. This matter-of-fact spirit of Zen is expressed in another paradoxical statement: "Before you have studied Zen, mountains are mountains and rivers are rivers; while you are studying it, mountains are no longer mountains and rivers no longer rivers; but once you have had Enlightenment, mountains are once again mountains and rivers are rivers." The stories of their arduous struggles for Enlightenment teach us that this matter-of-fact spirit of the Zen masters is not a thing easily come by: they are indeed awesome figures who have crossed the mountains and rivers, floods and fires of the spirit in order to come back sole and whole to the most banal things of daily life. The nearest thing to this, so far as I know, that the West has produced is Kierkegaard's wonderful comparison of the Knight of Resignation and the Knight of Faith: the former all fidgets and romanticism, aspiring after the infinite but never at home with the finite, while the Knight of Faith sits so solidly in his existence that from without he looks as prosaic and matter-of-fact as a tax-collector. But this ideal of being in direct and unmediated relation to ordinary reality was something that poor Kierkegaard, who waged a feverish lifelong struggle against the mediating and devouring power of his intelligence, could only aspire after but never realize.

In this striving for an unmediated relation to reality, as well as in its doctrine of an enlightenment (satori) that goes beyond reason, Zen would seem to be a form of Mysticism. But Zen is not mysticism as the West understands mysticism. The mystic, as defined by William James in *Varieties of Religious Experience* (James did not know about Zen), is one who pierces the veil of the natural or sensuous world in order to experience direct union with the higher reality. This formula holds for most of the great Western mystics from Plotinus onward, but it would not hold of Zen, which would reject this kind of mysticism as dualistic through and through, since it divides reality into lower and higher worlds. For Zen, higher and lower are one world; and in the records of Zen enlightenment which Suzuki sets before us there does not seem to occur anywhere the blurring of consciousness, the trancelike or semi-hallucinated state, which you will find among Western mystics. Even where it seems to move closest to mysticism, Zen remains supremely matter-of-fact. Nor is Zen to be confused with anything like pantheism, even though the Zen writings abound in statements that the Buddha-nature is to be found everywhere, in the dried up dirt-scraper, the cypress tree in the courtyard, etc. etc. Pantheism involves a division between the God who penetrates nature and nature itself as the phenomenal garment of God. But this too is a dualism that Zen leaves behind.

Neither a philosophy, then, in the Western sense, nor a mysticism, not Pantheism and not Theism, Zen might seem to the reader at this point so much a matter of subtlety and nuance as to be devoid of all practical value. On the contrary; for the greatest contemporary tribute to the practicality of Zen comes not from philosophers or artists, but from two prominent *practicing* psychiatrists, C. G. Jung and Karen Horney, who became passionately interested in Zen for its therapeutic possibilities. Jung has written about Zen, and before her death Karen Horney visited Japan to observe the life of a Zen monastery at first hand. What attracted Jung to Zen was its remarkable pursuit of psychological wholeness. Horney saw something similar, but in terms of her own psychology: namely, the search for self-realization without either the false image of an idealized self ("We are saved such as we are," says the Zen master), or without the resigned and dependent clinging to external props like family, social group, or church (after his enlightenment the disciple slaps the Master Obaku's face, remarking "There is not, after all, very much in the Buddhism of Obaku," and the master is pleased, for the disciple shows he can now stand on his own two feet). Certainly the Zen masters, as we read of them in Suzuki's pages, give us the powerful impression of fully individuated individuals, carved out of one whole and solid block. What is most incredible to the Westerner is that this demand for the individuation of the disciple should be made by a *religion!* Western religions have always been willing to settle for less, very much less, from the believer—his filial obedience or docility, let him be a miserable psychological fragment otherwise. The reason is that Western religion has always placed the weight of emphasis upon the religious object outside the individual—God beyond the world, the Mosaic

SENGAI

In the Zen sect, the circle symbolizes enlightenment, fulfillment, the attainment of human perfection.

The verse beside the circle relates to cherry blossoms, a flower of which Sengai was particularly fond.

The first three lines of the poem read:

"They blossom and fall.
Their blossoming after falling too
Is but last night's dream."

Law, the Church, the divine personality of Jesus. One can hardly imagine a Western religion producing a saying like the Zen Master's to his monks, "When you utter the name of Buddha, wash your mouth out." Zen is individualistic, and so iconoclastic and antinomian in its individualism that it will seem irreverent to many Westerners; but this is only because Zen wishes to strip the individual naked in order to return him to himself; in the end he cannot lean even upon the image of Buddha. Here precisely is the aspect of Zen Buddhism which is the greatest challenge to Western religions, and which needs to be studied most by us Westerners; for the march of our own history, as the great world of medieval religious images recedes ever further from our grasp and an increasingly secularized society engulfs us, has stripped Western man naked and left no rocklike security anywhere to lean upon. Here there looms before the frightened eyes of the Westerner what Buddhism calls the Great Emptiness; but if he does not run away in fear, this great void may bloom with all manner of miracles, and heaven and earth, in consort once again, engender effortlessly all their ancient marvels.

. . . But there is one final misgiving I imagine taking shape in the reader's mind, because it has been taking shape in mine as I write, which needs to be faced before we are done; and it is this: Must not Buddhism forever remain an alien form to the Westerner? something he cannot appropriate and make his own? Are not the conditions that make ourselves and our lives what they are such that something like Zen could never be lived here? The question cannot be shirked; Zen itself would insist upon it, since Zen holds that it is not the abstract or bookish truth but the lived truth that counts. Indeed, the question looms so intensely before my mind that it seems almost to take on the imaginary body of some Zen master shaking his stick, threatening thirty blows and crying, "Speak quick, quick!" Well then, quickly: I would agree with Suzuki when he holds that Zen is the living fact in all religions East or West; or, a little more modestly, that Zen touches what is the living fact in all religions. For the readers of this book the question will hardly arise of becoming a Buddhist, but that does not lessen the importance of Zen to them: for however small the fragment of Zen that makes live contact with the Westerner, its influence is bound to work through, and he will never be quite the same again. In the beautiful words of the Master Hoyen: *When water is scooped up in the hands, the moon is reflected in them; when flowers are handled, the scent soaks into the robe.*

Index

Abode of Fancy (*see also* Tea Room), 138, 144

Abode of the Unsymmetrical (*see also* Tea Room), 138, 145

Abode of Vacancy (*see also* Tea Room), 11, 130, 138, 139, 145

Abraham, 49; Christ's declaration, 229

Absolute (*see also* One Mind), 66*ff*

"accidents" in art, 336*ff*; "controlled," 337

"Achilles and the Tortoise," 212

Adler, Alfred, 198

"Adonais" (poem), 272

"Afterwards" (poem), 279

Aion, 240

"Ajanta" (poem), 272

Alice in Wonderland, 184, 238

Aloneness, 92, 94

Americans and Zen, ix, 3, 4–5, 7, 15, 17, 28, 328

American way of life, 334, 346

"Among School Children" (poem), 264

"Analysis, Terminable or Interminable?," 199

Ananda (Buddhist disciple), 23, 141

Anesaki, M., 269

Anglo-Saxons, 331

anshin ("repose of mind"), 60

"Antigonish" (poem), 238

anxiety, 225; as driving force, 204

archery and Zen, 8, 264, 289, 290, 299*ff*, 340

architecture, Japanese (*see also* art, gardens, Tea Room), asymmetry in, 95; Buddhist types, 95, 141; compared to European, 144*ff*

Architecture of Japan, 108*n*

arhats, 105

Aristotle, 343

Armitage, Merle, 293

"Ars Poetica" (poem), 279

art, modern Western, outside influences, 345; space in, 345

art and Zen (*see also* landscape painting, painting, *sabi*, space, Tea Ceremony, *wabi*), 10, 31; aims of, 90–91; aloneness in, 94; asymmetry in, 95, 97, 108; imperfection in, 93–94; incompleteness in, 103; new *vs.* old, 11; "one-corner style," 93, 95, 96; place of man in, 11; place of religion in, 101; space in, 95

Art of Japanese Gardens, The, 107*n*

"art of living," 198–199

"ascending the hall" (*jodo*), 20

Asvaghosha (Indian teacher), 228, 231

asymmetry (*see also* unsymmetricality), 10, 145

Auden, W. H., 256

"Auguries of Innocence" (poem), 263

Auw, Ivan von, xiv

Avatamsaka Sutra, 174, 324

Awakening, 17, 19, 339

Awakening of Faith, The, 231

Awareness, 10, 202, 289

Bach, Johann Sebastian, 101

Baishitsu (*haiku* poet), 264

bamboo, 90, 106, 107, 127

Bangkok, x

Bankei (Zen master), 83–84, 340; on "miracles," 83–84; stories of, 75, 79; on "temper," 83

Barrett, William, xiii, 341*ff*

Basho (*haiku* poet), xi; frog poem of, 107, 122, 168; quoted, 117, 118, 125, 240, 250, 264, 265, 278, 280, 286

Bayen (Ma Yuan) (painter), 92, 332

"beat generation," 4, 331*ff*